THE PEOPLE UNITED

The People United is a crucial and fascinating testimonial to how regular people organized, sacrificed, and built real power in defense of American democracy. A vital account from someone who truly was on the inside and made it happen.

—Leah Greenberg, co-executive director of Indivisible

A thoroughly compelling saga. . . . Obviously, this is an anti-Trump saga – but beneath the surface of these movements and experiences lies the beating heart of individual engagement and democracy in action. It's these features, combined with Pickett's personal involvement and reflections, which make *The People United* such a powerful documentation of struggle and hope.

—D. Donovan, *Midwest Book Review*

Chris Pickett's daughters will never have to ask their father what he did to protect democracy in the United States because they and their mother, Katherine, were with him all the way. ... If you believe that democracy is not a spectator sport, that the renewal of hope in this country lies in its grassroots activists, you couldn't read a more illuminating text than this one.

—Lynn Litterine, author of *River Town Girl* and
Indivisible Montgomery member

Chris Pickett takes us through the "fly the plane while building it" work that gave the resistance structure and stability and made our successes possible. Reading through *The People United*, you can't help but feel empowered to stand up and fight for what is right today.

—Barbara Noveau, founder and former director of DoTheMostGood

Chris Pickett's memoir stands out for its grounded, firsthand perspective and its focus on ordinary citizens who chose sustained civic engagement over outrage alone. This is not a pundit's account or a sweeping history; it is a personal narrative rooted in lived experience, local organizing, and the emotional toll of activism. . . . A thoughtful, measured account that preserves an often-overlooked side of recent history—the people who showed up, week after week, believing their efforts mattered.

—Scott Olsen, *Seattle Book Review*

THE PEOPLE UNITED

A MEMOIR OF HOPE AND RESISTANCE
DURING TRUMP'S FIRST TERM

CHRIS PICKETT

HOP ON PUBLISHING

Silver Spring, MD

Hop On Publishing
Silver Spring, MD 20901
www.HopOnPublishing.com

Book Layout © 2017 BookDesignTemplates.com
Cover design by Paul Nylander, Illustrada Design
All interior photos courtesy of the author.

The People United: A Memoir of Hope and Resistance During Trump's First Term / Chris Pickett. — 1st ed.
ISBN 979-8-9940240-0-3 (paperback)
ISBN 979-8-9940240-1-0 (epub)

The only people who've ever held Trump meaningfully accountable ... have been ordinary Americans.

—Osita Nwanevu, contributing editor at
The New Republic

Foreword

By Evan Glass, Montgomery County Councilmember

IN MOMENTS OF NATIONAL upheaval, it is easy to fix our eyes on Washington. Cable news, social media, and campaign cycles train us to believe that the most consequential battles for our democracy are fought on the largest stages, by the loudest voices. But anyone who has spent time in local government knows a quieter truth: while national politics may dominate the headlines, it is at the local level where democracy is most tangible, most accessible, and most capable of changing people's lives.

This book is a testament to that truth and to the power of committed, organized neighbors who turned their shared values into real-world progress. Chris Pickett's leadership of Indivisible Montgomery is a story not just about resistance, but about responsibility. About showing up. About understanding that democracy is not something that happens to us, but something we actively build together.

When Indivisible chapters began forming across the country, many people saw them as a reaction to a moment, a surge of grassroots energy sparked by national events. What Chris understood, and what this book makes clear, is that movements only endure when they take root locally. Indivisible chapters across the country became far more than protest organizations. They became civic forces that educated residents, mobilized voters, held leaders accountable, and strengthened the relationship between communities and the institutions they meant to serve.

I have had the privilege of working alongside Chris and the members of Indivisible Montgomery, and I have seen firsthand the impact of their engagement. They showed up not only when it was easy or fashionable, but when it was difficult and necessary. They asked tough questions. They demanded transparency. They reminded elected officials—myself included—that our authority comes not from titles, but from the trust of the people we represent.

Local government rarely inspires the same passion as presidential elections, yet it shapes the outcomes that matter most in daily life: whether families can afford housing, whether our schools are inclusive and strong, whether transportation is accessible, whether people are safe, and whether communities feel seen and heard. Chris and Indivisible understood that if you want to protect democratic values, you don't start by shouting into the void—you start by organizing your neighbors, attending council meetings, knocking on doors, and learning how decisions actually get made.

That work is not glamorous. It requires patience, persistence, and a willingness to engage across differences. It requires translating big ideals—justice, equity, dignity—into budgets, zoning codes, and committee hearings. And it requires leaders like Chris, who can bridge the gap between moral urgency and practical action.

What makes this story especially powerful is that it is not about one individual alone. This book captures a collective effort—a reminder that movements succeed when leadership is shared, when people are empowered rather than directed, and when participation is broad and inclusive. Chris cultivated a culture of engagement that welcomed first-time activists and seasoned advocates alike, proving that democracy grows stronger the more people see themselves as part of it.

At a time when cynicism about politics runs deep, Indivisible Montgomery continues to offer something radical: hope grounded in action. That belief has sustained real victories in our community and strengthened the democratic habits that will carry us forward.

As you read this book, I hope you see it not only as a chronicle of one organization or one leader, but as an invitation. An invitation to look beyond the noise of national politics and recognize the extraordinary power that exists in your own community. An invitation to participate, to organize, and to hold fast to the idea that local action is not small action—it is the foundation of our democracy.

Chris Pickett's leadership reminds us that when people come together with purpose and persistence, local government becomes not a distant bureaucracy, but a shared project. And in that shared project, we find the most meaningful, lasting impact of all.

Preface

What we did mattered.

The resistance to Donald Trump from 2016 to 2021 was an incredibly successful movement, preventing, or at least slowing, his erosion and destruction of American institutions and our way of life. Trump's reelection in 2024 led some to declare our efforts a failure, but that's only true if our movement was supposed to banish Trump from American life. That's not what we were built for.

I wrote this book to tell the story of the resistance to Donald Trump, and the ordinary Americans who held him and his administration to account. We were the people marching in the streets, from the 2017 Women's March to the 2020 Marches for Black Lives. We protested the Muslim ban, the repeal of Obamacare, the family separation policy, and the Kavanaugh nomination. We stood up to Trump and his actions to end American democracy. We were the volunteers who worked on political campaigns that built the 2018 Blue Wave and delivered the White House to Joe Biden in 2020. We donated to Democratic candidates, knocked on doors, made phone calls, wrote letters, and did everything we could to turn out voters. This book is about us and all the work we put in.

I wrote this book for my family and me to remember how our lives were upended resisting Donald Trump and defending American democracy. At the end of 2016, dejected and searching for a way to resist the incoming administration, I read the newly published

Indivisible Guide. The Guide was a blueprint for local activism, including urging members of Congress to resist normalizing Trump. I was so inspired that I founded Indivisible Montgomery, a local grassroots activism organization that recruited over 1,700 people to resist the Trump administration in our community and as part of the broader national movement of opposition. Along the way, my family made many sacrifices while I led this resistance organization. And there were a number of times when I wanted nothing more than to walk away and leave Indivisible Montgomery behind.

I wrote this book because our stories haven't been told. After Trump's election in 2016, I wanted to stand up for my country and the people who would undoubtedly be harmed during the Trump presidency. I wasn't the only one. People across the country had hope—a positive vision about what the future could hold and the urge to work for it. What we were lacking was direction. Once I read the Indivisible Guide, though, I realized my years of experience in science policy and working with volunteers gave me the tools and experience necessary to make a real difference. I founded Indivisible Montgomery to give direction to the directionless and to resist the Trump administration. We formed a tight-knit community that celebrated our successes and supported each other through the difficult times. The 1,700 people who made up Indivisible Montgomery, and those in similar groups across the country, made their own sacrifices as we worked toward our goals. The reelection of Donald Trump in 2024 did not erase our history. Our stories of resistance are still worth telling. What we did is worth remembering.

When I launched Indivisible Montgomery in the waning days of 2016, I had no idea our broad national movement to resist Trump and the GOP would be both successful and underreported. Media outlets repeatedly dove deep attempting to understand Trump voters and their motivations, while offering comparatively little attention to those resisting the administration. Trump rode the grievances of America's white racial majority all the way to the White House and amplified and fed those grievances in a destructive, self-serving attempt to cling to power. But he and his GOP were deeply unpopular. Trump decisively lost the 2016 popular vote, his approval rating never reached 50%, and most Americans disapproved of him in nearly every way that was important for leading the country.

Because the media failed to engage with our opposition movement in a meaningful way, most people don't know who we are. We aren't the right-wing caricature of resistance members—Marxists who loved MSNBC and made themselves feel better by writing *tRump*. We aren't antifa, con artists, or self-made social media celebrities who craved attention. None of us was paid to protest. Our movement was formed of Americans from all walks of life, and it comprised small acts and big. These acts—minor and major, raucous and quiet, one-off and long-lasting—defined American activism in response to the 2016 election. Our actions were modeled on the Tea Party's efforts to block or derail the efforts of the Obama administration. We organized, we called, we marched, we donated, we protested. We stood shoulder to shoulder with people and groups who had been in this fight much longer. We took the opportunities available to stand up and speak out. And it worked.

This is what I did. This is what we did.

THE PEOPLE UNITED

Prologue

DECEMBER 17, 2019

Leader. Activist. Firebrand.

These words describe me now, but they didn't three years ago. Back then, I was more accustomed to *husband, father,* and *policy specialist.* The 2016 election changed that. Donald Trump's ascension to the presidency and the imposition of his bigoted views on the country required a nationwide, grassroots response. I stepped up.

Now, as I walk back to my car on this frigid December night, the crunching of frozen grass punctuating each step, I am a changed man. In 2016, I founded Indivisible Montgomery. In 2017, I became a leader in my community and spoke out against the actions of the Trump administration. In 2018, I led our efforts to build the Blue Wave. Now, in 2019, I am about to address a rally in a local park, demanding the impeachment of President Trump for his illicit attempts to corrupt the 2020 election.

I reach the car and open the driver's door. Katherine, my wife, looks over. "It's time," I say. "I'll get Nancy."

"All right," Katherine says. "Hazel, you're with me."

I close the driver's door and open the rear passenger door. My nearly seven-year-old daughter looks up at me and brushes her wavy blond locks out of her face. "Don't forget your hat, Nance. It's cold out here."

Nancy puts on her knit hat and gets out while Katherine unbuckles three-year-old Hazel from her car seat. "Daddy, I see your breath," Hazel says from across the car.

Katherine holds Hazel as we walk around the trunks of large oak trees that rise into the darkness. We're too cold to talk, but I'm glad to have my family here supporting me and being a part of the event. Becoming an integral part of the nationwide resistance to the Trump administration meant weaving this work with my responsibilities to my family. Sometimes that meant keeping resistance time and family time separate. Tonight, it means packing a picnic dinner and bringing the family to a nighttime rally to support impeaching a corrupt leader.

We approach where the speakers are gathering, and Katherine realizes she's on the wrong side of the event. She scans the crowd, lit by yellow streetlamps. "We'll be in the audience over there," she says, pointing to a concrete bench 20 feet away. I nod and give her a kiss. Still holding Hazel, she takes Nancy's hand and explains to the girls where they are going.

I step into the small group of invited speakers—local politicians and other resistance leaders—and introduce myself to the few folks I don't already know. The organizer of the event, a woman in her early 60s, says to us, "Let's get started!" She picks up a microphone attached by a cord to a bullhorn and begins making announcements to the crowd of 80 people in heavy coats and caps. The mic/bullhorn setup is awkward, but I used it at a protest 10 months ago, and I was comfortable with it. The trick, if you want people to hear you, is to hold the mic close to your mouth and the bullhorn overhead in a Statue of Liberty pose. The organizer finishes her announcements and hands off the mic and bullhorn to the first speaker. I'm third. She doesn't tell him how to use the bullhorn. He speaks loudly with the bullhorn at chest level. There is some clapping and cheers, but the people at the edges strain to hear him. The second speaker is worse, forgetting she needs to project. The organizer should have briefed the speakers on how to use the equipment. Or maybe the speakers just needed more time at protests like I had.

The second speaker finishes and hands me the mic and bullhorn. The people farthest away from the center are getting restless. If I can't get them fired up, the cold is going to drive these people away. Well, firing up the crowd is what I came to do. I bring the mic to my lips, raise the bullhorn in the air, and close my eyes for a split second to remind myself how to do this: Relax. Slow your speaking. Enunciate. Project.

Hello, Montgomery County! I am Chris Pickett, and I am the director of Indivisible Montgomery.

Welcome to this celebration of American democracy!

2016 | FROM BRIGHT TO DARK

A Good Year

I WALKED INTO MY daughters' room and over to the crib. It was still dark out, but the bedroom night-light shone bright enough for me to see five-month-old Hazel kicking off her swaddle from the night before. This morning was a bit of an anomaly in our house—of the two of us, I was the one who had woken up crying.

The night before, Katherine walked into the living room to find me watching election returns. "I didn't think I'd be this nervous," she said. Normally upbeat, she had been in an even better mood than usual since the Chicago Cubs won the World Series five days earlier—their first since 1908. Katherine was born and raised in St. Louis, so it was a minor scandal in her family that she was a fan of her hometown team's archrival. She chalked her Cubs allegiance up to being the youngest of eight children and wanting to do something different from the rest of her family; the eight years she'd spent living in Chicago had cemented her feelings. The Cubs' win continued a streak of what had been a good year for us—I started my dream job in March, and our family grew to four in May as we welcomed Hazel.

"I'm sure it will be fine," I said. "It's too early for any pivotal states to have been called." This was November 8, 2016. We'd find out soon whether Hillary Clinton or Donald Trump had won the presidency.

The night was young and the early states to watch were North Carolina and Florida. There were rumors Clinton could win North

Carolina. Barack Obama won it in 2008, but it flipped Republican in 2012. Still, with Trump on the ticket, some solid Republican states may have been up for grabs. In my opinion, Trump shouldn't receive 100 actual votes, much less 100 electoral votes. But ever since I had started voting in 1996, a large portion of the American voting public voted for either the Democrat or the Republican, regardless of the individual's qualities or policy proposals. That meant every election was likely to be close. So I reminded myself that winning North Carolina was aspirational. Trump was doing better in some parts of the state than had been expected. Running strong in a somewhat reliable red state wasn't that big of a deal. I was confident the true toss-up states would turn out for Clinton.

Our attention turned to Florida. Florida was a must-win for any Republican to have a chance at winning the presidency, and polling indicated a close contest. Clinton winning Florida would slam the door shut on the likelihood of Trump winning. But a Trump win in Florida portended a difficult night for Clinton across the rest of the map. Chuck Todd, NBC's political director at the time, was discussing vote returns across the state. The winner wasn't yet clear, but Todd was frenetically highlighting specific counties and turning to talk to the other hosts about the number of votes that remained to be counted. Todd kept circling counties and talking about Trump over-performing expectations in certain Republican strongholds, then cycling through Democratic strongholds to show that there weren't enough potential Clinton votes left to overtake Trump. Todd's co-hosts barely concealed their shock and horror at the scene playing out in front of them, but Todd was almost gleeful as he geeked out

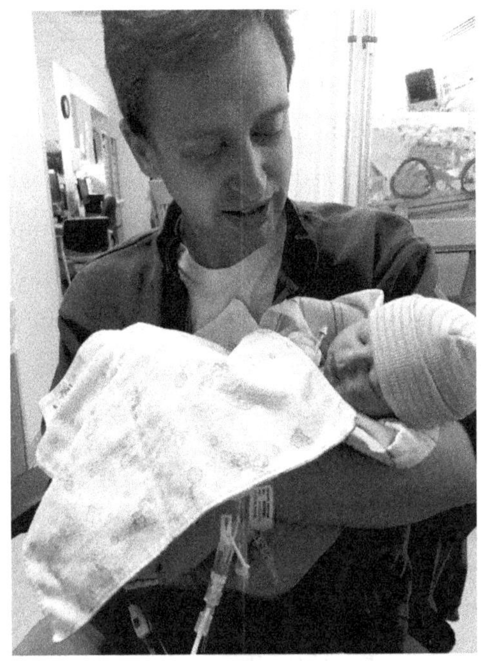

Top: Holding one-day-old Hazel, still in the hospital. *Bottom:* Katherine sits on our couch with five-day-old Hazel and three-year-old Nancy.

over the vote tallies. Unreasonable or not, I've never forgiven him for that.

It was during the discussion of Florida that I started pacing. I noted that the Blue Wall strongholds of Pennsylvania, Michigan, and Wisconsin hadn't been called yet. This was a concern. A Republican winning these states was a fantasy in 2008 and 2012, and they were never seriously contested. But what if cracks were forming? Clinton losing one Blue Wall state would be bad but not the end of the night. Losing all three would mean she had no path to victory. In the last week of the campaign, Clinton visited Michigan to shore up her support. Should she have also gone to Wisconsin? Much like in Florida, Trump was performing above expectations across the Blue Wall. I tried to calm down by telling myself there were plenty of votes left to be counted and later votes tended to break toward Democrats.

The night wore on and the clock slowed as we waited for updates from the swing states. Florida was called for Trump. That didn't give him the win, it just gave him a path. The election would come down to the Blue Wall states. Not too long after, Todd took what he had said about Florida and applied it to the Blue Wall—there may not be enough Democratic votes left to deliver the states to Clinton. I became nauseous.

Katherine and I went to bed after midnight. Neither of us slept well. We woke up at 6:00, well before the girls. I don't like checking my phone early in the morning, but I did that day.

"Well?" asked Katherine.

"It's Trump."

We cried.

By the time I finished changing Hazel's diaper, her three-year-old sister Nancy came out of their room, brushed her wavy blond hair out of her eyes, and took my hand as the three of us went downstairs for breakfast. Katherine was in the shower. I fixed Nancy's cup of milk and Hazel's formula. Once Nancy had taken a few sips, I knelt next to her.

"Nance, do you remember yesterday, when we went to vote?"

"Yes. You voted for the woman, not the bad guy."

"That's right." My voice cracked. "I wanted to tell you that even though we didn't want it to happen, the bad guy won. And he's going to be the president in a couple of months."

I wiped away the tears welling up in my eyes. Nancy wasn't sure how to respond. She didn't understand national politics, but she knew her dad crying at breakfast was not normal. "You don't have to be concerned," I told her. "Mom and I will worry about the president." I cleared my throat. "Would you like some toast?"

Foreshadowing

TRUMP WAS A JOKE when the presidential primary started. He rode a golden escalator down one level to his own campaign launch, yet claimed his opponents were low energy. Once he won the nomination, I still didn't think he could win the general election, but I had to admit that even being in the race meant it was possible. I ran through what-if scenarios in my head, imagining what the country would be like if Trump won. I became increasingly concerned as the election drew closer, and then the *Access Hollywood* tapes of Trump bragging about sexually assaulting women became public. He was toast, I thought. No one, especially a bumbling idiot like Trump, could recover from such a devastating scandal.

And then he was elected, and everything was upended. A yawning uncertainty hung over the nation. How much of what Trump said during the campaign could he make reality? Would he ban Muslims from entering the country or work to overturn *Roe v. Wade*? Who would he surround himself with? How would a government fully controlled by Republicans rule the country? How much of the power of the federal government would be brought to bear during the Trump years? Against whom? And to what end? These questions, fanciful fearmongering yesterday, now weren't just legitimate. They were pressing.

I felt lost. The day after the election, I was working "from home," which meant I gave Nancy a hug goodbye as Katherine took her to preschool, I dropped Hazel off at daycare, and I took my laptop to the local Starbucks. The shop was full of people but lacking in commotion. Instead of the usual buzz of conversation and the calls of the baristas, conversations were muted. Customers walked up to get their drink and shuffled out or sat down with their friends to talk in dejected tones. I got my own coffee and picked up snippets of conversation as I weaved through the crowd.

"Trump will moderate his positions as he starts to lead the country," one guy said. "There's no way he could govern like he campaigned."

"He had a bunch of idiots around him in the campaign," his friend responded. "He'll have better people in his administration, so we'll be fine."

I had been in denial about Trump's chances of winning, but these guys were delusional. Trump launched his campaign calling Mexican people drug dealers and rapists, and he regularly said worse during the campaign. He never walked back any of these comments. Trump's campaign was run by people like Steve Bannon and Paul Manafort, who were known for their bigotry and corruption. There was no moderation to be had. There were no "good people" to surround him with.

I found an empty table and set up my laptop. I tried to focus on work, but I was too consumed by fear. I read the news to understand what had happened the night before. I looked at the precinct-by-precinct breakdowns of votes in critical states, though this ended up being unsatisfying and ultimately useless. How last night happened was less important than what the future held. My attention was drawn to the opinion pieces of people who were as devastated as I was but had somehow mustered the ability to write insightful articles. Contrary to the attitudes of some of those I heard around me, there were some clear, no-holds-barred articles on just how bad the Trump presidency would be. One of the best was by David Remnick:

> The election of Donald Trump to the Presidency is nothing less than a tragedy for the American republic, a tragedy for the Constitution, and a triumph for the forces, at home and abroad, of nativism, authoritarianism, misogyny, and racism. ... On January 20, 2017, we will bid farewell to the first African-American President—a man of integrity, dignity, and generous spirit—and witness the inauguration of a con who did little to spurn endorsement by forces of xenophobia and white supremacy. It is impossible to react to this moment with anything less than revulsion and profound anxiety.[1]

These articles forecasted a grim future for our country because they did what a lot of people, including political pundits and people in this coffee shop, would not. They took Trump at his word. With Trump, what you see is what you get. And a lot of people saw a cynical, bigoted con man.

I turned my attention to social media. My Twitter feed was split between people crying over the election results and those getting ready to fight the Trump administration. On Facebook, friends were pouring their hearts out in anguish. I took a couple of hours to absorb those stories and posts and to sort through my own feelings about the election. I rejected the naïve urge to assume we'd all somehow be fine. But acknowledging reality meant admitting that specific groups of Americans were now under greater threat. And acknowledging this spurred me to take action to fight against these threats. I needed to say something. I'm not sure for whom. For me? I finally posted on Facebook:

> This morning, my wife said it felt like someone died. What died was our perception that we actually lived in Obama's America—an imperfect country with boundless potential and relentless optimism in the face of adversity. That despite our problems, we have the capacity to tackle important and complex issues and make real change. We thought we lived in a place where insistent racist and misogynistic demagoguery from a serial liar and confessed sexual predator would disqualify that person from the highest public office.
>
> This is not where we live.
>
> The forces of hatred and self-serving disaffection marshaled by Trump propelled him to victory. But the biggest defeat would be to buy into despair, concede that the bleak vision shopped by Trump is accurate, and let go of the vision of what this country can be. This election illustrates how much is left to be done in our efforts to make our country a more perfect union.
>
> Now it's time to get going. On behalf of everyone who is left exposed and vulnerable due to this morning's result, I have work to do.

False Starts

I HAD NO IDEA what to do.

I knew I needed to do something to protect those the Trump administration would target, but I had no idea what that meant in a practical sense. My Facebook post was something I needed to get off my chest, and it was also something I needed to hear. I wasn't going to shrink from this fight. But I needed direction.

As the days slipped into weeks, Katherine and I put on a brave face for the girls while searching frantically for effective ways to resist the incoming administration. I read plenty of articles about recognizing the country's descent into authoritarianism. Some even suggested packing a bag in case we needed to flee the country. I didn't want to flee. I wanted to fight. But few sources discussed what ordinary Americans could do to stand against the changes Trump would bring.

Being directionless was at odds with my deeply ingrained sense of duty to my country. I am the son and grandson of US Air Force officers. For 18 years, the Air Force ruled my life as we moved eight times before my senior year of high school. We lived in the upper Midwest, the Mountain West, the heartland, the South. Every place we went, one of the few constants was my dad leaving for work every morning in his light blue uniform shirt, dark blue slacks and hat, and polished black shoes. Even at an average height and weight, my dad was imposing in that uniform. When I was six, I remember my mom leading me through a maze of people and telling me to sit in an uncomfortable, adult-sized chair with my sister so we could watch my dad's boss pin a new rank on his collar. Those were the captain's double bars. A few years later it was the major's gold oak leaf. My dad clearly loved his job, and he was proud to do his duty to his country. But with his rising rank came rising hurdles. He dutifully did his job, but mismanaged disagreements with his superiors landed him in hot water and left him passed over for promotion. After serving 20 years, he left the Air Force, disillusioned.

For as long as I can remember, I wanted to serve my country with the same pride as my father did. After witnessing his struggles in the military, though, I looked for another way. While in college at the University of Colorado, Boulder, I committed to putting my interest in molecular biology to use serving my country and humanity. I pursued biomedical research as a career in the hopes that I might contribute to a discovery that would improve human health. After I finished at Boulder in 1999, I went to grad school at the University of Utah. Seven years later, I earned my PhD and, still intent on a research career, moved to St. Louis to work in a lab at Washington University.

My time in St. Louis was momentous. It was where I met Katherine. There was something about her as she walked through the doors of Kaldi's coffee shop, the way her dark brown hair fell around her shoulders and the smirk on her face when she recognized me from my online profile. I found her stories about her large family and her editing career fascinating. She wanted to know more about my small family and career in biomedical research. As our dates went by, it was clear she was the one for me. We wanted to go on the same adventures together—in the world and in life. After we dated for two years, I proposed. She said yes, and we married in 2010.

St. Louis is also where I became an activist. I was frustrated by the structural problems inherent in academic graduate student and postdoctoral training systems that favored the lucky and the few. I spoke out about these problems in formal and informal settings. In a minor epiphany, I realized I could improve training conditions for biomedical research trainees by changing my career from bench research to science policy. I was scared to make such a change—what if I switched careers and hated the new job? This slowed me down, but eventually my optimism about the positive difference I could make in a policy position won out over my fear of moving away from research. After a lot of networking and an extensive job search, I landed a position as a science policy fellow with the American Society for Biochemistry and Molecular Biology in 2012. A few months later, Katherine and I bid farewell to St. Louis and moved to Silver Spring, Maryland, just north of Washington, DC. In this new role, I was introduced to the inner workings of Congress, the National Institutes of Health, and more. I organized scientists advocating for federal funding for research, I taught them how to hold effective meetings with members of Congress, and I learned to write about policy for a lay audience. I was making a difference and I loved it.

BUT IN DECEMBER 2016, I was out of sorts. Counteracting Trump meant going beyond my training and experience in science policy. Shortly after Thanksgiving, I was working at a coffee shop, and I caught a glimpse of the computer at the table next to me. The background image was of the Maryland General Assembly. "Excuse me," I said to the computer's owner. "Are you part of the General Assembly?"

"Hi, yes," she said, smiling and extending her hand. She was at least ten years younger than me, with shoulder-length brown hair and wearing thin, plastic-rimmed glasses and a business suit. "I'm Maricé Morales. I'm a member of the Maryland House of Delegates."

"Really? That's great." I shook her hand and asked which district she represented. I was thoroughly embarrassed when she told me hers was the district I lived in, but that's what I got for ignoring state politics. Morales was getting ready for the upcoming General Assembly session. Even though we had just met, I took the opportunity to talk about my plight. "With Trump's election, I want to get involved in politics and activism. To do what we can to stop what Trump wants to do. I just don't know how."

"Why don't you come to the Montgomery County Young Democrats Christmas party in a couple of weeks," she said with a smile. "I won't be there, but I'm sure there will be people there who could help you."

I didn't have any other leads on how to stand against Trump, so I said, "Sure."

And that's how, about ten days later, I walked my 40-year-old self into a party for the Montgomery County Young Democrats (read: Dems under 35) without hesitation. About 30 of us nibbled on small plates of hors d'oeuvres while meandering and mingling in the basement of a blandly painted and sparsely decorated townhome community center. We exchanged pleasantries and discussed what we had done during the campaign. I realized quickly that this party was full of people looking for a way to resist rather than already knowing how to resist. Fifteen minutes after I arrived, I decided I'd rather be with my family. As I moved to get my coat, the rest of the party moved in the other direction, toward Rep. Elijah Cummings, who had just arrived. The longtime congressman and veteran of the Civil Rights Movement worked his way down the stairway to us. He came about halfway down the steps looking exhausted, his cheeks drooping, overworked from a lifetime of speaking to crowds and smiling for photos. He kept his overcoat on as he began speaking. He started with what we all knew: no one could predict what the coming four years held. And he reminded us that the answer to Trump's corruption and malice was in this room. Those who cared for this country couldn't sit back and wish for what might have been while Trump stripped the country for parts and profit. We needed to do what we could to uphold the ideals of our nation.

"Yes!" I thought. "That's what I want to do. I couldn't be more on board."

But how?

Indivisible
Montgomery

ON DECEMBER 14, I was on a moderately full Metro train on my way into my actual office in downtown Washington, DC. I found a seat to myself and checked Twitter to catch up on the previous day's news in science and politics. I noticed several people I followed were tweeting about something called "The Indivisible Guide." The more I read, the more intrigued I became. It apparently dealt with resisting the Trump administration, but my investigation ended as the train entered a tunnel and I lost internet connection. I flagged it as something to check out later that evening.

I walked into my office 20 minutes later. As I sat down, my phone buzzed. It was Katherine. When I answered, I could immediately tell she was excited.

"Hey, did you see this thing called the Indivisible Guide?"

"Um, I saw something about it on the train but didn't—"

Katherine cut me off. "There's a Google Doc," she said quickly. "It's a guide. A guide for fighting back against Trump. This is what you've been looking for!"

"Uh ..." I was confused. Katherine was moving a little fast for me. "What's the website?" She told me and I typed it in. "I'm not getting anything," I said slowly. "Maybe their site crashed?"

"I thought that might happen," she said. "I already downloaded their Google Doc. I'll email it to you. Give me a call once you've gotten through it."

I refreshed my email and Katherine's message popped up. I opened the attachment immediately. And. It. Was. Awesome! I was riveted. Here it was, a day-to-day, week-to-week guide to effectively resisting the Trump administration. Katherine was right. It was exactly what I had been looking for.

Written by Ezra Levin, Leah Greenberg, and friends, the Indivisible Guide was a manual that appropriated the tactics the Tea Party had used to oppose President Obama's policies and turned them around to resist Trump. It detailed how acting locally to hold our members of Congress to account could build a massive, nationwide movement. The work proposed in the Guide was familiar to me because it was what I did in my job. Most of my days were spent writing newsletters, blog posts, press releases, and more, all meant to engage readers in a way that helped them advocate for the causes they were passionate about. I knew how to organize volunteers and direct their energy in an effective way; what to say when calling and writing Congress; how to conduct a meeting with a member of Congress; and how to navigate that meeting should it turn contentious. And more importantly, I knew the pace at which the government worked. The Indivisible Guide made it so clear to me that I simply needed to take the skills I had learned over the past four-plus years in science policy and apply them to the nascent resistance.

The tactical foundation of the Tea Party was local chapters of activists spread across the country. This made sense to me. A widespread, community-by-community effort to put pressure on elected officials to stand against authoritarianism and hatred and to fight for American values was the correct way to frame a long-standing resistance to the Trump administration. Rather than getting directions from a national organization, each group was empowered to fight the fight in front of them: the individual groups would work to hold their own members of Congress to account.

From that day on, whenever I was alone with my thoughts, my mind went to the Guide and came up with practical ideas for implementing its suggestions. I wanted to do this. I wanted to lead this. A few days before Christmas, I was full of adrenaline when I walked into Katherine's office. "I want to launch an Indivisible chapter," I blurted. Katherine and I had talked about Indivisible a lot over the past week, but this was the first time I said I wanted to take such a big leap into it. And I knew this might be a tough sell. Katherine had recently finished a two-year stint as the president of the Montgomery County chapter of the Maryland Writers' Association. To an outsider, running the chapter meant putting on monthly meetings, with invited speakers discussing the ins and outs of book writing and publishing. But behind the scenes, Katherine hustled every month to keep her volunteer board on task and pick up the slack when needed. Before MWA, Katherine spent two years writing, publishing, and marketing her award-winning book about navigating the book-publishing process. She was looking forward to taking a break from volunteer work and spending time with our family. Nancy was three, Hazel had just turned seven months, and these girls were growing up fast. Trump's election gave us pause, though. Katherine wanted to resist Trump, but she was interested in volunteering with established organizations, like National Popular Vote, without losing family time. Having a new group form under her roof would put a crimp in that plan. But forming a group such as Indivisible felt so right for me that I had to pursue it.

I had prepared myself for this to be a long conversation, and I was ready to explain what I saw as the benefits of founding an Indivisible group. Katherine gave me a crooked look, let out a long sigh, and said, "I know." Her shoulders slumped. After our discussions over the past week, she realized even before I did that I wanted to be a part of what the Indivisible Guide proposed. Still, I knew Katherine had reservations and I wanted to give the decision some space.

I gave myself a week to see if the urge to found an activist group would wear off or if I could discover a group already operating nearby. During that time, I tried every keyword search I could think of and scoured social media to find a local organization. I kept coming up empty, so my thoughts drifted to what I might name my own group. I wanted it to be short and memorable. I wanted it to be inclusive of our metro area without listing out every city and town just north of DC. And I wanted to make sure people looking for an Indivisible group would know we were a part of that network. Indivisible Montgomery fit all those criteria.

December 27, 2016, was seven days after I announced to Katherine I wanted to start an Indivisible group. And because the urge was still strong and Katherine was supportive, that was the day I did it. Once the girls went to bed, I created an Indivisible Montgomery Mailchimp account, WordPress website, Facebook page, and Twitter feed. I emailed a dozen friends, telling them what I was doing and asking if they wanted to be a part. Eleven of the twelve said yes, and I added them to the newsletter mailing list. Indivisible Montgomery had its first members.

Indivisible Montgomery Newsletter: Week 1

THANK YOU FOR JOINING this group. Events will probably move pretty quickly for the next several months so I thought it best to do some introductory tasks before the real work begins.

Our Focus

Donald Trump is America's first autocratic, narcissistic president, but he is not the first autocratic narcissist to run a country. For those that have lived under such rulers, they suggest the best way to defeat an autocratic narcissist is to attack his policies, not his persona. This group will focus on policies.

Our best way to influence policy is through our representative and two senators. By clearly and consistently expressing how we expect our members of Congress to fight the destructive agenda of Donald Trump and the Republican-controlled Congress, we can ensure we have strong voices speaking on our behalf. And should those voices falter, we will take them to task for their complicity.

Our Tactics

As demonstrated by the Tea Party and laid out nicely in the Indivisible Guide, holding accountable our elected representatives is critical to ensure they are representing us properly. We will voice our opinions, satisfaction, and displeasure with their policy positions over the phone, at town-hall meetings, and other avenues of opportunity.

This newsletter will provide a script for you to follow with pertinent information to convey to our elected representatives. In subsequent newsletters, there will also be information for Indivisible Montgomery meetings, town-hall meetings, and other events.

Our Work Starts Next Week

Donald Trump's inauguration may be three weeks away, but the new Congress is sworn in on Jan. 3. Hundreds of bills are introduced in the first days of a new Congress, but this Republican-led Congress will be anxious to have bills ready for the new president's signature on the day of his inauguration. It may take a couple of days to identify which of the bills we will need to target immediately. Until the next newsletter comes out, you can keep tabs on our efforts by following @IndivisibleMCMD on Twitter.

2017 | RESIST!

New Year, New Fight

As the calendar flipped to 2017, I had only questions in front of me. How far would Trump follow through on his divisive and revanchist campaign rhetoric? How drastically would his administration change this country? And by far the biggest question: what the hell was I supposed to do with this organization I just founded? I, and Katherine somewhat reluctantly, brought an impressive array of experiences to running the organization. For the past four years, I taught scientists how to effectively advocate to federal officials on behalf of biomedical research. I understood how Congress worked and the speed with which government moved. Katherine had just finished her two-year stint with MWA, so she knew what it was like to run a small organization on a shoestring budget. We had many skills to draw on, and this gave me confidence.

In those first days of January, I evaluated where Indivisible Montgomery was: an organization with 11 members, a newsletter, and a presence on social media. And then I considered where I wanted us to be: an organization of experienced grassroots activists dedicated to resisting the new Trump administration and defeating President Trump in the 2020 election. This formed the frame for all the decisions made in setting up the organization.

I knew these early decisions would define Indivisible Montgomery for the next several years. One misstep could doom the organization before it even got off the ground. Aside from launching the organization, how we would communicate was my first major decision. I needed a platform that was equally effective in regular times and in times of crisis, and it needed to be accessible to all members. The Mailchimp email newsletter fulfilled these needs. This would allow me to control Indivisible Montgomery's messaging without the interlocutors found on social media. All other forms of communication would amplify the takeaways from the newsletter and funnel newcomers to the newsletter sign-up.

Next, to keep people participating for the long term, we needed an action plan that would engage our members on a regular basis and provide opportunities for success, all while guarding against burnout. Considering what I knew from science policy and the suggestions in the Indivisible Guide, I chose weekly phone calls to members of Congress as our regular action. Weekly phone calls, with scripts delivered by me to keep us on topic and effective, would give our members an outlet for their energy. Traveling to the offices of senators and representatives, attending protests, registering voters, and participating in other activities could be added in as they cropped up. To ensure members' routine engagement, I established a newsletter schedule: Monday's message previewed the coming week and disseminated relevant news stories; Tuesday's provided the phone scripts for our weekly calls to Congress; and Thursday's wrapped up the week and discussed any response to our Tuesday calls.

These decisions provided the frame for running the organization. Now I needed to clear the next hurdle: grow the membership.

Let's Talk

Without many members, Indivisible Montgomery wouldn't be much of a force. Where would I find prospective members? I quickly realized that was the wrong question. Assuming there were other people in my community like me, I needed to ask how I could get prospective members to find us. Indivisible Montgomery's Facebook and Twitter feeds were already directing people to our newsletter sign-up. But what about the people who wanted to resist the current administration but didn't obsessively search the internet for opportunities to do so? Here, I was stumped. I was building a community of local anti-Trump activists. But where do these people hang out? I told Katherine about this brick wall I had run into, and she responded, "Doesn't that make it easier for you?" I was confused. "If there never was a community before," she continued, "that means your prospective members are everywhere. Design a flyer, and we can hang it up in public places around the county."

When our first set of actions went out on Thursday, January 5, the first day of the 115th Congress and nine days after Indivisible Montgomery's founding, it was sent to 25 people. Katherine and I hung flyers at coffee shops, at libraries, and wherever we went that had a bulletin board, and I encouraged others on the group's email list to do the same. The flyer advertised the upcoming Indivisible Montgomery–wide phone call on January 11. This call was a way to explain my vision for the group, to hear from members about our actions, and to brainstorm new recruitment methods. The newsletter I sent the morning of January 11 reminding members of the phone call went to 50 people, double the number when we started hanging flyers and four times where we were at the founding.

As the time of the call approached, I set up my computer and phone in the dining room. Once Katherine was done helping Nancy and Hazel to bed, she went into her home office. By joining the call separately, we'd both be able to listen and comment when we needed without talking over the other. I started the call, and there were so many pings indicating people joining that I couldn't count them all. Once the pinging stopped, I introduced myself, thanked everyone for coming, and explained the agenda for the call. I paced while I spoke to dissipate my nervous energy. I laid out my plan for the organization's operations, including how we would spread out our actions and focus our communications through the newsletter. I also introduced the attendees to our first effort beyond our weekly calls to members of Congress—delivering a petition to Congress imploring it to impanel an independent commission to study Russian interference in the 2016 election. The petition had just gone live on our website, and I encouraged everyone to sign it and distribute it far and wide.

After making a few dozen laps around the dining and living rooms, I asked for questions and invited discussion. I was encouraged to hear that everyone had just as much energy about this work as I did. We talked about the newsletter schedule, how to contact members of Congress, and opportunities for working with fellow resisters in other groups and states. Everyone was on board with the plan I had laid out so far and seemed to want more. Toward the end, one person asked, "When are we going to have an in-person meeting?"

I paused for a beat. Katherine and I had discussed this. "In two weeks. The last Saturday of January." This was not what Katherine and I had discussed. "I'm still working on getting that set up. Once I get that situated, there will be a new flyer going out through the newsletter, and I encourage each of you to print it out and post it in a public place to recruit more people to our cause."

Ten minutes later, our call ended. Katherine came out of her office with her arms spread wide and a mix of a smile and a look of incredulity on her face. "What was that? I thought we agreed to get the group together every other month."

"Ha, I know!" I finally sat down after an hour of pacing. "But come on. Those people were never going to wait an entire month before the next meeting. There was too much energy on that call. So I adapted," I said with a shrug.

She laughed and agreed. We compared our notes and recapped. Thirty people had joined the call, and the discussion could not have gone better. We were building our community of like-minded activists committed to resisting Trump and the GOP. Suddenly we were two weeks away from our first in-person meeting. I needed to find a space that would hold a sizable group and design a new flyer for members to post. I started a to-do list for the meeting but decided I could finish it the next day. The adrenaline from the call was finally ebbing, and it was time for bed.

Indivisible Montgomery Newsletter: Week 4

THANK YOU ALL FOR the great work this week! Having watched some of the Senate confirmation hearings, I'm pleased to say that Sens. Cardin and Van Hollen are doing their part to expose the inexperience, corruption, and inappropriateness of Trump's cabinet nominees. I'm hopeful that some of them will be blocked.

The past three weeks have been a great way for us to get ourselves accustomed to being active advocates. As of noon on Friday [Inauguration Day], our work will have more serious consequences as we actively work to resist the Trump agenda. I look forward to doing this work with such a committed group of neighbors.

The Women's March

IT WAS THE SATURDAY after Thanksgiving, which we had celebrated with some family friends, and I had just set Hazel down for a nap. I came down the stairs and walked by Katherine's office, where she was catching up on some work and social media. "Hey, did you hear about this?" she said. "There's going to be a Women's March the day after Trump's inauguration."

I walked in and looked at her computer screen. "Huh. No, I haven't heard of that," I responded flatly.

"My friends are already making plans to go. I'm going, too," Katherine said.

"That's cool." At the time, I hadn't found the Indivisible Guide and was still looking for a widespread, long-term form of resistance to Trump and the GOP Congress. There was no way a simple march could achieve all that.

That wouldn't be the last time I was wrong.

Excitement about the march built through December and into the new year. After launching Indivisible Montgomery, at least half of my interactions with members had something to do with the Women's March: Was I going? Would Indivisible Montgomery have a meeting place? Did I know who was speaking? I couldn't help getting swept up in the excitement. This was the first event where those opposed to the Trump administration could gather shoulder to shoulder and raise our voices, and I wanted to be there. But could I go? We didn't have any family nearby and our friends were all headed to the march, so if I went, our three-year-old and eight-month-old would have to go, too. We tried our best not to let our kids limit what we did, but this was different. Neither Katherine nor I had ever been to a protest, and we had no idea what to do with two young kids at an event like this. Food, bathrooms, naps, and all the other calculations parents of young children consider just when leaving the house came with additional question marks in the context of a protest march. Even more, this was a well-publicized event. Did that mean pro-Trump counterprotestors would be there? Would they incite violence? With so many unknowns, we decided it was best for me to stay home with the girls. I was disappointed, but it was clearly the best option for the family. The program would begin with a rally starting at 10:00 a.m. and was scheduled to turn into a march around 1:15 p.m. So that I could take part in some of the festivities of the day, we invited Indivisible Montgomery marchers to our house after the march to warm up, enjoy some hot chocolate, and keep building our Indivisible Montgomery community.

On January 20, the cascade of events that started on November 8 came to fruition: Trump was sworn in as president. I had watched Barack Obama's first inauguration and attended his second. I had even watched parts of George W. Bush's inaugurations, but I couldn't bring myself to watch Trump's. Nothing about his early positions had changed during the post-election period, and he repeated all his hateful campaign rhetoric on a regular basis. His "American Carnage" inauguration speech was a continuation of his campaign, setting the tone for his presidency. There was no walking back. There was no moderation. Our resistance had begun.

Katherine holds her protest sign and poses with the girls before
heading out to the 2017 Women's March.

That night, after I helped the girls to bed, I came down to the living room to find Katherine working on her protest sign. After a brief chat, I sat on the couch and logged on to Twitter. I hadn't been on much that day because I was trying to avoid being overwhelmed by inauguration news. As I opened the app, I was astonished. "Holy shit, babe. Have you checked Twitter or Facebook this evening?"

"Only briefly," she said. "There were a ton of pictures of women on planes, buses, trains, and cars headed to their nearest metro area to join a march."

I nodded. "I think I underestimated how big this is going to be."

Interspersed among the photos was information on marches in different locations across the country—who was marching when, where to meet, and so on. The Women's March website registered several hundred marches planned across the country for January 21. Even that night, as I saw the buzz generated online, I still didn't grasp how big the day would be.

The next morning, we were all up early to have breakfast and spend some time with Katherine before her big day. Katherine bounded around the kitchen, full of adrenaline, as she talked to us about what she was eating, what she was going to bring with her, where she was meeting her friends. She was thankful that, while cold, at least it wasn't going to rain or snow. Nancy, Hazel, and I were still working on our breakfast when Katherine went off to brush her teeth and get ready to leave. As she began to bundle up, the three of us gathered around to give her a hug. Katherine opened the front door to leave, and I brought over her protest sign and handed it to her. "Do you have everything? Are you ready?"

Katherine turned and looked at me, her eyes full of anger and adrenaline. "I. Am. Livid." Here were all her emotions around Trump's election funneled into a single point of rage.

"Give 'em hell, babe," I told her. She gave me a kiss and was out the door.

Whenever I wasn't changing a diaper, making a snack, or playing with the girls, I was checking on the march. One time while her sister napped, Nancy cuddled up with me on the couch to look at picture after picture of packed Metrorail cars and people carrying protest signs to the National Mall. When we saw the aerial footage of the DC march, we couldn't believe how many people there were, and we were excited that Katherine got to be a part of this historic event. When we saw footage of what was going on across the country, I nearly choked up. Boston, St. Louis, Miami, and other cities were inundated with protestors in pink hats carrying signs. As the day rolled on, more and more cities boasted photographs of large protests that consumed parks and major roads. Some of the most inspiring pictures from the day were the handful of women holding protest signs while standing amid snowbanks in their small rural towns. No part of the country was untouched by this movement, and we were all ready to resist. This wasn't just an American phenomenon. People in London, Paris, and cities across the globe turned out to protest Trump and everything he stood for. To have such a stunning visual indication of how many people were in this fight with us made me so proud and brought me to tears.

Nearly half a million people attended the DC event, Katherine and her friends included. That was about 300,000 more people than the organizers expected. Nearly 400,000 people marched in New York City, and Los Angeles was estimated to have three-quarters of a million protestors. Upwards of five million people turned out across the US for the Women's March, and another two million people protested across the world.[1] At that point, it was the largest single protest event ever. What an incredible thing to be a part of.

Sometime around lunch, Katherine sent a text saying the program for the rally was so far behind schedule, she didn't know if they'd have time to march. But there were also so many people around her that she didn't think she'd be able to leave if there wasn't some movement. The program ended mid-afternoon after Madonna, the surprise musical guest of the day, finished her set and the march began. Katherine eventually made her way back to the Metro station and arrived home just before dinner. No Indivisible Montgomery members joined us for hot chocolate that day, which was completely understandable given how exhausted Katherine was. During dinner she regaled me and the girls with stories of uplifting chants, fun music, and energizing speeches, along with the ambient excitement of being around so many people feeding off each other's energy. Three-year-old Nancy was entranced by her animated and charismatic mother. The 2017 Women's March was an uplifting and unifying counterpoint to the doom and gloom of Trump's inauguration the previous day.

The Women's March made it clear to me that this resistance to the Trump administration was primarily a women's movement. It would be an effort largely led, organized, and conducted by women. I found it fitting and appropriate, despite realizing I would forever be a man in a women's movement. This didn't bother me. Indivisible Montgomery members might turn out to be predominantly women (they did), and Indivisible Montgomery might fail as an organization because it wasn't woman led (it didn't). I encouraged our members to find the group that best fit their interests, and if that meant they wanted a group led by a woman, they'd leave Indivisible Montgomery. What mattered more was that they continue the work of resisting Trump and his GOP sycophants. I didn't much care if it was with us or with another group. We just needed to get the job done.

Our First Meeting

"How many people do you think will show up?" Katherine asked as she helped Nancy into her seat.

I finished strapping Hazel into her car seat and sighed. "I really have no idea."

We were about to meet Indivisible Montgomery members face-to-face at our first in-person meeting, and neither of us had any idea what to expect. I had advertised the meeting extensively in the newsletter, and Katherine hung flyers and posted the meeting on online calendars. But would people show up? We had asked simple things of Indivisible Montgomery members so far—sign up for a newsletter and call your senators and representatives. Taking time to join us in the basement of the Kensington Park Library and talk politics for two hours on a Saturday morning was a much bigger commitment.

We pulled out of our driveway. "I'd be happy with 20," I said.

"Come on," Katherine said. "Ten percent of the mailing list? I'm going with at least 40."

"I don't know," I responded. "A week after the Women's March and the day after the airport protests? How does that affect people coming out?"

The night before, chaos consumed international airports across the country. Trump made good on his campaign promise to issue an executive order barring anyone from specific countries from entering the United States. All the countries listed in the EO were majority-Muslim countries, but, the administration argued, this was about national security, had nothing to do with religion, and was definitely not the ban on Muslims Trump had talked so much about during his campaign. Uh-huh. In response, people across the country flooded international airports in protest. Members of Congress went to their nearest international airport demanding to meet with federal immigration authorities to clarify how the ban was being enforced. They couldn't get straight answers because most of the authorities tasked with enforcing the ban didn't even know it was coming until they heard about it through the news. Confusion reigned.

As we drove to the library, Katherine and I continued chatting about attendance and protests. The four of us arrived to see one of the library workers opening the building. We followed them in and set up our Indivisible Montgomery sign, which happened to be the sign Katherine took to the Women's March the week before. I tried the door to the meeting room, but it was locked. While we waited for an employee to unlock it, a couple of grandmotherly women in their 60s with graying hair made their way down the stairs and tried the door as well. One turned to me. "Are you here for the Indivisible Montgomery meeting?"

"Yes, I'm Chris Pickett. I'm the leader of Indivisible Montgomery."

"Oh, fantastic! I'm Nina Liakos."

"And I'm Betty Dooley."

If I had known then that Nina and Betty would be two of the most reliable, longest-lasting volunteers for Indivisible Montgomery,

I would have hugged them. Instead, I introduced my family and continued the introductions as more people made their way down the stairs. A few minutes later, the door was unlocked, and we rushed in to set up the room. We didn't need a lot of creativity with the meeting space. It was a large rectangular room with white-painted cinder block walls and a vinyl floor. There were several stacks of chairs in one corner, a couple of tall, empty bookcases against one of the long walls, and, in another corner, a baby grand piano. I told Nina, Betty, and the others there that we would set up the chairs to face the wall with the bookcases. I started to help, but I turned around and was surprised to see that people just kept coming. I found Katherine to make sure she was OK with the girls—she had planted herself at a corner near the entrance for an easy exit if the girls needed it—and I told her I was going to position myself up front. I introduced myself to as many people as possible as I made my way to the front of the room, but I couldn't get to everyone. By the time we started at 10:30, there were 90 people joining us. Fifteen minutes later, there were 120.

Most of the chairs had been taken and people were standing where they could find space. Most attendees were women, and there was a lot of gray hair in the room—Katherine and I were among the youngest adults there. We didn't have a mic or a sound system (it hadn't even occurred to me that I would need one), but I raised my voice and was able to get everyone's attention. I started the meeting by introducing myself and followed with a surefire way to get things off on the right foot: "How many people were at the Women's March last week?" The room erupted in applause. I then launched into my vision for Indivisible Montgomery. I spoke about how resisting is

Me (*far left, standing*) in front of Indivisible Montgomery at our first meeting.
Kensington Park Library, January 28, 2017.

a long-term effort. We needed to build ourselves into an electoral force in time for the 2020 election to limit Donald Trump to a single term. We would take consistent, weekly actions to call on our members of Congress to resist normalizing Trump and his actions.

Before opening the floor to questions, I made two points. First, I encouraged everyone to sign our petition encouraging Congress to impanel an independent commission to investigate Russia's role in the 2016 election. Second, I wanted to be clear about the realities of full GOP control of the government and what we should expect of our resistance. Montgomery County was represented only by Democrats in the House and Senate, and Republicans didn't need Democratic votes to pass their agenda. Our leverage was limited. "We will fight for what is right," I said, "but we're going to lose. That's the reality of the GOP holding all the levers of power. Defeats can be demoralizing. If we are going to last for four years, we need to be able to accept and move past these losses and keep working toward the ultimate goal of getting Trump out of office."

"I don't want to wait until 2020," shouted one woman. "I want Trump out of office now!" she said, eliciting murmurs of agreement across the room.

"We will pursue every legitimate opportunity to get Trump out of office," I responded, "but in the meantime, we must focus on consistent methods to resist his plundering of our country. Our immediate task is to make sure our members of Congress stand up against Trump and his policies."

"Democrats need to grow some balls!" shouted a woman from the back.

Once we all stopped laughing, I said, "That's exactly right, and it's our job to hold them to account when they normalize Trump and his actions. Our members of Congress need to be as passionate about resisting the Trump agenda as we are, and their votes need to reflect that."

"How are we doing that with Trump's appointees? Why aren't we calling to oppose Jeff Sessions?" asked the first woman. Sessions was Trump's nominee for attorney general.

"Yes, I forgot to mention this in the beginning. Part of conserving our energy is making sure our actions are as effective as possible. That means calling when our congressmen and senators are about to vote on something critical. It just happens that our senators aren't on committees voting on Trump's worst nominees. Once the nominations move out of committee and to the Senate floor, though, we will absolutely call to tell them to oppose Sessions and others."

"Trump has been in office for only a week, and I'm already exhausted." This came from a man in front. "How long can we keep this up?"

I had been hoping someone would ask this question. "The reason to come together in a group like Indivisible Montgomery is to build our community. For each and every one of us to realize that there are people just like us taking action across our county and country every week. And because of that, it's OK if we need to take a week or two off. The others in this room will still be doing the work. But this is a community, so if you take time off, please come back. Because this won't end the way we want if I'm the only one still doing this work in November 2020."

After another hour or so of discussion, I was relieved to see the end of the meeting. Have you ever tried shouting while remaining calm? It's not easy. The adrenaline from being in front of this crowd carried me through. I had given public talks before, but it was nothing like this. Anyone who has spoken in front of a crowd loves that person in front who nods at their good points and is clearly engaged. Now imagine half the room doing that.

The discussion that morning highlighted that everyone wanted to resist Trump, but each person had an issue they wanted to be heard on. I seized the opportunity and asked people to sign up for topic-specific committees. What these committees would do and how they would fit into Indivisible Montgomery's goals was still a mystery to me. But I wasn't going to pass up the chance to harness the energy of the people in this room. After passing around sign-up sheets, we had a dozen proposed committees—including environment and science, elections, women's issues, and gun safety—and at least a dozen people signed up for each.

What a whirlwind morning. I officially ended the meeting and was mobbed by people wanting to talk more about the organization. A few minutes later I broke free and found Katherine and the girls so we could leave. As we got in the car, I couldn't help making fun of myself. "I'm never making a prediction again. 'I'd be happy if 20 people showed up.' Ha." Katherine laughed. The only way it could have been better was if I had had a microphone. As we drove home, I was surprised when Katherine asked what happened at various points of the meeting. I hadn't realized at the time, but she missed almost an hour of our two-hour meeting because Nancy needed the bathroom and both Nancy and Hazel needed a snack and some playtime. As I filled her in, I explained that our setup of Indivisible Montgomery was working the way we'd hoped. We had a web presence and the flyers recruited people to the meeting. We asked very little of people: sign up for the newsletter. Acting beyond that was up to the individual subscriber. I was unlikely to get ironclad four-year commitments from members, so we made it as easy as possible to remain a part of the organization and be a part of our work as members were able and available. We made this vision clear in the newsletter, on our phone call two weeks prior, and at the meeting. Based on their enthusiasm, our members bought in. Indivisible Montgomery was in the best position possible to operate at a high level for the next four years.

A Disconnect

At the end of 2016, the authors of the Indivisible Guide launched a national Indivisible organization to act as an information hub and provide resources for the new local groups springing up. In early January, national Indivisible announced a strategy call for all Indivisible group leaders nationwide on January 30, which happened to be two days after that first Indivisible Montgomery meeting. The call was advertised as an opportunity to learn how to organize and run a group. Indivisible Montgomery already had a successful launch and a successful meeting, and we were gaining members. But there is more than one way to run an organization, and I was happy to hear how other leaders were managing their growing pile of responsibilities.

I signed up for the call but became concerned when I received the confirmation email. The email came from Move On, not Indivisible. Move On was an organization founded nearly two decades earlier and was synonymous with the progressive wing of the Democratic Party. As I looked through the message, it became clear the call was a collaborative effort between Move On, Indivisible, and other notable progressive groups. Personally, my politics are aligned with progressivism, but my understanding of the original Indivisible Guide was that our resistance to Trump and the GOP should be a pro-democracy movement rather than a progressive movement. I didn't fault the leaders of national Indivisible for aligning themselves with

Move On and the others. Those groups were well-established organizations with existing infrastructure that could support our fledgling efforts. But it did put me in a bind. Indivisible Montgomery accepted anyone who rejected Trump and his brand of authoritarianism, whether they supported progressive policies or not. Because of our shared name, I was concerned that the alignment of national Indivisible with progressive organizations would limit Indivisible Montgomery's ability to recruit everyone we would need to do the work.

The evening of the call, I sat at the dining room table and logged on with several questions and concerns about the relationship between national Indivisible and Indivisible Montgomery. Ezra Levin and Leah Greenberg, the authors of the Indivisible Guide, started the meeting. They explained they were now co-executive directors of the Indivisible Project, a nonprofit organization that would be a resource for resistance groups across the country.

And then I got kicked out of the call.

I dialed back in. Nothing.

It took me about five minutes to reconnect. Once I was back on, Ezra and Leah were apologizing. They had to add capacity to the conference call system because more people called in than the 1,000 the original system could handle. I wasn't terribly surprised. The last time I checked Indivisible's tool to find local resistance organizations, there were nearly a dozen groups in Montgomery County alone, most of which sprang up after the Women's March.[2] If we were anywhere close to average for a large county in a metro area, it was possible thousands of group leaders were on the call.

Ezra and Leah continued discussing their plan for the national group. They were staffing up, including hiring regional liaisons to connect the various resistance groups to national Indivisible. And while they would suggest actions groups could take, national Indivisible was not going to require groups to support specific progressive policies or priorities. I found this acceptable. It meant I could chart Indivisible Montgomery's path as a pro-democracy organization regardless of the path taken by national Indivisible. The rest of the call was group leaders asking for materials and best practices for running their organization. I had hoped this part of the discussion would be useful for me, but it wasn't. Most of the groups represented on the call were around a week old, whereas Indivisible Montgomery had been around for five weeks. That may not sound like a big difference, but the problems of a week-old organization—establishing an organizational structure, setting up communications channels, and contacting other local activist organizations—I had already solved for Indivisible Montgomery. Not because I was a wunderkind, but because Katherine and I had a four-week head start and experience running volunteer organizations. As a result, the resources provided by national Indivisible in response to this phone call likely helped many groups, but the materials were not of much use for me.

National Indivisible's liaison system did come online and offer assistance, and Leah even called me out of the blue once to ask if there was anything Indivisible Montgomery needed. I appreciated the outreach. But that was months down the line. Until then, there was often a disconnect between what national Indivisible offered and what Indivisible Montgomery needed.

An Independent Commission

"Russia, if you're listening ..." These infamous words were spoken by Trump in July 2016, at a news conference where he invited Russian intelligence to hack the Clinton campaign's email system.[3] Inviting a foreign power to interfere in American elections was abhorrent and reprehensible. It was widely suspected that the Trump campaign had been cultivating foreign contacts to help win the presidency. And these suspicions grew greater as we moved closer to the election.

In June 2016, it was revealed that Russian intelligence had hacked email accounts of the Democratic National Committee, elected Democrats, and members of the Clinton campaign.[4] The Russians released the information through WikiLeaks at opportune times, often when the Trump campaign was experiencing a bad news cycle. News organizations breathlessly reported on the leaked documents, even though they contained little of importance, with the effect of minimizing negative stories about the Trump campaign. It was so obvious the Russians and the Trump campaign were working on parallel tracks that, in their final debate, Clinton called Trump the puppet of Russian dictator Vladimir Putin. Trump responded, "No puppet! You're the puppet!"[5] Clearly here was a master of the witty comeback.

With Trump's election, the investigation of Russian interference in the 2016 election became paramount. Had a foreign adversary installed in the White House someone sympathetic to their interests? Had an American campaign, wittingly or unwittingly, worked with a foreign power to win the highest elected office? In years past, this was the stuff of fiction. This time, there was sufficient compelling public evidence that the possibility could not be discounted. The hitch was that Trump would have the power to determine who ran every federal intelligence agency and would have limitless opportunities to put undue pressure on any investigation that might endanger his presidency. To be free of Trump's influence, an investigation needed to be independent of any executive branch agency.

My personal goal, beyond building up Indivisible Montgomery, was to get Congress to investigate Russia's role in the 2016 election. We had a chance to apply some real pressure. While still in the minority, Sen. Ben Cardin of Maryland was the ranking member of the Senate Foreign Relations Committee (SFRC), and he had some say in the direction of the committee. At the start of the new Congress, Indivisible Montgomery launched a petition campaign to pressure the SFRC into investigating Russian interference in the 2016 election. Our ask was for Congress to appoint an independent commission, not a congressional committee, to investigate Russia's actions affecting the presidential election. It was a long shot, but our country's electoral integrity was at stake, and we had to take every opportunity we could. To boost the Maryland signatures, I reached out to each of the eight to ten resistance groups in Montgomery County that I had contact with, asking them to spread the petition to their own members.

We needed to catch the eye of the majority as well. The chair of the SFRC was Sen. Bob Corker of Tennessee. For this petition to be relevant to Corker, I needed a boatload of Tennessee signatures. I found contact information for all the Tennessee Indivisible groups through national Indivisible's group locater tool, wrote each of them an email explaining my plan, and asked for their help. The response was fantastic. Twelve out of the sixteen groups I wrote to responded positively.

We collected nearly 800 signatures over a two-week period, with an eye toward delivering the petitions to Corker's and Cardin's offices on January 31. Even though we coordinated only with groups in Tennessee and Maryland, people posting the petition on their social media pages led to people in 31 other states signing as well. At the first Indivisible Montgomery meeting, I advertised a trip to the Capitol to deliver the petitions and told anyone interested in joining where to meet. On the morning of January 31, the day after the group leadership call with national Indivisible, Katherine and I dropped off Hazel at daycare and Nancy at preschool and then hopped the Metro to Union Station. From there, we walked to the Hart Senate Office Building and found about a dozen Indivisible Montgomery members in the atrium ready to advocate for an investigation of the 2016 election.

As we approached Ben Cardin's office, I stopped the group in the hall just outside the office doors and asked how many of them had been in a meeting like this. Two people raised their hands. "OK, here's how the meeting will go," I said. "If we're able to meet with a staffer, I'll start by explaining that we're all a part of Indivisible Montgomery in Montgomery County, Maryland, and we're here because we want the senator to support efforts to investigate Russia's role in the 2016 election. Then we'll do a round of introductions—we'll each say our name and what city we're from. After that, I'll explain and present the petition, and then it will be a free-flowing conversation. Any questions?"

They all looked at each other, then Katherine turned to me and said, "That was good. I think we got it."

I walked into Cardin's office and explained to the staffer in the reception area who we were and why we were there, and I asked if there was anyone we could speak with. A few minutes later, a young staffer told us their conference rooms were in use. He invited us into the hallway to talk. The discussion went exactly as I had told the group. Once I was done explaining the petition, I faded back and let the members guide the conversation, stepping in only to smooth over any confusion. It went well. Everyone joined the conversation and made cogent points, and no one forced the conversation in a direction it wasn't already going. I was proud.

We shook hands with Cardin's staffer and made our way to Bob Corker's office. While I had been fairly certain Cardin's office would produce someone to talk to us—members of Congress pay attention when a group of constituents shows up—without anyone from Tennessee in our group, I wasn't so sure about Corker's office. I took the same approach as in Cardin's office, asking to speak with someone. We milled about in the waiting area for 10 minutes as they checked to see if anyone was available to meet. Eventually they informed us no one had time in their schedule. I explained why we were there, mentioned the significance of our petition, and handed the staffer in the lobby the petition with signatures. We didn't get our meeting, but we delivered our message.

This was a big success. I was happy we delivered the petition to the Cardin office first. That gave our group a positive experience to start the day. Our group of inexperienced activists went to Capitol Hill and made a difference on a critical issue. It would take more than one set of signatures to see the change we wanted, but this was an important step.

Meet and Greet

INDIVISIBLE MONTGOMERY WAS THE first resistance group in Montgomery County to register with Indivisible's group locater tool, but we were not the first or only resistance group in the county. Between the Indivisible tool, people reaching out to me, and information I came across myself, I tallied around a dozen resistance groups in Montgomery County by the time Indivisible Montgomery held its first meeting at the end of January. I made it a priority to talk to the leaders of each of these organizations. Most of us were fledgling groups, and we would be more effective if we understood each other's focus and worked together when appropriate. Open communications also meant we were less likely to unnecessarily duplicate efforts when it wasn't beneficial.

Effective outreach with these organizations would take time, and time was one commodity I was running short of. Even before the first Indivisible Montgomery meeting, I had been looking for someone to take over outreach activities. I had had a few email exchanges with Kyle Benton, who seemed keen on knowing more about how Indivisible Montgomery was being run. I offered him the chance to lead our outreach, and he agreed. I was thrilled. I suggested we should convene the local leaders, and he took the reins organizing the gathering. I met Kyle, a thin guy with wire-rimmed glasses and shoulder-length black hair, at the first Indivisible Montgomery meeting. We briefly discussed the plan for the group leaders meeting, and I said I'd see him there.

On a brisk, slushy February morning one week later, I arrived at Kyle's parents' upscale house in the middle of the county. Kyle invited me in and explained that he spent most of his time in college in western Maryland, and he stayed with his parents when he came back to Montgomery County. Kyle walked me through the living room full of mismatched furniture and odd trinkets from travels abroad. It was quirky, but it had what every meaningful collection of people dedicated to fighting for their country needed: a bunch of chairs.

By the time everyone had arrived, there were 15 of us representing a variety of resistance organizations, including DoTheMostGood, Rockville Resistance, Indivisible Cabin John, and Takoma Park Mobilization. We made brief introductions, and I connected with some of the people I had already spoken to on the phone as we grabbed pastries and coffee. When we took our seats, I kicked off the meeting. After introducing myself and thanking Kyle and his parents for the use of their house, I continued, "We're all here because we're leading organizations dedicated to resisting Donald Trump and the GOP. The goal of this meeting is to meet each other and figure out how we might work together to amplify our efforts while minimizing duplication."

We worked our way around the circle introducing ourselves, and it became evident working together was going to be a challenge. Each group was in some different level of organization. Takoma Park Mobilization had been around well before 2016 and had an established structure. DoTheMostGood, Rockville Resistance, and Indivisible Montgomery formed shortly after the election and had some degree of leadership and committee structure to speak of. A handful of groups were still in the beginning stages of building up their leadership and formalizing their methods of outreach. Others formed in the wake of the Women's March two weeks prior and didn't even have a formal membership to speak of at that point. Beyond organizational structure, we also each had a different focus for our activism. Indivisible Montgomery focused on federal issues. Takoma Park Mobilization and DoTheMostGood addressed state issues as well. The rest hadn't decided yet what they wanted to work on. We said some good things about working together, but the differences in the structure and maturity of the groups made this more difficult than I originally expected.

With one exception. We agreed we should all host a town hall during the February congressional recess. The nationwide resistance had circled the end of February as a moment of opportunity. This would be the first congressional recess of the session, and many members of Congress had already started publicizing town halls in their districts. Except ours hadn't. This was an opportunity for us to organize an event, invite our representatives and senators, and express ourselves directly to them.

We spent the last half of the meeting discussing everything that needed to be done. Reserving a venue, recruiting volunteers, inviting speakers, and other tasks were assigned. Even with this level of coordination, getting everything set for an event three weeks away was going to be a tight turnaround. Takoma Park Mobilization took the lead—they had organized events like this before, knew the venues, and had contacts with elected representatives throughout Montgomery County and the state of Maryland. The rest of us would play our parts, from setting up the schedule, finding volunteers to work the event, and publicizing the event to our own members.

Despite the complications that the varied structures across organizations presented, the meeting went better than expected. My goal was to forge the beginnings of fruitful partnerships with others. We did that. And we launched ourselves into a complex effort to hold a town hall meeting in three weeks. It would be challenging, but we were all driven and had our specific tasks. I enjoyed being with other group leaders. We were all going through many of the same things, from launching our organizations to juggling work and family life. Unfortunately, this would be the only time we got together. After the town hall, about a third of the groups either folded into larger groups or faded away. Such was life in these first few months of resistance.

Finding Time

I LEFT THE MEETING at Kyle's house excited and with several new additions to my to-do list. The past week had been busy: our first Indivisible Montgomery meeting, a phone call with national Indivisible, our trip to Capitol Hill, and the meeting with the other group leaders. Along with my job and time with my family, the only other thing I had time for that week was writing the Indivisible Montgomery newsletters. My schedule was a little clearer for the next couple of weeks, leaving me free to tackle some of the necessary activities that had slipped down the priorities list.

I was looking forward to relaxing with my family for much of the day, but I had a 20-minute drive home, so I used that time to figure out how I'd organize the Indivisible Montgomery committees. These committees were going to be the centerpiece of volunteer engagement, expanding the breadth of topics our organization could engage on. I couldn't personally oversee the work of each committee, so I decided I would email the people who had signed up for each committee asking them to identify a leader who would organize the group and report to me. This would remove the pressure I felt to focus on every issue the Trump administration was acting on, as well as give our volunteers some leeway to pursue the topics they were most interested in and to develop events that furthered Indivisible Montgomery's goals.

I also needed an overall leadership team to provide opinions and advice on how the organization should be run and how to approach different issues. While I could make all the decisions, I didn't want my blind spots to lead to a boneheaded error that would forever taint the organization. Because Kyle Benton had already proven himself as a liaison to other resistance groups, he became our director of outreach. Gracie Dominguez and Lois Hampton reached out to me asking to be part of Indivisible Montgomery's leadership. Gracie stepped in as our director of communications. And a while later, Loid volunteered to be the director of administration and coordinate Indivisible Montgomery activities. I felt good about having a leadership team I could trust to shoulder some of the load. Because that load was building. Fast.

A few days later, as the committees were working themselves out, I was complaining to Katherine that I had another coffee meeting with a leader of a group interested in Indivisible Montgomery's work. Our group's public presence, which had brought our membership up to 1,400 people by mid-February, also brought a variety of folks eager to talk to me about the organization and how we could effectively resist the current administration. I met with leaders of religious activist organizations, other resistance group leaders, and even a representative of the Montgomery County Democratic Party. (She was trying to figure out if I had ambitions to run for public office. I didn't, but I also didn't feel like I owed her or the party anything, so I played coy to keep the mystery alive.)

I took most of the meeting requests, often driving to far-flung parts of the county to talk in person. It was while I was complaining about these drives that Katherine stopped me: "This is the last meeting." I didn't fully understand what she meant. These people wanted to talk to me, and if that would improve Indivisible Montgomery's actions, I should take their meeting. She knew what I was thinking. "No more in-person meetings. You're driving all over the county losing time from your work and your family. And you're not being paid for any of this."

She was right. One way to save time in my busy week was to cut out unnecessary travel. After lunch, I converted every upcoming activism-related meeting I had to a phone call. My shoulders immediately relaxed when I realized how much time that would save. Not only did this give me more time to spend with Katherine and the girls, but it also kept me from burning out much faster than I would if I kept trekking all over the county.

Town Hall

Within a week of sending out the initial emails, Indivisible Montgomery had six committees with leaders, and further email pestering found leaders for another three a week later. By mid-February, we had committees on Conflicts of Interest, Women's Issues, Environment and Science, Health Care, Communications, and more. Some committees we planned, like gun safety, never got off the ground because no one stepped up to lead. While I regret these missed opportunities, I had too much on my plate to lead them myself so I had to let them go.

The upcoming multi-organization town hall quickly became the largest part of my resistance work in February. I had been tasked with finding a venue, but I was getting nowhere. We wanted a place that could hold a few thousand people, and there just weren't that many places in the county fitting the bill that we could rent on short notice. However, my colleagues at Takoma Park Mobilization heard that the Silver Spring Civic Center was available the night we wanted. It's a fantastic spot in the middle of Silver Spring, and it even gave us the option of having events inside and outside at the same time. Takoma Park Mobilization submitted a deposit and, voilà, we had a venue.

Two weeks out from the event, though, we had made little progress with invitations to our representatives. We invited each of the federal elected representatives covering Montgomery County—

Representatives Jamie Raskin, John Sarbanes, and John Delaney, and Senators Ben Cardin and Chris Van Hollen. Raskin agreed right away, Delaney never responded, Sarbanes declined as he was going to be out of the country, Van Hollen said he'd get back to us, and Cardin's office explicitly told us the senator would attend only if Van Hollen did. I think the elected officials didn't know yet what to make of our nascent resistance. Days ticked by and, with only Raskin confirmed, we invited some members of Congress from outside Montgomery County, along with elected state and county-level elected officials. Most of them accepted.

A week later, videos were all over the news showing Indivisible and associated activists confronting members of Congress in other districts. CNN reported, "Anger erupts at Republican town halls."[6] The stories didn't do justice to the frustrated and angry constituents taking Republicans and mealymouthed Democrats to task for not standing up to Trump. It was invigorating to see people across the country doing what we were doing—getting in front of their elected representatives and holding them to account. We had staunch Democrats representing us here in Montgomery County, so we didn't expect our town hall to produce these kinds of confrontations, but we were still ready to make sure our representatives weren't going to normalize Trump and his GOP. Shortly after these stories aired, Van Hollen accepted our invitation. When we went back to Cardin with that information, he also accepted. As news of our momentum and our growing list of top-notch speakers circulated, Sarbanes realized that, actually, he would be in the country and that he was available. We had almost every elected federal official from Montgomery County attending our town hall.

As part of the organizing committee for the Montgomery County Town Hall on February 26, 2017, I had backstage access and met my congressmen, Rep. Jamie Raskin (*right*) and Sen. Ben Cardin (*facing page*).

ON THE DAY OF the town hall, I left for the Civic Center shortly after dinner. It was just me that night. My whole family had attended the second Indivisible Montgomery meeting the day before, and we were still trying to get our schedule settled for the upcoming workweek. Besides, the town hall was too late for the girls to attend. So if Katherine were going to attend, that meant hiring a babysitter. It wasn't as if she and I would get to hang out at the town hall, because I would be working in the background to ensure a smooth event. Katherine preferred to spend the night with Nancy and Hazel rather than sitting alone in a crowd listening to politicians speak. I didn't blame her.

As I approached the Civic Center, I saw the finishing touches being put on the outdoor stage. I joined the other resistance leaders inside and was happy to see the indoor stage complete. Because we expected a large turnout, we had reserved the indoor area for people

who needed to sit, people with children, and others who couldn't be outside in the cold February night. The outdoor area was for everyone who could handle the elements. We had only one program, though, which meant speakers would shuttle between stages, and we needed separate schedules for each stage. My job was to escort Senator Cardin from stage to stage. I met some of his staffers, and Cardin arrived maybe 15 minutes before the event began. He and I spoke only briefly. Cardin seemed to be more interested in talking to the other elected officials or his own staff than in meeting his constituents and the people hosting the event. I also introduced myself to Representative Raskin, my newly elected representative from Maryland's Eighth District. He seemed excited to meet me and the other leaders of the various "Tocquevillian groups," as he called us.

Cardin and I started the evening outside. The program began with some local officials, followed by Van Hollen and then Cardin.

It quickly became evident that was the wrong order. Van Hollen was so much more dynamic than Cardin that he should have finished the program. Cardin didn't say anything wrong; he just lacked Van Hollen's charisma. By the time the two senators started speaking, there were 500–600 people surrounding the outside stage. When they finished, we took the elected officials inside, where I was surprised to walk by Rep. John Delaney. Despite the fact that he never acknowledged our invitation, I guess someone alerted him to the big event happening in Silver Spring and he needed to attend. The inside stage was running a little behind, which turned out great for me because I got to hear Raskin spit fire about Trump and his GOP enablers to the 300 or more people gathered there. He got the crowd to go along with the chant he had made up at the Women's March: "No Trump! No Pence! Impeach them on emoluments!" It was fantastic.

We repeated the outdoor program inside, and vice versa, and then the town hall ended. It had no viral moments but was undoubtedly a success in turning people out and spreading the message about resisting Trump. The energy level from the attendees had not waned since the first Indivisible Montgomery meeting a month ago. Raskin was the clear star of the event—he was the only one who spoke to the passions of the attendees. Van Hollen came close. The other star of the event was Obamacare. Health care was the only topic touched on by all our speakers as they promised to do what they could to protect President Obama's signature accomplishment from repeal. The other organizers and I all agreed that the first major coalition effort of resistance groups in Montgomery County was an unmitigated success.[7]

Dine-Arounds

From the inception of Indivisible Montgomery, a constant refrain was that members wanted a way to come together. I was juggling so many activities that I couldn't give sufficient thought to this. Katherine and others suggested forming an email list for discussion. I wasn't supportive at all. I felt that these groups were often dominated by a vocal minority pushing an agenda that may not have been the same as Indivisible Montgomery's. This would be the opposite of building community, and it would also put me in the position of moderating content. I should have said as much to Katherine. Instead, I dragged my feet until the issue went away and people stopped asking for it.

Another of Katherine's ideas, which I supported enthusiastically, was dine-arounds. In one weekend, Indivisible Montgomery members would host small potluck brunches or dinners at six to eight homes across the county, spaced out geographically so members could attend an event close to them. These events provided a more personal experience of community. In the middle of February, I sent out a call for hosts through our newsletter. I forwarded the volunteers' contact information to Katherine, and she took it from there. She worked with potential hosts and identified the first weekend of March as the best option for the event. And then she coordinated all aspects of the dine-arounds, including determining who welcomed kids, who had pets, and how to set up a form for attendees to indicate what they were going to bring. After the sign-up deadline passed, the host would communicate with everyone who planned to attend at their house, providing their address and any last-minute instructions. To entice more people to attend, Katherine suggested that a member of Indivisible Montgomery's leadership show up at each dine-around event so attendees would have access to and could get information from leadership.

This was a problem.

The senior leadership team that had come together just a month ago had fallen apart. Gracie wanted to resist the Trump administration in ways other than what Indivisible Montgomery was doing. Kyle stopped responding to emails, and I had no other way to get a hold of him. I never heard from him again. That left me, Lois Hampton, and Katherine (even though she wasn't officially leadership) to speak for the organization. A few days before the planned dine-arounds, Lois volunteered to go to two events, Katherine would go to one, and I agreed to go to four.

On Saturday night, I left home at 5:00 for my first event, interested to see how the dine-around experiment would turn out. This was a dinner in northern Montgomery County. As I walked in, guests were chatting in front of floor-to-ceiling windows that looked out on a field and pond. I was lost in the view when the host startled me by asking to take my coat. We laughed it off, I picked out a bottle of beer, and I walked over to mingle and introduce myself. One woman in her mid-50s with graying hair looked at me with side-eye and said, "Wait, are you *that* Chris? The one from the newsletter?"

"Um, yeah."

"Oh, well hello!" and she shook my hand with a big smile on her face.

That might be the closest I ever come to knowing what a celebrity feels like.

A handful of attendees arrived after me, and once we finished introductions, the host turned to me and said, "Should we get started?" She was referring to the discussion topics Katherine provided to the dine-around hosts to make sure the evening was productive. I wasn't sure whether hosts intended to start with the discussion topics or leave them for after dinner. This group wanted to jump right in, talking about how Indivisible Montgomery could improve our resistance and how we were going to stop the GOP's attempt to repeal Obamacare. It was a good conversation, though I had to leave partway into it because I had several more dine-arounds to attend that night. They understood, gave me some food, and sent me on my way.

The next venue was Tamara Prince and Alan Crane's house. Tamara and Alan would become two of our most consistent volunteers through the entirety of my time leading Indivisible Montgomery—hosting dine-arounds, attending meetings, working on get-out-the-vote efforts, donating, and more. When I walked in, I was equally amazed at their house, even though it was quite different from my first stop. Ornate tables and other furniture were sensibly scattered throughout the surprisingly spacious rooms. Small groups of three or four people were spread out across the living and dining rooms. The intense conversations of my first dine-around were absent, replaced by people laughing and picking at the food on their plates. I must have looked lost because Tamara walked up and introduced herself, recognizing me from the in-person meetings. She went straight to business. "Should we call everyone together for the discussion topics?"

I was still taking in the scene when she asked this. "Uh ..."

"I'll let you get something to eat and drink, and then I'll call everyone together." So I filled my second plate of the night while Tamara gathered the group. The conversation we had was a blast. Everyone was energetic and, just as at the previous dine-around, wanted to know how we would defend Obamacare from repeal. As we finished the last discussion question, I checked my phone. It was time for me to leave if I wanted to get to all my events that night.

The third event was at Linda McMillan's house, and this was a big question mark. After signing up to host, Linda had gone AWOL. Katherine did everything she could to connect with her, to no avail. The day before the dine-arounds, Katherine sent word to the people signed up for Linda's event that we had to cancel. Linda then emailed a few hours later with a long explanation of what had gone wrong. We relayed the change in information to the people who had planned to attend, but most of them had already switched to a different event. Because of this, I didn't know what to expect when I arrived. I knocked and Linda welcomed me into a dimly lit house that smelled amazing. She apologized again, and I said that these things happen, that I appreciated her offer to host, and that I hoped it would go smoother next time. Only one of the people to sign up for her house showed up. The two of them had never met before, but they were having a great time chatting. It made me happy that, even with the canceled/uncanceled event, these folks were still able to do the work of building our community. I was getting tired from all the driving and conversation, so I excused myself after only 20 minutes.

But my night wasn't done. After those three stops, I headed over to the home of Jessica Flint, a friend of mine and Katherine's.

Shortly after we sent out the dine-around information a few weeks back, I received an Evite from Jessica inviting my family to a potluck at her house on this Saturday night. She hadn't offered to host a dine-around, but she was an active Indivisible Montgomery member. She was on the newsletter list and at our meetings. She knew when this event was happening, and Katherine and I were confused that she was having a dinner party on the night of the dine-arounds but not actually taking part in the dine-arounds. On the other hand, finishing the night at a friend's house sounded fun and relaxing. I arrived at Jessica's, grabbed a samosa and a beer, found a chair, and settled in to listen to some random conversations. I had just taken a bite of my samosa when I realized the conversation had mostly stopped and about 20 people at the party were looking at me. My first thought was, "Am I supposed to be using a fork?"

As I started looking for silverware, a person across the table asked me a political question. Wait. So I go to a random social gathering with a bunch of people I don't know, and we're going to start talking politics? Certainly not impossible. But waaait. This question wasn't just about politics. It was about activism. So Jessica told some of her friends I'm leading Indivisible Montgomery and they want free advice on resisting? Also not impossible. But waaaaait a minute. Jessica planned a dinner party on dine-around night and invited me to an event to talk politics—goddammit, she was hosting a rogue dine-around. Thankfully, the realization didn't make me choke on the samosa. I composed myself, and we had a great conversation. It wasn't the unwinding experience I had expected but still a good time.

The next day, Katherine, the girls, and I packed up and went to the final dine-around. I was happy to not have to take more time away from my family. But attending the same event didn't mean we were spending time together. Young children require a lot of attention, especially in a house owned by people who like kids but don't want kids touching their things. While I was being leaderly with the dine-around attendees, Katherine was in the kitchen rolling a car to Nancy and trying to keep Hazel happy. This was the first time Katherine attended an Indivisible Montgomery event without taking part in it. It was not anywhere close to the last.

These dine-arounds were our heaviest lift so far as an organization. Katherine was the backbone of the effort, arranging everything ahead of time. I was busy with so many other things that I was thankful I could trust someone as capable as Katherine with this. While I enjoyed all the events I went to, I was exhausted by the end of the weekend. Katherine was understandably wiped out, too. It seems ridiculous that we'd do these events quarterly. But that's what we did.

Fighting Obamacare Repeal

THE KEY TO LONG-TERM, constant resistance, in my opinion, is consistent communication. Having a coherent message helps, yes, but also sending the message at the same time each week. That's why, on the evening of the final dine-around, I sat on the couch with my laptop composing the Monday morning newsletter. Just because I was exhausted from a weekend of resistance work didn't mean the next week would take care of itself. The discussions from the dine-arounds made clear what I needed to write about: protecting Obamacare from GOP repeal efforts. Much like at the town hall a couple weeks before, health care was the only policy to come up at every event I attended. Since Republicans won the House in 2010, they had passed dozens of bills to repeal the law, but because President Obama held the veto pen, these GOP bills were political statements rather than policy solutions. With the House, Senate, and White House now under unified GOP control, the least surprising action Republicans would take in 2017 was attempting to repeal Obamacare.

Republicans said they had good-faith concerns about the government playing an outsized role in the medical insurance industry. This was a lie. The fact is that many of the policies in Obamacare had their foundation in Republican policies proposed or enacted at the state level. In an actual good-faith effort, those portions would have served as a foundation for negotiations on a compromise bill. Instead, Obamacare served as a proxy for everything Republicans hated about Barack Obama and the Democratic Party. However, now in complete control of the government, Republicans found themselves painted into a corner. By 2017, the Affordable Care Act, the formal name for Obamacare, had been in effect nearly seven years and its benefits were felt by people in every state. Repealing the bill meant taking health care away from millions. To follow through on their promise without causing a catastrophe, they needed to repeal Obamacare while replacing it with something that would leave unharmed those who benefited from the law. This seemed an impossible needle to thread.

At the beginning of March, freshly back from being hammered in town halls across the country, the GOP unveiled its bill to repeal and replace Obamacare. It was breathtakingly destructive. And they knew it. GOP leadership knew there was no real way to improve the bill, so they decided to try to rush the repeal bill through and deal with the fallout later. But the entire Indivisible movement and related groups, ready for this, had mobilized. The previous two months of learning to resist primed our members for the first real legislative battle of the session.

The Indivisible Montgomery Health Care committee, led by Martin Trocki, crafted our efforts to stand against the GOP bill. I took Martin's suggestions and translated those into our weekly actions. His committee also kept us apprised of rallies and other events around the area where we could demonstrate and show our opposition to Obamacare's repeal. We worked alongside national

Indivisible as they and other groups set up phone banking networks, connecting activists with people in other states to encourage them to call their members of Congress. We were taking every avenue we had available to save this law.

The public pressure was so intense that rumors emerged only a few days after the bill was unveiled, suggesting that some Republicans were telling colleagues they wouldn't vote for the bill. Rumors weren't votes, though, and we didn't relent. Between the GOP leadership's intransigence and the continued efforts of grassroots activists across the country, it took about a week for vulnerable Republican members of the House to publicly announce they would not vote for the Obamacare repeal bill. Here was more than rumors; this was a real commitment. House leadership thought the naysayers were either bluffing or could eventually be won over. Leadership served notice the House would vote on the bill on March 24. A showdown was set.

Our work went into overdrive as we continued to use every lever available to pressure the House to abandon its efforts to repeal Obamacare. I impressed on our members that the only people we should be calling individually were the people who represented us. Calls to a representative who wasn't our own would be ignored by their office and may edge out a call from an actual constituent they would listen to. I kept directing people to post on their social media feeds, contact their relatives in other states, and use the Indivisible phone banks to encourage people in other states to tell their members of Congress to vote against repeal. The House went into session on Friday, March 24, and leadership informed members they would vote on the repeal of Obamacare sometime that day. Publicly, a few dozen Republicans indicated they would oppose the repeal effort, and many more had not committed. Where would they land when it came time to vote?

We never got a chance to find out. Mere hours away from the vote on the repeal bill, leadership withdrew the legislation from the calendar before the House could vote on it.[8] Too many Republicans had signaled they'd vote against the bill, and rather than suffer a humiliating defeat, GOP leadership abandoned the vote.

We won!

I was stunned. Republicans came into the year holding every lever of power in the federal government. I expected us to lose for a long time—every nomination, every rule change, every vote. But here we were at the end of the third month of this administration with an improbable legislative victory. I was also proud of how quickly we had matured as an organization. We started with a dozen people who had little to no activism experience, and now we were a community of 1,400 seasoned, successful activists. We effectively worked together with groups from across the country, and we had notched an unexpected victory.

The Indivisible Montgomery meeting the next day was jubilant.

Indivisible Montgomery Newsletter: Week 12

March 23, 2017

Yesterday, [Rep. Devin] Nunes informed the media that he received a leak of classified information from an unnamed source concerning the inadvertent surveillance of Trump aides working on the transition team. Now, the only reason there would be inadvertent surveillance of Trump aides is if they were speaking to foreign operatives already under surveillance or if foreign operatives were speaking about them. But then in a bizarre turn of events, Nunes went and told the White House about it.

Let's unpack that a little: The leader of [the House Permanent Select Committee on Intelligence] investigating the White House for potentially colluding with foreign powers during the presidential campaign (1) took leaked, confidential information and (2) without verifying it (3) let the people whose communications were captured by covert surveillance know that their communications were captured by covert surveillance. Even Sen. John McCain is now saying the House can't conduct an unbiased investigation.

I have to agree. Not sure how you run an independent investigation when you tell the targets of your investigation that you have confidential information on them. But apparently, that just happened.

My Double Life

OUR FIRST PETITION URGING Congress to impanel an independent commission to investigate the 2016 election was successful in that Indivisible Montgomery ran an effective signature-gathering campaign. There had been no congressional movement on an independent commission, though, and we needed to do more. Our next step would be to get signatures from the constituents of everyone on the Senate Foreign Relations Committee, not just Senators Corker and Cardin.

In mid-February, I asked three Indivisible Montgomery members—Catherine Schupp, Mollie Ferguson, and Lauren Petersen—to take the lead on a new committee I was calling National Engagement. This group would serve as our liaison to Indivisible groups across the country and help align our efforts. Their first task was to contact those groups in all the SFRC-represented states. We would launch a new petition for people from all the states represented on the SFRC to sign. That would make the petition relevant to every senator on the committee.

I thought finding other groups to work with would be easy. When I founded Indivisible Montgomery, I worked very hard on our group's branding. I wanted people in the community to know who we were, which meant we had to present ourselves the same way every time members, prospective members, and the community at large interacted with us. Our website and our newsletter had "Indivisible Montgomery" in a banner across the top. My email address was indivisiblemontgomery@gmail.com. Every time one of our organization members called their member of Congress, I encouraged them to say they were with Indivisible Montgomery. Outside of conversations with Katherine, I couldn't bring myself to even abbreviate our name to "IM."

When asking the National Engagement committee to contact other Indivisible groups, I pointed them to the national Indivisible website. The site had a handy tool for visitors to type in a zip code and find all the contact information of all groups within a specified range, such as 25 miles. This was the same tool I'd used to gather Tennessee signatures to present to Senator Corker. What the committee found was that there were often knots of similarly sounding groups within a small area. Were these the same group listed in multiple ways or several individual groups whose leaders all had the same idea? I was surprised but shouldn't have been. Despite ours being the first Indivisible group in Montgomery County to register with the national Indivisible tool, that didn't keep such groups as Indivisible MoCo and Indivisible Montgomery County from forming with names obnoxiously close to ours.

Mollie, Catherine, and Lauren agreed to divide the states we were targeting equally and do their best to reach all the resistance groups we could find contact information for. Once the National Engagement committee had made positive contact and explained our plan to contact the SFRC, all the groups were on board. Thanks to their tireless efforts, the petition gained well over 10,000 signatures in two weeks. We specifically partnered with a few dozen resistance groups in SFRC states, but social media and word of mouth expanded our reach to the point that we had signatures of people from over 190 Indivisible groups and residents of all 50 states.

In the middle of March, I led a dozen Indivisible Montgomery members to Capitol Hill to deliver the petitions. About half of the group had attended our previous trip to the Capitol. Katherine, busy at work and having already been, skipped this iteration. The meetings themselves were effective but unremarkable. Cardin's staffer told us there wasn't much Cardin could do as part of the committee minority, and he encouraged us to keep up the pressure on Republican offices. Corker's staff said launching a new investigation would be counterproductive because this commission would interfere with investigations already underway at the FBI and the House and Senate Intelligence Committees. This was bunk. Nothing was keeping these investigations from cooperating or having witnesses testify multiple times. We may not have been able to change minds in the Corker office, but we held our own and made the forceful argument we intended. We walked out of the meetings feeling we had done some good work to push for an independent investigation.

Somewhat abruptly after the Corker meeting, I said, "I need to leave." The outing had run slightly long and I needed to find a secluded place to make a call. I worked for a volunteer organization called Rescuing Biomedical Research (RBR) as the inaugural director, and my job was to guide the organization in its work to make positive reforms benefiting trainees and researchers across the country. I had a regularly scheduled call with Shirley Tilghman, former president of Princeton University and now my boss, to discuss progress on RBR projects.

Why have a work call with my boss directly on the heels of activist meetings on Capitol Hill? Because I hadn't told Shirley that I founded and was leading Indivisible Montgomery. I hadn't told her because I was scared. If I asked to reschedule our standing call, she may have asked why, and I didn't want to lie to her. Over and over, I played what-if scenarios in my head of telling her about Indivisible Montgomery. Maybe she would be supportive—the entirety of RBR and I were aligned politically. But it was also likely she would see the same conflicts I did. RBR's work was to advocate for changes to federal biomedical research policy. Indivisible Montgomery actively opposed most policies of the Trump administration. Could one person effectively lead an organization working through the system to make real change and, at the same time, lead another organization built to oppose the administration running that system? I felt I could keep my RBR and Indivisible Montgomery lives separate, but what if Shirley thought differently? Would she make me choose between Indivisible Montgomery and RBR? I didn't want to find out.

I called Shirley and apologized for the background noise, letting her know I was on Capitol Hill. RBR had multiple ongoing projects, but none had made much progress during the past week so I expected it to be a short call. I was about to say goodbye when she asked, "So what takes you to Capitol Hill today?" She sounded genuinely interested.

Even though I had done so much to prepare for this call and still protect my role with Indivisible Montgomery, I had not anticipated this glaringly obvious question. And now I was forced into the position I was trying to avoid: either lie to Shirley or plunge headlong into the conflicts of interest problem.

"I'm helping some friends from my last job talk to senators about NIH funding." The lie was the easiest way out. I didn't feel good about it, though.

"Oh, sounds like fun! Have a great time."

On the Metro ride home, I was replaying my conversation with Shirley. Now I had more scenarios to run through. How does this lie play out? Should I come clean or let it slide? What if she asked about this Capitol visit next week?

While deep in thought, I received a call from a number I didn't recognize. Given all the new people I was talking to as the Indivisible Montgomery director, this was a regular occurrence. I answered, and the caller identified himself as a TV news reporter. I bolted upright, startling the woman sitting next to me. Apparently, an active and engaged Indivisible Montgomery member told one of his friends about our petition, and this friend happened to be a reporter for the local CBS affiliate. He wanted to talk about our goals with the petition effort. My lie to Shirley moved to the back burner as I realized he was suggesting he and his cameraman come to my house for an interview. I ran some quick calculations of how long it would take me to get home, and we agreed the CBS team would meet me at my house in an hour. Once the train pulled into my station, I rushed out and ran to the car. I burst into the house, roughly setting down my messenger bag, tossing my suit coat aside, and babbling to Katherine about the reporter. After she got me to stop moving and take a breath, I was able to explain clearly what was going on. She gave me a big hug and then said, "We have a noisy dog and two small children. Do the interview outside."

I walked down our front steps and sat down to catch my breath. A few minutes later, the reporter and his cameraman arrived. I explained about the noisy house, and they agreed outside was better. The reporter and I walked along the sidewalk as he asked me questions. I thought I did a pretty good job. The cameraman also did a close-up of the letter we brought to Capitol Hill while I explained its contents. The whole experience took 10 minutes, but I went back inside completely exhausted. It had been one hell of a day, and we hadn't even had dinner yet. Katherine and I watched the 10:00 p.m. news that evening and were excited when "Indivisible Montgomery" showed on the upcoming stories ticker. Woo-hoo! We didn't get cut! The anchor introduced our story, and there I was on TV! They showed me walking up the sidewalk chatting with the reporter and then cut to me discussing the letter and why it was important. It was a 30-second spot, but my name and our organization were on TV, along with a description of what we were doing. I couldn't ask for better advertising than that.

As I went to bed that night, I reflected on the day. The signature drive and petition delivery went better than I expected. Getting Congress to act requires many small nudges from activists like us, and we did some good work in that regard. And topping it off with a TV spot was more than I thought possible. As we lay in bed talking, Katherine said, "Well, it's good Shirley lives in New Jersey. If she had seen your spot on the Maryland evening news, your lie would have been for nothing."

Family

THE 2016 ELECTION BROKE a lot of families, and mine was no different. Politically, my dad was a non-voter, my mom and sister voted Republican, and I voted Democrat. How we ended up this way, I'm not sure. When I lived at home, the political conversations we had were odd. Find the right historical political question, and my dad would go on at length, often going off on tangents that only he could follow. As for current affairs, conversations in the family were often short and superficial.

My mom was the person in my family I was closest with. When I was growing up, she was a stay-at-home mom and part-time Mary Kay consultant until I was in high school, when she dropped the cosmetics and got a full-time job. In retrospect, this was the first step in her steady gain of confidence and independence, integrating her best interests into those of the family instead of sacrificing them. Several years later, as I started my second year of college, my mom recognized that my dad was in a depressive spiral dealing with the demons from his Air Force career, and rather than getting caught up in it, she decided to make a new life for herself. They separated, and a year later they were divorced. Since the early 2000s, my mom and I had spoken every Sunday. We talked about our weeks and if we had anything exciting coming up. Once Nancy and Hazel came along, I gave her updates on the new things the girls were doing. We never lived in the same city after she left my dad, but we saw each other once or twice a year.

My mom and I kept up our weekly calls after the 2016 election. Without her saying anything, it was clear she had held to her Republican voting pattern. Despite his rank misogyny and blatant anti-Semitism (my mom is Jewish), she voted for Trump. This grated on me, but I didn't bring it up directly. I knew that if I precipitated a direct confrontation, she would shut down and stop talking. So I didn't ask about her motivations, but there was nothing keeping me from expressing my feelings. I didn't hide my despondence at Trump's victory. I made very clear my concern about the direction of our country under the incoming administration. The conversation never went anywhere, though, as she never engaged.

In mid-January, I was riding the high of launching Indivisible Montgomery and watching the organization gain members. Indivisible Montgomery's first in-person meeting was a week away, and I was boosted from the excitement of the Women's March. The Sunday after the march, my mom called me as she normally did for our weekly call.

"Well, Chris, how was your week last week?"

"Yesterday was pretty exciting. Katherine spent the day at the Women's March so I was with the girl—"

"How was the rest of your week?"

She cut me off. She didn't like where my answer was leading so she changed the subject without letting me finish my sentence. It was then I realized that my family's superficial treatment of politics was not a quirk but the rule. I talked about politics all the time with Katherine and my friends long before launching Indivisible

Montgomery. My family's rule against talking politics had never been explicitly stated, but her cutting me off from talking about the Women's March made me realize she was going to try to enforce this rule even now. This wasn't acceptable. I wasn't talking about politics as abstraction. My life had become inextricably tangled with it through Indivisible Montgomery and our resistance work. Because Indivisible Montgomery took up so much of my time, excising it from what I did during the week left little else to discuss. I found it galling that, if I tried to broach the topic of how the resistance was taking over my life, she would change the subject and expect me to steer clear of political issues. This did not sit well.

In March, one week before our trip to Capitol Hill to deliver our second petition asking for an independent investigation of the 2016 election, and amid House Republicans' efforts to repeal Obamacare, matters with my mom came to a head. Over a series of texts, she asked why I had been distant on our calls. I was honest. I was leading Indivisible Montgomery. It was a major part of my life. I recognized she didn't want to hear about it, but I wasn't going to spend our phone calls pretending everything was fine for the sake of her comfort. I went further, saying that setting boundaries for yourself is perfectly reasonable. I never broached her boundary by asking about her politics. However, she asked about my life, and, instead of listening to the answer, she wanted to tell me how I should respond.

I've looked back through this text exchange several times, and it is clear now that my mom wanted the illusion of being a part of my life while ignoring the parts that made her uncomfortable. In my last message, I told her Indivisible Montgomery was too much of my life to continue pretending it wasn't there. I told her she could stop dismissing what was happening in my life, or she could prioritize her own comfort.

We haven't spoken since.

Fundraising

Despite the troubles with my family, the end of March was a heady time for Indivisible Montgomery. We had delivered our second petition to launch an investigation into the 2016 election, and we protected Obamacare. Compared to how these two-plus months could have played out, we all felt pretty good. I mean, we didn't feel great, what with Trump's Muslim ban still in effect and the possibility he might start World War III with a tweet, but we had proven ourselves as an organization that could marshal the resources necessary to make a positive difference.

Up to this point, I had put off one major aspect of running a volunteer organization: fundraising. But money was becoming an issue. We needed to reserve meeting rooms for our monthly in-person meetings, our newsletter subscriber list grew large enough that we no longer qualified for a free Mailchimp account, and website hosting cost money. I had been paying these expenses out of pocket, but that wasn't tenable. Raising money would take the pressure off my personal checking account and give Indivisible Montgomery the flexibility to support more events. Money also introduced complications though. How do we raise money? Where do we keep it? Who has access to it, and how do we track it so that no one, namely me, goes to jail? The answers weren't always straightforward, and I hadn't had the bandwidth to deal with them before.

Indivisible Montgomery existed as a mailing list with social media outlets and a website. We hadn't filed any paperwork to have a formal tax, nonprofit, or business designation. I would have loved to have talked these things through with other members of leadership, but Lois, our remaining leader, said the demands of Indivisible Montgomery were too much and she left. Katherine was supportive, but she was busy with other things, resistance and non-resistance related, and wanted to leave much of the running of Indivisible Montgomery to me. I researched how to set up Indivisible Montgomery as a nonprofit, but there seemed to be more headaches than maintaining the status quo. Instead, I set up a bank account for Indivisible Montgomery under my name. For transparency and security, I created the Indivisible Montgomery account at a bank different from the one Katherine and I used for our personal finances. I also created a GoFundMe page so we could receive donations.

With that set, I strategized how to raise money. I limited our fundraising drives to once per year—I didn't want Indivisible Montgomery to be like a political campaign, where we constantly sent emails asking for money. I figured $1,000 would cover our needs for 2017, so I set that as the initial GoFundMe fundraising goal.

I told Katherine I was going to launch our first fundraising campaign at the beginning of April, and I told her my goal. "Is that enough?" Katherine asked. "Have you calculated how much you'll need for the rest of the year?"

Of course I had anticipated this question. "Uhhh ..."

OK, I hadn't anticipated the question. After scratching out some figures and assuming there would be incidental expenses, I bumped the goal to $2,000.

I launched the fundraising campaign at the end of March with a special message to Indivisible Montgomery asking for donations. To make sure we hit our goal, I planned to send fundraising messages every few days over a two-week period. If we didn't hit $2,000 in that time, then we'd just have to make do with whatever we raised.

The first fundraising message went out in the morning as I was getting on the Metro. Every time I checked my Indivisible Montgomery email that day, about once an hour, I had at least one message indicating a new donation. When I checked in after the girls went to bed that evening, we had already reached $2,000. I was stunned. Catherine Schupp and one other person donated $250 apiece, and several others donated $100 or more. I raised the GoFundMe goal to $3,000, and we hit that two days later.

One thing I love about Indivisible Montgomery members is that we put our money where our mouths are.

March!

APRIL WAS MARCH MONTH. I would have chosen March as march month, but I wasn't in charge of march planning. After the wild success of the Women's March, a variety of well-organized groups put together additional marches to harness the same energy. The Tax Day March, to focus on President Trump's tax evasion and corruption, was April 15. The March for Science on April 22 and the People's Climate March on April 29 focused on the Trump administration's rejection of sound science to further partisan objectives. I did not have much bandwidth to advertise these marches while we were running our petition drive and fighting the House's Obamacare repeal efforts. But once the calendar flipped to April, I was happy to change the subject to marches. Indivisible Montgomery had been making calls every week for three months, holding meetings on Capitol Hill, and creating our own in-person events to grow our community. Three straight weekends of marches provided a break—I didn't have to plan anything and I could choose when and how I participated. I encouraged Indivisible Montgomery members to attend as many of the marches as they felt they could make. I didn't expect anyone to go to all three, but I had underestimated the resistance community before, so I felt it better to let everyone know about all the protests.

Katherine and I strategized our march attendance. The Indivisible Montgomery Conflicts of Interest committee was attending the

Tax Day March, so Katherine, as the committee chair, led the group there. I knew some of the organizers of the March for Science from Twitter, and I attended that event to support their efforts. Because Katherine and I thought we could each stomach only one march per month, we attended our marches individually and we'd skip the Climate March.

Katherine reported the Tax Day March was fine. Her only other comparator was the Women's March, so it was no surprise this was a bit of a letdown for her. I hadn't attended a march yet, and I was excited to go. But the March for Science didn't meet my expectations. This was an opportunity to link sound science to the opposition to Trump administration policies and to clearly state how the policies Trump was proposing would gut American research and cede global science leadership to the Europeans and the Chinese. But the organizers and speakers misread the situation. They chose to deliver an apolitical "Science, rah!" message, while every so often slipping in veiled digs at the Trump administration. They did not rise to meet the moment. On a positive note, I saw several Indivisible Montgomery members, and with Katherine's committee having attended the Tax Day March the week before, I was pleased with my organization's effort to do what we could to make these marches successful.

To encourage Indivisible Montgomery members' attendance at the People's Climate March the following week, I canceled our monthly meeting scheduled for the same day. Besides, I needed a breather. We had met in person in local libraries at the end of January, February, and March. We had been active for four months, during which time our membership exploded from 12 people to over

Me at the March for Science, April 22, 2017. The speakers were just OK, but the protest signs were excellent.

1,400. We delivered two petitions to Congress alongside the more than 10,000 signatures we collected, had a major legislative victory, hosted a well-attended town hall, launched dine-arounds, created over a dozen committees, started building a leadership team, and raised over $3,000. And in the background was me—writing three newsletters each week, arranging and hosting monthly in-person meetings, and making connections with other groups while trying to make time for my family and work commitments.

I thought I deserved a Saturday off.

Crisis at the DOJ

With the start of May, I began brainstorming our next efforts to encourage Congress to impanel an independent commission to study the 2016 election. I wanted to move on from another petition, but I didn't know what to do. Turns out, I didn't have to think about it long. On May 9, a political firestorm erupted as President Trump fired FBI Director James Comey.

The FBI began investigating Donald Trump and his campaign in July 2016 for allegedly accepting support from the Russian government to beat Hillary Clinton.[9] Because of the sensitivity of the investigation, James Comey, director of the FBI, oversaw the investigation and all matters related to it. Shortly after Trump's inauguration, Gen. Michael Flynn, Trump's pick for his national security adviser, was interviewed by the FBI to determine what he knew about the campaign's interactions with Russia. Flynn lied during the interview—a federal offense—and was forced to resign about three weeks into the Trump administration, making him the record holder for shortest national security advisor tenure.[10] But let's take a moment to fully appreciate this. Trump's inner circle of advisers was so corrupt that the man originally picked to advise the president on national security issues was himself a security risk because he lied to the FBI. The day after Flynn resigned, Trump invited Comey to a one-on-one dinner. In their conversation, Trump pressured Comey to drop the Flynn investigation and asked for Comey's loyalty.[11]

Comey reportedly stated his loyalty was to the Constitution, and he would pursue the investigations where they led. On May 9, Trump fired Comey,[12] likely in an attempt to derail the Flynn and Russia investigations. It had the opposite effect.

Trump was so erratic in office there was something new to be outraged about daily, but the act of firing Comey rose above it all. It was a demonstrable abuse of power. Comey's firing refocused the country on the Russia investigation and Trump's attempts to quash it. Democrats immediately called for a special counsel to be appointed and, short of that, for an independent investigation to be impaneled. Republicans sat on their hands.

Even more brazen was that Trump then invited and hosted the Russian foreign minister and Russian ambassador in the Oval Office one day after dismissing Comey.[13] One day! Even more bizarre was that we only knew this happened because the Russian press released photos of the event. Trump had barred US press from the meeting.

To be clear: under investigation for his campaign's interactions with Russian operatives, Trump fired the guy running the investigation, then secretly hosted high-ranking Russian officials in the Oval Office. And we were supposed to believe that Trump didn't have a soft spot for Russia? OK. Republicans tried the "Trump is a novice at politics" excuse, but no one was this stupid. Certainly his aides, who knew the president's schedule, were not nearly this dumb. Trump hosted this meeting precisely to flaunt his power. Presidents shouldn't interfere in investigations targeting them, even if they have the power to. It's been part of the public trust, at least since the Nixon administration, that no one, not even the president, is above the law. By firing Comey, Trump asserted that he was. Through the weekly newsletter during this time, I directed Indivisible Montgomery to call our members of Congress to keep advocating for an independent investigation.

Nine days after Comey's dismissal, former FBI director Robert Mueller was appointed special counsel overseeing the Russia investigation and related matters.[14] This felt like a victory. Mueller was highly respected in Congress, and, for much of the public not acquainted with Mueller himself, having a former FBI director take over the Russia investigation seemed the best possible way to ensure it would be thorough and independent. He was supposedly a no-nonsense man who would safeguard his independence and hire accomplished people who knew what they were doing.

Mueller's appointment also meant there would be little appetite on Capitol Hill to establish an independent commission. No member of Congress wanted to touch the investigation of the 2016 election any more than they had to. I still thought the independent commission was a good idea, but since it clearly would never happen, that gave Indivisible Montgomery space to focus on any one of the many other ongoing dumpster fires.

Internal Stability

The beginning of June gave me time for a small breather. Mueller's appointment meant our work encouraging an investigation of the 2016 election could be moved to a back burner. The Senate was weeks away from considering its version of Obamacare repeal, and we didn't have any major resistance marches or events on the calendar. But rather than having time to spend with my family or my hobbies, I had to deal with Indivisible Montgomery personnel and structure. I no longer had a leadership team. Kyle Benton, Gracie Dominguez, and Lois Hampton stepped up early on, but they had each left the organization. We also had two webmasters leave, and two or three committee leaders no longer had time for the work. None of the work these people did was optional to the functioning of Indivisible Montgomery. The work needed to be done, and if the volunteers doing it weren't around, it fell to me to complete their tasks. This amounted to an existential threat to the organization, as it was far too much for me to take on. For the past few months, I had been accomplishing my duties and fulfilling the roles of a leadership team, webmaster, and committee leaders, but poorly.

On the plus side, Indivisible Montgomery had several committees with good leaders—Katherine leading Conflicts of Interest, Angela Hvitved leading Environment and Science, Nina Liakos leading Administration, Martin Trocki leading Health Care, and Carol McShea leading our Women's Issues and Community Outreach committees. Jennifer Thompson took over our Facebook page, Jeff McShea became our webmaster in April, and Teri Blandon was our ace at Twitter. This was a solid team. And these committee leaders had found ways to make their committees effective. Angela's Environment and Science committee was full of current and former federal employees who led Indivisible Montgomery's efforts to write responses to environmental regulatory changes. Nina's Administration committee implemented a system to set up the room for our monthly meetings and streamline the inclusion of new members. And Katherine's Conflicts of Interest committee was planning an event for early November focused on the GOP's emerging legislation to cut taxes for rich people.

What I really needed was a group of five or six people that I would meet with once a month to discuss the higher-level functions and events of Indivisible Montgomery. These folks would know about the work of the committees so they could help me integrate our volunteers' efforts into effective events that provided value to our members. I asked Nina Liakos, Karen Sultan, Mollie Ferguson, and Jeff and Carol McShea to be a part of the steering committee.

One night in early June, I told Katherine that those I invited to the steering committee accepted and how relieved I was to have a leadership team in place. "Did you ever set up a communications team?" she asked. As part of our community engagement efforts, Indivisible Montgomery needed a team to write press releases about upcoming events, list our events on local calendars, and identify opportunities to write letters to the editor regarding issues of importance.

"No." I sighed and rubbed my eyes. "We set up this committee in February, but no one stepped up to lead. Lynn Litterine and David Kameras have said they're still willing to do the work, but neither of them wants to lead."

Katherine bit her bottom lip and shook her head. "I think comms is just too important. You need to have a functional committee." A brief pause. "I'll lead Comms."

"But you're already leading Conflicts of Interest," I responded. Katherine wouldn't be the first person to lead more than one Indivisible Montgomery committee, but I knew how thin she was stretched.

"Yeah, well ... Let's try it for a few months," she said. "Once we get things rolling maybe Lynn or David will take over."

To no one's surprise, the plan to have Katherine step down from Comms after a few months didn't work out, and she would lead the committee for the next four years. To their credit, she said Lynn and David were the most reliable, responsible, and professional people she ever worked with in the entirety of her volunteer career. "They're a dream," she said.

With a steering committee and a communications team in place, Indivisible Montgomery gained some internal stability for the first time since its founding. Committees and leaders would come and go during my time with Indivisible Montgomery, but from then on we always had a core group of people covering the essential functions of the organization.

And There It Is

Back in May, the House had narrowly passed a bill to repeal and replace Obamacare, and all our time in May and June was spent working to stop the Senate from doing the same. The entire resistance was so focused on saving Obamacare from the GOP that no other major story broke through the noise in that time.

Except one.

In early July, I had put the girls to bed and was sitting outside their room to make sure they were asleep. I pulled out my phone and scrolled through Twitter. On this night, everyone was discussing a story from *The New York Times* about Donald Trump Jr. and something related to Russia. Rather than decipher tweets to piece the story together, I found a link to the *Times* story. I started reading and my jaw hit the floor.

The June 3, 2016, email sent to Donald Trump, Jr. could hardly have been more explicit: One of his father's former Russian business partners had been contacted by a senior Russian government official and was offering to provide the Trump campaign with dirt on Hillary Clinton.

The documents "would incriminate Hillary and her dealings with Russia and would be very useful to your father," read the email, written by a trusted intermediary, who added, "This is obviously very high level and sensitive information but is part of Russia and its government's support for Mr. Trump." ...

He replied within minutes: "If it's what you say I love it especially later in the summer."[15]

I don't know how many times I said "holy shit" reading those paragraphs. It was a lot. I walked downstairs and read the opening paragraphs of the story to Katherine. It took a while to get through because she also kept saying "holy shit."

It didn't get clearer than this. The Russian government made clear efforts to help the Trump campaign and suggested meeting Trump Jr. to discuss the parameters of this help. It is illegal to accept foreign assistance in any form for a political campaign in the United States. The Russians were, in effect, saying, "Let's crime!" And Trump Jr. responded, "I'll crime with you!" The Trump campaign had been briefed by federal law enforcement agencies on the perils of foreign influence in campaigns. But even if Trump Jr. didn't get that information, accepting the meeting demonstrates corrupt intent and a willingness to work with foreign powers to get Trump elected.

The Trump camp explained this away, saying there was never any explicit agreement with the Russians. As if the only proof of guilt would be a video of Trump Jr. shaking hands with a representative of the Russian government and saying, "We've agreed to crime!" Come on. The Trump campaign said the Russian representative only wanted to talk about adoptions. To understand this apparent non sequitur, it took only a little digging to find stories explaining that, during the Obama administration, American sanctions against Russia and Russia's retaliatory actions limited American parents' opportunities to adopt Russian orphans.[16] This caused a diplomatic schism between the two countries. By talking about adoptions with Trump Jr., the Russians were making clear they wanted sanctions relief and an American foreign policy favorable to Russia. And while Trump Jr. may not have been smart enough to understand what the Russian attendee was talking about, surely Paul Manafort knew. Paul Manafort, the Trump campaign chair who also attended the meeting, was well connected with Russian oligarchs and had extensive experience working for pro-Russia political organizations across Europe.[17]

This was a stunning revelation—that members of the Trump family and campaign were willing to entertain the possibility of foreign aid in a presidential campaign. Any campaign accepting such an offer meant that administration would be beholden to this foreign power rather than to the American people. Whether this meeting or additional revelations about Trump's ties to Russia would lead to indictments, we didn't know at the time. However, Trump's Russia-friendly foreign policy and fawning over Vladimir Putin made it clear that the Russians got what they wanted out of their meeting with Trump Jr.

Indivisible Montgomery Newsletter: Week 28

July 13, 2017

WE ARE MORE THAN six months into this resistance, and over this time, some people have mentioned to me that they don't really understand the point of Indivisible Montgomery's continued action. Have we done anything that matters? Does our voice make a difference? The short answer is yes, but let me take a moment to describe what I see as Indivisible Montgomery's biggest success.

With Democrats in the minority in the House and the Senate, their power is incredibly limited. To blunt the GOP's ability to ram through their agenda, Indivisible Montgomery had to (1) demand unified opposition from our senators and representatives and (2) do whatever we could to amplify the many scandals surrounding the Trump campaign and presidency as a way to distract and delay the GOP's disastrous agenda.

We have been successful in getting our senators and representatives to oppose the administration and congressional GOP. Public pressure and discussion on a variety of scandals including Trump-Russia and the administration's conflicts of interest gave important indications to media outlets and elected representatives that there was public interest in these issues. And now, six months in, the Trump-Russia scandal has blown up in the faces of the GOP to the point that even the most ardent Trump supporters are voicing concern.

Yesterday, Sen. John McCain said that the constant string of revelations around the Trump-Russia affair "sucks all of the oxygen out of the room," and makes it difficult for Congress to work on anything else. Look at #2 above—this is exactly the goal of Indivisible Montgomery! Thus, our work on the Russia investigation, in collaboration with others across the country, has been our most impressive success by far.

Of course, we must keep going. There is a very real possibility that the GOP will leave for the August recess without a single, major legislative victory. For that to happen, we have to stop the Senate GOP's health care bill. Let's get to it!

Fighting Obamacare Repeal, Again

IT WAS JULY 27 and everyone in my house had gone to bed. I was awake because I needed to write a newsletter. For the past three months, the message had been one-note: Save Obamacare! This night's newsletter was different. This was one of defeat. The Senate GOP was about to repeal Obamacare and take health care away from millions of Americans.

This wasn't the House GOP's bill passed at the beginning of May. The Senate GOP had dismissed that bill almost the moment it had passed the House. Called "skinny repeal," the bill about to be passed was a significantly pared-down version of what the House passed, but it would still remove many benefits Obamacare had provided Americans. Once the Senate passed skinny repeal, it would have to go to the House for another vote and then to the White House for Trump's signature. The real hurdle was the Senate. If it made it through the Senate, the House GOP would find the votes necessary to pass skinny repeal. After months of grueling effort, the Senate was poised to vote on its bill.

The Senate would consider skinny repeal under budget reconciliation rules, meaning they could pass the bill with only 50 votes. The Senate GOP had a 52–48 advantage over Democrats, though Senators Lisa Murkowski and Susan Collins had already said they would not support skinny repeal. The rest of the GOP caucus was either publicly on board with the bill or had kept quiet to avoid public backlash. Still, with no one whispering that they might vote against the bill, we were looking at a 50–50 vote, with Vice President Mike Pence ready to break the tie and pass the bill. I decided to get a start on writing a message to Indivisible Montgomery explaining the situation, praising the members for their work, and encouraging them to recover and stay active despite this deep disappointment.

We would need to recover, because once the Senate started considering Obamacare repeal in May, the nationwide resistance had elevated our activism to a completely new level. Half, if not more, of the 1,400 Indivisible Montgomery members opened every email I sent, and we got reports of our senators' phones ringing off the hook and full voicemail boxes. Activists from across the country poured into DC to protest in the offices of senators who had pledged to repeal Obamacare. Since June, I didn't need to search for where protests were planned. I told people to go to the Senate office buildings, where they would undoubtedly find a protest they could join. Videos went viral every day showing activists pushed to the ground, and some pulled out of wheelchairs, to be arrested by Capitol Police for trespassing in the senators' offices.

All the while, the Senate GOP worked to repeal and replace Obamacare. At the end of July, the stage was set for the GOP's coup de grâce. But before getting to skinny repeal, we first had to deal with the political theater of it all. Over the course of a week, Sen. Mitch McConnell, the GOP leader in the Senate, put different Obamacare repeal bills on the floor. The first was the House bill, which everyone knew to be dead on arrival. The bill failed a procedural vote and the

Senate moved to the next bill. That bill would have repealed almost all of Obamacare, and while it passed the procedural hurdles, it garnered only 45 votes—five short of passage. Finally came skinny repeal, which would have repealed Obamacare's mandate that people must buy health care and other popular provisions but would have left a fair amount of the law in place. Make no mistake: this bill would have wrecked Obamacare and left millions without health insurance, but it was the least destructive of those proposed. Skinny repeal was the last arrow in the GOP's quiver, and Senate leadership had put all its effort into passing it. Collins and Murkowski were opposed, but pundits who knew how the Senate worked assured us all that McConnell would never move forward with skinny repeal if he didn't have the votes necessary to pass it.

The vote on skinny repeal was happening late at night, and I was determined to watch the proceedings regardless of when it happened. This was one of the most pivotal moments in our resistance. Losing Obamacare wouldn't be the end of our fight, but it would be a significant blow. I needed to witness it.

After giving Katherine and the girls a hug good night, I went down to the dining room, opened the computer, turned on C-SPAN, and listened to the Senate go through its pre-voting procedures. I finished my draft message to Indivisible Montgomery at about the time the Senate clerk started going through the roll to record everyone's vote. Some senators were missing when their name was called, but when they came in, they simply caught the clerk's attention and indicated their vote. It was tense but also mind-numbing waiting for the clerk to read out 100 names. I checked in on Twitter, and my feed was full of people nervously bored like me. Folks were tweeting about Pence presiding over the Senate and how he would eventually break the tie.

After 10 minutes, the vote stood at 49 senators in favor and 50 opposed. It is common for senators to be late to a vote, even an important one, and we all waited for the final senator to appear and cast their vote. Once the time of the vote reached 20 minutes and our mystery senator hadn't appeared, those of us still watching started wondering who the missing person was. It turns out the missing vote was from Republican Sen. John McCain. McCain had been cagey on his vote on skinny repeal all week long. Several other Republican senators had also been cagey but they ended up voting for the bill. Why hadn't McCain? Even more importantly, where was McCain? He had been spotted leaving his office for the vote, but no one had seen him enter the Senate chamber. Eventually a reporter got a bead on him and indicated that McCain was in a cloakroom adjacent to the Senate floor and involved in intense discussions with small groups of GOP senators. What was there to discuss? McCain would vote in favor, Pence would cast the tiebreaking vote, the bill would eventually head to Trump's desk, and Obamacare would be dead. The only reason for any discussion was if McCain's vote wasn't nailed down. There was no way McCain would submarine the GOP's best chance to quash Obamacare. Would he?

After another 10 minutes, Pence left the dais. The senators talking to McCain apparently hadn't made any headway, and it was Pence's turn. Well, now. This seemed serious. Bringing Pence in to talk made it look like McCain might vote against skinny repeal. Then Pence walked away because McCain was on the phone with Trump. That would only happen if McCain was actually considering voting against skinny repeal. For Pence and Trump to be talking to him meant they were in serious negotiations to win him over.

These conversations dragged on. It ticked past 1:00 in the morning on July 28, with the vote on skinny repeal having been open for well over an hour. I was determined to see this play out. My Twitter feed was excited about a potential McCain no vote. I didn't buy it. There was almost no concession Trump, Pence, or McConnell wouldn't make to win McCain's vote.

Then the impossible became possible. Pence left the Capitol, which would happen only if he had already cast the tiebreaking vote, or if there wasn't going to be a tie. Could it be? Was McCain really about to bring down the GOP's Obamacare repeal effort?

We didn't have to wonder long. A few minutes later, McCain entered the Senate chamber. I switched back from Twitter to C-SPAN and watched as McCain approached the clerk and got her attention. "Mr. McCain," she said. McCain then gave a clear and emphatic thumbs-down. I jumped up, punching the air, and nearly knocked over my chair. He voted no! Obamacare repeal failed 49–51!

Once I calmed down and got my head straight, I had to rewrite my newsletter. I congratulated the members on their efforts. Because of them, Obamacare persisted and people across our country would continue to benefit. I was elated. Instead of having to pick people up after a defeat, we would celebrate a win.

I have no idea how I got to sleep that night.

Very Fine People

By the time August rolled around, I was exhausted. In addition to the work we were doing on Obamacare and keeping up with the Mueller investigation, I was still writing three newsletters a week, hosting monthly meetings, and coordinating efforts with other resistance groups in the county. And we had just finished our second dine-around weekend. Despite my exhaustion, I was proud of how far Indivisible Montgomery had come. The committees set up in February were progressing on projects to help Indivisible Montgomery members make their voices heard. The summer was also a busy time for Rescuing Biomedical Research, where my double life remained secret. We had recently gathered a group of university officials to discuss a plan to collect and publish data on the career outcomes of PhD alumni—a 20-year-old recommendation to improve biomedical research that had never been fulfilled. Our meeting was a huge success and led to multiple publications as well as the formation of a coalition of universities committed to continuing this work on career outcomes. After the RBR meeting, which was a few days after the GOP's Obamacare repeal efforts collapsed, I felt like I could sleep for a week.

I needed a vacation. I wasn't the only one.

Katherine's editing business required constant attention, and she had taken on several Indivisible Montgomery responsibilities alongside her own work. In addition to leading both the Conflicts of Interest and Communications committees, she convened an Administrative Board composed of the chairs of Indivisible Montgomery committees focused on the functioning of the organization. Since July, Katherine and the Admin Board had been organizing a membership drive for the coming September and October. She also shouldered a heavier load of the caretaking for Nancy and Hazel while I was busy leading Indivisible Montgomery. My wife needed a break more than I did.

Back in January, I had circled August on my calendar because Congress went on recess for about five weeks during August and September. With no legislation being considered, I could take a break from writing the newsletter, and Katherine and I could plan time with our family. There was a rumor that Trump would vacation for much of August, too. Not that he couldn't tweet us into a war from any location, but I was vaguely optimistic the fire hose of awful news that characterized the first seven months of the year would slow down a bit. I was determined to take two weeks off from the business of activism and relax and spend time with the family.

To that end, we took a mid-August vacation to St. Louis to visit Katherine's family and introduce them to Hazel. I was going to take a break from RBR, Katherine would take a break from editing, and we would both take a break from Indivisible Montgomery. I was looking forward to enjoying time with my girls. Nancy was four and about to embark on her final year of preschool. Hazel started walking a month before, so there was no shortage of mischief in the house.

Once I wrapped up the RBR meeting, I was eager to pack and get out of town. I was even taking a break from Twitter during this vacation. The only news I read was *The Washington Post*'s news alerts in my email. This is why it wasn't until we were in the middle of the first day of our two-day road trip that I found out that, the night before, the Ku Klux Klan, neo-Nazis, and other far-right hate groups converged on Charlottesville, Virginia, in a sign of unity and support for President Trump. In advance of their Unite the Right rally, these hateful white men marched across the University of Virginia campus carrying tiki torches and chanting Nazi slogans. When we stopped for the night, I read about the white supremacists in Charlottesville being met by ardent counterprotestors. Clashes between the groups had been limited, but one of the white supremacists rammed his car into a crowd of counterprotestors, killing a woman named Heather Heyer.[18]

Sitting in our hotel room after the girls were asleep, I said to Katherine, "Do you think I should write to Indivisible Montgomery? Say something about how we stand on the side of the counterprotestors?"

"I think Indivisible Montgomery understands we're against Nazis," she responded flatly. "Do you have something to say that would add to the conversation?"

I thought about it for a moment. "Not really, no." I decided to skip the newsletter, happy to have not turned on my computer, and we continued our trip.

The next day we drove to St. Louis. We took our time on the drive, stopping on our way at our favorite cozy pie shop in Terre Haute, Indiana. A few hours later, we pulled into St. Louis at the perfectly sized Airbnb apartment Katherine had found for us. The place was near a huge park, where we had planned a picnic with Katherine's

Family time at Forest Park in St. Louis on August 15, 2017, as we take
a break from work and resistance.

family the afternoon we arrived. All seven of Katherine's siblings
and their kids were there, so it was a party. The day was beautiful.
Everyone had a great time. Nancy and Hazel had a chance to play
with their cousins, and Katherine and I were able to de-stress and
speak to adults about something other than politics.

A couple of days later I was pulled back in to politics as Trump
offered his own comments on Charlottesville. Trump responded
to a reporter's question, saying there were "very fine people on
both sides" of the protests.[19] Very fine people. The president of
the United States called neo-Nazis and Klan members "very fine
people." Unbelievable.

Trump's comments were a step too far. I was furious that anyone would ever describe neo-Nazis and Klansmen in such a way.
Katherine had also seen Trump's comment and was as upset as I

was. I thought through a message to Indivisible Montgomery. Once I had it right, I told Katherine I was going to write to the group and that I already knew what I was going to say. I know she wasn't happy about it, but she understood. And I was true to my word. I sat at the foot of the bed, wrote the message while Nancy and Hazel played, reread it once, and pressed send. It was the only newsletter I had written in less than 10 minutes. While I was furious about our president calling neo-Nazis "fine people," I was also furious that I couldn't take a break from the resistance. I couldn't take one simple vacation without Trump intruding.

This episode crystallized just how complicated my feelings toward Indivisible Montgomery had become. Founding the organization was essential to fighting Trump's agenda, and I was glad I did it. Leading people against Trump, the GOP, and white supremacists was righteous and necessary. It was invigorating and fulfilling. But this event made it clear I would never be able to take a vacation from Indivisible Montgomery. If I wasn't actively leading the organization, I was always on call. Always.

This was when I started to resent Indivisible Montgomery.

Indivisible Montgomery Newsletter: Week 33

August 16, 2017

Indivisible Montgomery HQ is still on vacation, but the events in Charlottesville this past weekend and President Trump's response require a comment. The Indivisible Project was started under the premise that Trump's racism, misogyny, xenophobia, and other bigoted views could be countered and overcome if we stood together as one, indivisible, against hatred and division. Indivisible Montgomery's mission, clearly stated from our inception, is to work, "… in defense of diversity, inclusion, fairness, transparency, and the empowering of all Americans."

The events in Charlottesville and President Trump's response have served to sharply remind us not only that racism and hatred are alive and well in the United States, but that they are alive and well in the highest office in our country.

Let's be clear, though: there are not two hateful sides to this issue. Nazis, Klan members, and members of other hate groups spew venom from a platform of white superiority and white domination over other races, thereby denying the humanity of those they denigrate. Claiming that there is an equally virulent form of evil on the left purposefully misunderstands the actions of those standing up for the basic humanity of one another and elevates the depravity of Nazi, KKK, and other groups to a level worthy of dialog. There can be no dialog with those who deny the rights of a person's or group's existence.

The Kensington Labor Day Parade

IN JUNE, CAROL MCSHEA, chair of Community Outreach and member of the steering committee, suggested Indivisible Montgomery march in the Kensington Labor Day Parade. I thought this was a fantastic idea. It was a chance to get our name out in the community, it was a new activity for us, and it was the kind of event I had hoped a steering committee member would suggest and lead. I was thrilled. The event gave me an excuse to do something I had been wanting to for a while: buy an Indivisible Montgomery banner and get T-shirts made.

Carol and her husband, Jeff, were some of the few people in Indivisible Montgomery we knew from before I formed the organization—Carol and Katherine were in the same book group. The book group was in political alignment—they all went together to the Women's March—but Carol and Jeff were the only ones to dive deep into resistance work. They attended our events, led committees, and took over running our website. They were dependable and a pleasure to work with. It's why I asked them to be part of the steering committee.

In mid-August, we returned from our St. Louis trip more relaxed than we had been before, despite the events in Charlottesville, and ready for Indivisible Montgomery's busy upcoming months. The

2017 elections in Virginia were just over two months away and our Elections committee would be involved with their get-out-the-vote efforts. The Conflicts of Interest committee was preparing a forum on tax reform and corruption for November. And Katherine was leading the Administrative Board in setting up a membership drive for October. And, of course, the Kensington Labor Day Parade in just a couple weeks' time.

Carol and Jeff took the lead in designing the Indivisible Montgomery T-shirts and banner. Once we agreed on a design, they also ordered and paid. The payment was the problem. In my and Katherine's experiences working with and running nonprofit organizations operating on a shoestring budget, no one received anything for free. My expectation was that I would reimburse Carol and Jeff for their expenses minus the cost of two T-shirts, assuming they wanted them. However, I had not communicated this policy clearly before Carol and Jeff started on this project. They took offense that I would make them pay for their shirts after they put in so much work.

Then I made it worse.

Instead of using my professional skills to smooth over the argument before it got off the ground, I sent a flip email to the effect of "I pay for my shirt. Katherine pays for hers. You pay for yours. We all pay for our shirts." To make a long story short, Carol and I launched long emails back and forth, our rift widening, until Katherine stepped in to patch things up. She calmed us all down, and everyone paid for their shirts.

The day of the Kensington Labor Day Parade was beautiful, and although it was going to be hot and sunny that day, I hoped our march would finish before the heat became unbearable. I parked my

Indivisible Montgomery, marching with the brand-new banner, at the
Kensington Labor Day Parade on September 4, 2017.

car in a neighborhood near the parade route and checked my email
before getting out of the car. In my inbox was a message from Carol.
I feared this was a message saying she and Jeff were bailing at the
last minute. They were supposed to bring the banner. Opening the
email, I was relieved I was only half right. Carol wouldn't attend, but
Jeff would, and he would bring the banner. Carol had a reasonable
excuse for missing the parade, but I couldn't help but wonder if she
wasn't still angry after our argument. However, we would have all we
needed to march, so I locked up my car and went to meet up with my
fellow marchers. Thirty Indivisible Montgomery members RSVP'd
yes, and twenty showed up. I felt a little awkward talking to Jeff at
first, but we got past it. The banner looked phenomenal and everyone
loved their brand-new T-shirts. We brainstormed a few chants for
the parade route, and I also brought leaflets to hand out along the
way explaining who we were, what we did, and how others could join.

Katherine and the girls weren't marching with Indivisible Montgomery, but they were joining the parade. Nancy's preschool was around the corner from where the parade started, and the school invited the families of students to join them for a potluck breakfast in the parking lot before marching. I would get to walk by my family at the preschool and wave to them before they'd join in and we'd all meet up at the end.

Our 20 members in matching dark blue Indivisible Montgomery shirts and banner made us look like a real organization, one that definitely wasn't flying by the seat of its pants. We started marching about 50 yards away from Nancy's preschool, and the route was packed with onlookers. Before we could even start our first chant, someone from the crowd yelled out, "INDIVISIBLE! YEAH!" What? I didn't know this guy or any of the dozen people around him who were all clapping for us. Our entire group looked at each other in surprise, but we cheered back and became more energized. I gave Nancy and Hazel high fives as we marched past and waved, saying I'd see them soon. Several more times people saw our banner and were cheering for us before we even got there. We handed out all the informational flyers in the first 10 minutes of the 45-minute parade, and we cycled through our chants the rest of the time, waving at onlookers. Once we finished the route, we congratulated each other on a fun event and said we'd all see each other at the Indivisible Montgomery meeting in a few weeks. I went off to find Katherine and the girls, who were, like me, exhausted but in good spirits.

At the end of the parade, Teri, who ran our Twitter account, said she lived just a few blocks away from the parade route and would be happy to help Indivisible Montgomery get involved in future

Kensington Labor Day Parades. She didn't know it at the time, but that was going to be incredibly helpful for me. I had no idea if my schism with Carol and Jeff was truly patched up or if we were in for bumpy times ahead.

Indivisible Montgomery Newsletter: Week 40

OCTOBER 5, 2017

OCTOBER IS MEMBERSHIP DRIVE month! We need your help to spread the word about Indivisible Montgomery. Although we are proud of our membership of 1,400 concerned citizens, Montgomery County has a population of 1 million. We have a lot of room to grow!

Over the next four weeks, please forward an Indivisible Montgomery newsletter to five people you think would like to join forces with us and invite them to subscribe.

The middle two weeks of the month, several of your fellow Indivisible Montgomery members will be attending farmers' markets across the county to hand out flyers about our organization and collect email addresses for the newsletter. If you would like to be part of that, sign up here. Volunteers are asked to stay for at least 30 minutes at their chosen market. A training phone call is scheduled for TONIGHT at 9 p.m.

In the last week of October we will "paper the town" with flyers for the final event of the month: the Indivisible Montgomery Open House, with guest speaker Ben Jealous. Saturday, October 28, 10:30 a.m. to 12:30 p.m. Committee tables! T-shirts! Raffle!

Our Best Marketer

Katherine's work for Indivisible Montgomery was indispensable. I had a long list of Indivisible Montgomery responsibilities, but her list was at least as long as mine. As co-leader of our Administrative Board, she helped ensure that the organization ran smoothly. She chaired two committees as well, Communications and Conflicts of Interest, and was co-organizing the tax forum hosted by the latter. She also led our dine-around planning.

During the summer, Katherine had proposed that we devote October to finding new members. She reasoned that people were still out there wanting to get involved but didn't know how. The Kensington Labor Day Parade and the subsequent bump in newsletter subscribers proved Katherine's suggestion prescient. We set a goal of increasing membership by 5% through October. Since Indivisible Montgomery had hovered around 1,400 members since the middle of February, we were looking to add about 70 new people to the mailing list.

Our efforts were two-pronged. Shortly after the Kensington Labor Day Parade, I made a big deal of our membership drive through the newsletter, telling recipients to forward it to friends and talk them into joining. Second, volunteers headed out across farmers' markets in Montgomery County in mid-October, armed with clipboards, sign-up sheets, and information to encourage people to join the group. The newsletter and farmers' market activities advertised our monthly meeting at the end of October, which would be an open house showcasing the work of our committees and highlighted by a discussion with Ben Jealous, a candidate for the Democratic nomination for governor of Maryland.

The Admin Board checked all the boxes necessary to make sure our members were prepared for the farmers' markets. They went out with their clipboards, spoke with scores of people, and signed up many of them for the newsletter. The most common frustration among the folks who went to the farmers' markets were those in the community who said they didn't get involved in politics and that it didn't concern them. Katherine said she wanted to run after them to argue that politics affected them whether they took part in it or not.

The end of the month brought the open house, which we held at the Montgomery County Executive Office Building in Rockville. Katherine and the Admin Board worked hard to get all of the Indivisible Montgomery committees on board with hosting tables to talk about their work and recruit new members. The Admin Board landed Jealous as a speaker, worked with the building managers to make sure attendees had access to the room, and coordinated the behind-the-scenes efforts to ensure the open house would be a professional and engaging event. Given the amount of effort that went into it and the fact that it was the culmination of our membership drive, this was the most important monthly meeting we had held since our first one in January.

So far I had led every monthly meeting, and for most of the ones Katherine attended, we had brought the girls with us. But while physically in the building, Katherine missed most of the meetings because our kids were four and one and didn't sit still very long to listen to adults talk politics. Rather, she was helping them use the bathroom, divvying up a snack, or letting them get their energy out running in the hallway. We had to do something different for the October meeting, though, since her presence was so integral to this event. Our families lived out of state, and we didn't want to wear out our welcome with our friends. So Katherine turned to Nextdoor, where she found a babysitting team of two sisters. The open house would be the first time they babysat for us.

After making sure the girls were set at home and the babysitters had things under control, we left for the meeting. We were the first to arrive, along with Nina, and we set off for the meeting room. The long, rectangular room had a short stage at one end. Since Katherine and I agreed the stage was the focal point, we would set up chairs to face it while positioning committee tables at the opposite end of the room. The rest of the Admin Board, which included Carol, Catherine Schupp, and Betty Dooley, arrived shortly after and we set up the room. This was the first time Carol and I had interacted in person since the T-shirt blowout. I was slightly apprehensive because I didn't know if she was harboring any ill will. It seemed fine though. We didn't have much of a chance to talk before other members started arriving, but it was enough to make me think we were back to our normal working relationship. I was then pulled into discussions about Indivisible Montgomery and the Trump administration with the new arrivals. I left Katherine, Nina, and the rest of the team to finish setup.

Two minutes before the meeting was supposed to start, my phone rang. When I saw it was the babysitter, I excused myself and went into the hallway. The moment I answered, I recognized the sound of Nancy throwing a screaming fit in the background. "Um, Nancy is just throwing a fit, and we don't know what to do. She's been screaming for five minutes and won't calm down." On one hand, I get it. Angry four-year-olds can be loud and intimidating. On the other hand, we hired a babysitter to watch our kids for us, good and bad, while we were away. I asked the babysitter to hand the phone to Nancy so I could talk to her, but she yelled louder as the babysitter approached. Now I was getting flustered because I needed to get the meeting started, and I didn't have the patience to think up other ways to help calm Nancy. I found Katherine, explained what was going on, and asked if she would try to help the babysitter through the tantrum. Before I could commence the meeting, I got waylaid by a member with a logistics question. Katherine came back to me, obviously angry for the same reason I was—we hired the babysitters to take care of our kids. But they were calling for help, and there was nothing we could do from where we were to calm our child down. Katherine said she would have to go home.

What I should have said was, "Kath, this open house wouldn't have happened without you, and you need to be here to enjoy what you put together. Besides, Nancy's fits burn out on their own. Maybe call the babysitter back in five or ten minutes to see how things are going."

What I actually said was, "I guess so? I can't think of anything else."

As I walked up to the stage, I saw Katherine gather her things and walk out of the meeting to head home.

Over 80 people showed up to the event, and about 20 of them were new. This was a change from our typical meetings, where we'd pick up a handful of new people. My remarks were well received, and we had a robust Q&A about Indivisible Montgomery activities. Jealous came in on time and gave a good speech. A gubernatorial candidate had spoken at two of our past three meetings, and Jealous was easily the most charismatic of the bunch. After he spoke, we asked the people to look over the tables in the back because our committees had turned out great materials describing the work they were doing.

As the mingling portion of the morning began, I worked my way through the crowd and greeted people I hadn't had a chance to talk to yet. One attendee introduced himself as the former mayor of Rockville. "You know, when you've done this as much as I have, you recognize people who would make a good elected leader. After hearing you speak, I wonder, when is Chris Pickett going to run for office?" he said with a smile. I laughed nervously. I had no interest in running a campaign, much less holding office. Besides, Katherine told me several times she'd divorce me if I did that. I responded in kind, smiling. "I have enough on my plate right now, but we'll see what the future holds."

That open house was one of the best monthly meetings we would ever hold. The new venue introduced a new energy, and committees were able to recruit new members. We tallied around 100 new members over the month, even more than the 70 we were hoping for. Katherine had pulled it off.

I had to wait to tell her that, though. Angela Hvitved, chair of Environment and Science, dropped me off at home once the open house was over. When I walked in, I found two happy children and a frustrated wife. Katherine filled me in on what happened after she left the meeting: Katherine drove home, and when she walked in the door, Nancy was playing nicely with Hazel and the babysitters. Five minutes after they called me, Nancy calmed down on her own. There had been no reason for Katherine to leave. She missed her big event for nothing.

Whenever Katherine and I reflect on our time running Indivisible Montgomery, it's clear the open house was one of the deepest wounds. For Katherine, this meeting was one more example of what was becoming a pattern: organize a complex event only to have the family responsibilities and my duties as executive director prevent her from fully, or even partially, enjoying the event. I realized there were times when I was so absorbed in Indivisible Montgomery that I didn't consider what was best for my wife and family, even while despairing how much the resistance took me away from them. It was a problem we never fully solved.

A Tax Forum

A WEEK AFTER OUR open house, we turned our attention to the GOP's efforts to enact tax cuts. Frustrated by a party in disarray, high-profile GOP donors told Republican leadership that their financial donations for 2018 campaigns could be withheld if the party couldn't pass any major legislation while holding complete control of the government.[20] After their colossal failure to repeal and replace Obamacare, the GOP moved on to their signature issue—cutting taxes for the wealthy. Since August, Republicans had plotted how to build their tax package. As details came out, of course they publicly touted the parts that were supposed to cut the taxes of most Americans. It was a lie. Any relief felt by low- and middle-income households was projected to be minimal.[21] It was a $2 trillion giveaway to the richest people in the country.

Katherine and I commiserated that it would be difficult to rouse the same passion to oppose the tax reform bill as there was to combat Obamacare repeal. Cutting taxes on the rich doesn't generate the same emotional response as trying to take away someone's health care, but we were committed to trying. The entire Conflicts of Interest committee—Katherine, Dawn Leaf, Susan Zengerle, Claire Robertson, and Debbie Coburn—did an incredible amount of work to lead Indivisible Montgomery in this effort. When firm details of the GOP tax plan started to emerge in September, their committee provided me with language and suggestions for our weekly messages and calls to Capitol Hill. We told our members of Congress that a president who owns roughly 500 limited liability companies (LLCs) should not be allowed to sign a bill that would dramatically cut taxes on LLCs.[22] The committee also organized a forum titled "Rigging Tax Reform: Who Benefits from Trump-Era Changes?" The event was intended to have tax policy experts make the GOP tax bill accessible to non-experts.

One person who would definitely attend the forum was Katherine. After the babysitting / open house debacle, we agreed I'd be the one heading home if the babysitters faltered again. Katherine was MCing the forum, and I had no doubt she and the Conflicts of Interest committee would put on a strong event. They had recruited a powerful list of speakers and encouraged our cosponsors—Indivisible MoCo, Rockville Resistance, DoTheMostGood, and others—to heavily publicize the event. The one thing we couldn't control was turnout, though, and we were all concerned. After all, we were asking Indivisible Montgomery members and others to come out one week after our open house for a discussion on taxes. No, a discussion on tax *policy*. On a beautiful Saturday morning in early November. Would anyone show?

As Katherine and I pulled up to the Cabin John Community Center, we were happy to see that our setup crew had already arrived. We followed the signs for the event and parked our car. We walked into a large room with sign-in tables near the doors, a lectern on the opposite side of the room, and 150 chairs in between them. As we approached the start, we were pleasantly surprised to have over 100 of those seats filled. The attendees all seemed eager to hear what our speakers had to say. Katherine welcomed everyone and introduced me for my opening remarks, and then she introduced our keynote speaker, Rep. Jamie Raskin. He was great! He roused the crowd and had us chanting about impeaching Trump and Pence for emoluments just as he had at the town hall eight months earlier. Once he finished, he shook Katherine's hand and headed out.

Then came the main event—our panel of tax experts and politicians talking about taxes and tax policy. The panel included people who knew quite a lot about this topic, including Stephen Spaulding, chief of strategy and external affairs for Common Cause, and tax scholars Karen Brown of George Washington University School of Law and Donald Marron of the Urban Institute. As the discussion started, it was apparent the panelists agreed on two issues: (1) tax reform was necessary and worthy of Congress's efforts, and (2) the GOP bill fell far short of making necessary improvements to America's tax system. Gauging by the quality and quantity of questions the audience asked, everyone was engaged and interested in the topic.

Katherine and I did our part to clean up afterward, in between thanking our speakers and cosponsors and congratulating the Conflicts of Interest committee for pulling off a nearly flawless event. And we didn't hear a peep from the babysitter.

A Blueprint

Several special elections occurred throughout 2017 as members of Congress took jobs in the Trump administration. Most of these people held seats in deep-red districts. The races to replace them in Congress were not supposed to be competitive. Nevertheless, the resistance worked hard to flip these seats. While the Democratic candidates generally did far better than any other Democrat had done in those districts previously, none of them won. Indivisible Montgomery had not played much part in these elections because our election apparatus had a major false start.

One thing I purposefully did not do during our first meeting was set up an elections committee. Working on elections would be a big part of Indivisible Montgomery's work, according to my plan. But I wanted to get Indivisible Montgomery members focused on how they could be effective activists—calls, protests, marches, etc. Without this basis, many of our members would tune out until election time rolled around. That might make us good at elections, but we'd be terrible activists.

In May, once we had clearly established our activist credentials, I created the Elections committee. Phil Harris stepped forward to lead. At the outset, I wrote to Phil explaining the committee needed to be a resource to educate our members on how to make a difference in the 2018 and 2020 elections. While Phil worked to build relationships with the elections-focused groups in the community, I suggested encouraging Indivisible Montgomery members to participate in get-out-the-vote efforts for the 2017 Virginia elections. That year, Virginia was voting for a governor and for their entire state legislature. Because these were elections we, as Maryland residents, could not vote in, this seemed a relatively low-risk way to test our partnerships and methods for engaging volunteers in elections efforts.

For many in Indivisible Montgomery, the Virginia elections would be the first we worked on. But what could we do? Political campaigns develop lists of voters, cultivate donors, design advertising campaigns, and work to spread the candidate's message. Indivisible Montgomery didn't have the resources or knowledge to do this. Instead, we amplified the Virginia campaigns' messages by phone and text banking, writing letters and postcards to voters, and canvassing—which meant knocking on doors to encourage Democratic supporters to vote in the election. We also wrote letters and postcards to voters on issue-specific, rather than candidate-specific, matters.

Phil had a different vision for the committee. He wanted the committee to delve into deep canvassing, which had become popular in the aftermath of Trump's election (and was the focus of a 2023 book, Anand Giridharadas's *The Persuaders*).[23] Deep canvassing entails volunteers having empathetic conversations with people of differing viewpoints with the goal of changing hearts and minds. Phil's idea was for Indivisible Montgomery members to travel to Trump-supporting areas of Maryland to deep canvass, attempting to turn these voters away from Trump. I balked. Deep canvassing has its place, but I felt that a nascent organization with people new to elections and activism was not it. Republicans had shown themselves to rally around Trump regardless of what he did or said, and I was convinced no amount of fine-tuning our messaging would break through to the level necessary to win back at least one house of Congress in 2018.

The elections-focused groups in Montgomery County specialized in voter registration and get-out-the-vote efforts, and that's what our members voiced an interest in at nearly every Indivisible Montgomery meeting and dine-around event to date. Ultimately Phil couldn't find the enthusiasm for this kind of work, so he stepped aside at the end of August. By then, the Elections committee had grown to 30 people, and I needed someone to step into the leadership role fast. I issued a call for a new committee leader. Steve Pressman emailed promptly, saying he was interested in leading the committee.

I didn't know him prior to this, but, as I would soon come to find out, Steve and I were the same person, just separated by about 25 years: We were in sync on every major issue that confronted Indivisible Montgomery during my tenure with the organization, sometimes agreeing word for word on our rationale for specific actions. Retired and in his late 60s with mostly white hair, Steve and his wife, Myra, joined Indivisible Montgomery in the spring of 2017 and became regulars at our monthly meetings. He was incredibly dependable, energetic, and diligent. On our first phone call to discuss the direction of the Elections committee, he agreed with me that deep canvassing was not the right effort for this group, and he was eager to connect with the elections groups in Montgomery County. I was thrilled.

Steve got right to work making connections with local elections groups, none more important than the J Walkers Action

Group—a group of seasoned veterans of multiple campaigns to elect Democrats. In September and October 2017, J Walkers led multiple phone banks and canvasses for elections all over Virginia each week, despite being centered in Montgomery County. I posted their events in our newsletter as a way for our members to gain campaign experience. These were incredibly popular events with Indivisible Montgomery, judging by the number of clicks on the J Walkers links. I checked in with Steve every so often, and it became clear quickly that Steve had the committee under control and was not shy about speaking up if he had a question. So I worked to advertise elections-related activities and support Steve when needed.

On election night 2017, a Tuesday, I was in a sports bar by myself having a beer and watching the results roll in. Back in 2015, Katherine and I had set up a system for each of us to get a night out of the house each week. We wouldn't have to deal with bedtime or baths or getting the girls ready for the next day. We each got a break and some personal space. My night out was Tuesdays, which is why I was at a bar rather than home that night. The polls suggested Democrat Ralph Northam would win the Virginia governorship by four to five points, and they forecasted Dems would close the gap but not take over the state House. Results started coming in around 8:00 p.m., and it became clear that the polls had underestimated Democratic strength across the ticket. Northam won by nine points, and Democrats lost the House of Delegates on a coin flip (really).[24] It was far better than any of us expected, and part of it was due to the work of our members to turn out voters. It was an amazing sign of the power we could wield.

I was excited. After Democrats lost special elections throughout 2017, the Virginia election demonstrated that, in races not heavily tilted toward Republicans, we could make a difference. Indivisible Montgomery had a capable person leading our elections efforts. By working with our partners in the area and announcing opportunities to get involved, we now had a path to training ourselves to be more effective in future elections. We were gaining the experience and knowledge needed to be an electoral force for the rest of the Trump years.

I wrote a message to Steve congratulating him and the entire Elections committee on their work. I also thanked him for establishing our blueprint for electoral work. My partnership with Steve would be the backbone of the electoral success of Indivisible Montgomery for years to come.

Closing Out the Year

BECAUSE 2017 HAD BEEN an incredible year for Indivisible Montgomery—we had done so much—I wanted to do something big for the last in-person meeting of the year. After the election, I approached Ailea Sneller, leader of Rockville Resistance; Barbara Noveau, leader of DoTheMostGood; and Jon Heintz, leader of J Walkers Action Group and suggested we have a joint meeting to close out 2017. The goal was to recap our successes and focus everyone on the year ahead and on the 2018 election. They agreed, and at the beginning of December, we convened our groups in the biggest room Gaithersburg Library had, which we filled with more than 250 people.

With all the seats taken and people lining the walls, the meeting kicked off with an opera singer, a member of Rockville Resistance, singing the national anthem. I offered her the microphone for the song, and she gave me an "Are you kidding me?" look. She could've sung to a space twice that size without a mic.

The leaders of the four groups stepped up to give a brief rundown of each group's biggest accomplishments over the past year. There was no air of competition among us. The message was the same as the one I had given at Indivisible Montgomery's first in-person meeting—local resistance groups are doing so many different things. Folks should join the group that best fits their own vision of how to resist the Trump administration. Just stay involved and do the work. This aligned with the message of our guest speaker, Sen. Chris Van Hollen. Van Hollen was finishing his first year in the Senate after serving as a congressman representing Montgomery County since 2003. He was warmly received, and he did a fantastic job putting the work we had done in perspective—we defended Obamacare and won major elections. But there was a lot of work to come, and we needed to stay engaged.

As Van Hollen spoke, I felt a pang of regret. I missed having Katherine there. After organizing and running the membership drive, town hall, and tax forum, she was ready for a break. But the fact that we were even having this December meeting, rattling off accomplishments, and possessing confidence heading into 2018 was, in large part, due to Katherine working just as hard at this as me. I wished she had been there to enjoy the moment.

Then I looked out across the audience. This meeting felt so different from the one I led 11 months ago. Back then, I knew almost no one in the room. Now, I knew almost everyone. There were people in the room I could depend on—Steve Pressman, Angela Hvitved, Nina Liakos, Teri Blandon, and more. People in the room had become regulars at our meetings, committee events, and dine-arounds—Tamara Prince, Susan Zengerle, Catherine Schupp, and others. This was the community I set out to build, a community dedicated to resisting the Trump administration that held each other up and supported one another. Many of those in the audience were the same people who had attended our first meeting. The energy of this meeting was different, though. In January, this was a group that needed direction. Now, we knew how to make real change. We had been tested and knew how to win. We were ready for 2018.

2018 | THIS IS WHAT DEMOCRACY
LOOKS LIKE

New Year, New Opportunities

THE YEAR 2018 WAS one of promise and singular focus on the November midterm. Our goal was to elect enough Democrats to flip at least one of the houses of Congress to Democratic control and to win back control of the Maryland governor's mansion from Republican Larry Hogan. Our 2017 victories in Virginia established a foundation for racking up electoral wins, but we still had work to do. We needed to be more in sync with the groups in our area and to integrate our work with campaigns across the country. From a leadership standpoint, 2018 would be completely different from 2017. I'd spent the previous year building Indivisible Montgomery from the ground up. With established committees, a stable steering committee, and income from fundraising, our work in 2018 could focus on expanding our message and influence.

Expanding Indivisible Montgomery's reach started right away. Shortly after the Kensington Labor Day Parade, I was contacted by Jane Barbara, a film producer who attended the parade. She had co-produced a short film called *Leia's Army* about the Women's March. She invited me to a screening just before the second Women's March in January 2018. I would then be part of a panel discussing the film and the larger resistance. I accepted immediately.

I was going by myself though. Ever since the November tax forum, Katherine hadn't attended any Indivisible Montgomery or broader resistance events. We couldn't pay babysitters every time Indivisible Montgomery had a meeting or in-person event. Hazel was nearly 20 months old and fully mobile, meaning Katherine chased two girls around instead of being part of the activities. If she had to focus on Nancy and Hazel, she might as well do it from home, where we had all their food and toys. So on a typical cold and gray January afternoon in the DC area, I hopped on the Metro to head into the city for the screening.

I walked through the doors and into the theater lobby. The lobby was dark, with various art house movie posters on the walls. I wasn't the first to arrive, and once I checked my coat, I mingled. Or I tried. After a year of Indivisible Montgomery meetings where people sought me out, I had forgotten how to walk up to others and become part of the conversation. People were kind but uninterested in talking to someone who couldn't jump into their conversation. So I enjoyed my anonymity and strolled slowly around the lobby until we filed into the theater. The theater itself sat about 150 people, and there was plenty of space for us to spread out. I grabbed a program and found a seat a third of the way from the front. I flipped through and saw we'd be screening three short films. The first two were enjoyable, and the last was *Leia's Army*. This movie was about three generations of women and how they responded to Trump's election. The central friction was the grandmother and granddaughter intent on attending their local Women's March while the mother was adamantly opposed. I enjoyed the movie and felt it touched on issues being dealt with across the country—how do you handle the Trump voters in your household when you're vehemently anti-Trump? The movie didn't have any answers. I don't think there are good answers.

When the movies ended, Jane invited me and four women to the front of the theater for the panel session focused on the moment we found ourselves in. The session lasted 30 minutes, and I don't recall any of the questions except one. A man commented that we must live in our country with Trump voters, and he asked the panel how we could reconcile our differences and live together peaceably. This question reignited a pang of disappointment in me about a recent development among the larger Montgomery County resistance. Ailea Sneller, leader of Rockville Resistance and a staunch ally of Indivisible Montgomery, moved her group away from the actions that had characterized our resistance to link up with Braver Angels. Braver Angels was trying to foster the reconciliation this movie attendee asked about by convening groups of left-leaning and right-leaning people to talk through the thorny issues of the day. "That's a fool's errand," I had told Ailea, but I wished her luck. I hoped she and the movement succeeded in moving our country forward. I just wasn't the person to do it. I didn't see what there was to reconcile. Trump voters thought it was fine to marginalize groups they didn't like—Black people, Hispanic people, immigrants, Muslims, Jews, LGBTQIA+ people. You don't reconcile with people like that. You don't barter and compromise when one side is questioning a marginalized group's right to exist. The other panelists answered his question in very considerate ways, and the moderator moved the

conversation along before I had a chance to respond. My answer—
"I don't much care to reconcile. That's for someone else to do."—
would have taken the conversation in a different direction, so it's
probably best we moved on.

The Second Women's March

After missing the first Women's March, I was excited to attend the second. The success of the 2017 march led to a second series of marches across the country in 2018. Now that Katherine and I were well-seasoned activists and rally-goers, the concerns we had last year about taking the family to a protest were gone. We were excited to take our girls to their first protest and to have the whole family attend a Women's March.

Our day started off by hopping on the Metro. The girls were thrilled. What kid doesn't enjoy riding a train? Metro cars the previous year were full to the brim, but ours had a lot of space to move around. We exited at the Metro Center station and walked out into a bright, cold January day. We walked toward a spot a couple blocks north of the National Mall. That's where we set up a rendezvous point for anyone from Indivisible Montgomery to meet up and walk as a group. About 15 others showed up, and as had been the case for much of the past year, Katherine and I were the youngest adults there and Nancy and Hazel the only children. We took a group picture and then made our way to the Lincoln Memorial to find a comfortable spot near the stage and the Reflecting Pool.

Once we settled in at the rally, Katherine and I started doing what every parent does when you want kids to sit still for a long

The Picketts at the second Women's March, January 20, 2018. *Top:* Katherine and Nancy. *Bottom:* Me, Hazel, and Nancy.

period of time when adults are talking—juggle. One of us would hold Hazel while the other talked to Nancy. Then Hazel would sit in the stroller and Nancy would be on my shoulders. Then they'd each have a snack. Then Nancy would stand and Hazel would walk around us. Endless variations and permutations to keep the girls happy.

The event itself was a bit of a letdown. How could it not be? There were 500,000 people at the march the year before, and the lineup of speakers and entertainers was top-notch. This year, there were maybe 20,000 people, and most of the speakers were politicians.[1] It was cool to hear Rep. Nancy Pelosi speak, but these weren't fire-you-up kind of speakers. This march felt like every other march after the original Women's March: it was fun to get together, but it wasn't a life-changing event.

Because we had expected a long day, we brought plenty of snacks. After about four hours of trains, cheering, and waving our Blue Tsunami sign, Hazel was near the end of her rope, so we called it a day. We had seen nearly the entire program, and Katherine and I were satisfied. We walked back to the Metro, which put off any kind of breakdown from the kids. They handled the entire day like champs.

The Last to Arrive

On February 14, a gunman entered Marjory Stoneman Douglas High School in Parkland, Florida, killing 14 students and 3 staff members.[2] This massacre was the deadliest high school shooting in American history. The next day, the country resumed its well-worn argument over the role of guns in our country. That conversation naturally continued 10 days later at the Indivisible Montgomery meeting.

Nearly 100 people packed into the meeting room at the Kensington Park Library that gray Saturday morning. The white cinder block room hadn't changed much since our first meeting 13 months prior, although we were much more methodical and efficient at setting it up. I walked around greeting attendees before starting the meeting. After my standard welcome and explanation of upcoming activism opportunities, the conversation turned to gun safety. The members dove in with anger at the National Rifle Association (NRA) and their GOP allies blocking commonsense firearm policy reforms. I let the conversation flow among the attendees, giving them a chance to vent. If there was a comment about Congress or gun policy, I reminded everyone that the GOP controlled Congress and the White House, so opportunities to make meaningful change would be limited until Democrats came to power. The first comment about something other than the NRA was about Indivisible Montgomery. "Look around," an elderly gentleman started. "There's so much gray hair in this room. That guy in Florida shot up a school. The kids are the ones with the biggest stake in this. How can we help them make their voice heard if they aren't here?"

This wasn't the first time someone had remarked on our lack of diversity. Indivisible Montgomery was mostly white, mostly female, and mostly older—I'd guess within 10 years on either side of retirement. As the person staring out onto the membership on a regular basis, the lack of diversity was obvious to me. It was one reason I had launched a Community Outreach committee charged with advertising that we exist and making connections with other advocacy groups. Montgomery County is one of the most diverse counties in the country. If we just let more people know we existed, I thought, we were bound to become a more diverse organization. That committee never gained traction though, and we never made headway.

To the gentleman's question, I relayed that a student at nearby Montgomery Blair High School contacted me in the past week with questions about community organizing and setting up protests, asking whether Indivisible Montgomery would support their school walkout. I gave the young man all the information I could and said they had our full support. "But why aren't they here?" he responded. "They should come here instead of creating their own group." There were some murmurs of agreement and nodding heads.

I smirked. "I've only had kids for five years," I said, "and if my experience is representative, kids are going to do things their own way, regardless of what older people think." This got some laughs. "The Blair student reached out to us for help, which means they know we're here. I told him they're welcome to join us. But they've chosen to organize on their own." I then moved to the broader context. "When our resistance started over a year ago, there were more than a dozen resistance groups in Montgomery County, Maryland, alone. Everyone wants to make their voice heard in their own way. That was true a year ago and it's true today. The other group leaders and I work hard to make sure we're amplifying each other's messages and not duplicating efforts. We'll do the same with the high schoolers. The important thing is they're engaging and making their voices heard. We will support that." The next hand went up, moving the conversation to a different topic.

An hour later, the meeting ended, we stacked the chairs, and I headed home. While driving, I turned over the exchange about Indivisible Montgomery's lack of diversity in my head. Despite my calm response to the issue during the meeting, I was deeply concerned about the lack of diversity in Indivisible Montgomery. Why didn't we have more Black people, more Latinos, or more young people in the group? The homogeneity wasn't just about Indivisible Montgomery. It was a resistance-wide problem. But if high schoolers knew we existed, I reasoned, it was likely that Black people, Latinos, and other marginalized groups knew about us, too. And if high schoolers were forming their own organizations, then these marginalized groups likely had their own, too. But where were they?

After going around and around with this conversation in my head, it finally clicked. People from marginalized groups weren't forming new groups. They were working with groups that already existed, like the NAACP, CASA, and GLAAD. These groups had track records of successful activism that stretched decades. Thinking in this broader frame of activism, the missing piece wasn't the activism of these marginalized groups. It was us: well-organized groups of mostly white people establishing a track record of working on behalf of and with the members of these more storied organizations to amplify their efforts and broaden the visible support they had in society. Did our national resistance signal a change in the dynamics of activist organizations? I had no idea. But this revelation did help me stop worrying about Indivisible Montgomery's demographics. Rather than working to recruit people from underrepresented backgrounds to our organization, we would support the groups that were already in existence. Indivisible Montgomery would amplify the work and events of these other organizations, and we would invite their leaders to speak to our group. We would be responsive to the comments and needs of groups not well represented in our organization. And all the while, we would still do our best to make Indivisible Montgomery as welcoming and inclusive as possible.

We Bought a House!

AFTER ARRIVING HOME FROM the February meeting, I didn't have much time to tell Katherine, Nancy, and Hazel how the meeting went because we were deep into trying to buy our first house. Katherine and I had been renting the same house the entire time we lived in Maryland. In 2012, it was a great house for a young couple starting to have kids. In 2018, it was a cramped house for a family of four. The bedrooms were too small for two growing girls, and we didn't want to have landlords anymore. We had been reluctant to look for a house though because we didn't understand the finances of buying a home. But over the past few months, Katherine had dug into the specifics and done quite a bit of research. After showing me the incentives Maryland had for first-time home buyers, Katherine convinced me we could do it. At the end of January, Katherine and I started house shopping. House searches are stressful, and ours was more so because we were up against a deadline. Our lease ran out at the end of March. If we didn't find a house to buy, we'd have to either extend our lease or find a new place to rent.

The first house we saw was nearly perfect, except for the extensive water damage. Another had a fantastic kitchen but a treacherous staircase to the upper level. Not so great for two young kids. As the days ticked by and we kept crossing houses off our list, we worried we wouldn't find what we needed in our price range. After three weeks of searching, Katherine and I were catching up on some work as the girls napped, and Katherine received an email. "The landlords just emailed to say we can't renew the lease. They're going to sell this house once our lease is up."

I stared at her for a moment. "Well, shit." Katherine and I had assumed that if our house hunting didn't go well, we could extend the lease a month or two until we found a place to buy. That was now off the table. Katherine and I laid out our options. We agreed that we'd give the house search another two weeks, until March 1. After that, we'd look for a new place to rent.

A couple days later, our real estate agent called. Katherine answered. "Oh, hi Emily. How are you today? ... Sorry, you kind of broke up. You said a house in our current neighborhood is about to come on the market? ... Yes, that's absolutely in our price range! Chris, do you have time Tuesday at 2:00 to see a house? OK, I'm getting a thumbs-up. OK, I'll look for your text with the address and we'll see you at the house on Tuesday at 2:00 p.m."

After Katherine relayed the other half of the conversation, we oscillated between giddy and merely excited. Our agent was going to show us a house in our same neighborhood, a short three blocks away. It was listed as a one-story house with four bedrooms, two bathrooms, a fixed-up basement, and a price that fit our budget. The house wasn't on the market yet, so no pictures had been posted online and we didn't fully know what we were walking into. We kept trying to talk ourselves down. It sounded great on paper, but any number of things could be wrong with the place. There might be irreparable damage. The seller might not want to move as fast as we needed to. We might get outbid.

Two days later, we toured the house. When I first walked in, I had a good feeling. At first glance, the house was in great shape. But we really wanted this to be the one, so we looked closer for any problems we couldn't overcome. We didn't find any. One of the bedrooms on the main floor could be Katherine's office, while Katherine and I could take the main bedroom and the girls could share the third. The "fourth bedroom" was in the fixed-up basement but wasn't much of a bedroom at all. Katherine and I agreed the basement would need a major overhaul for us to live in the house, but we were up for the renovation. It wasn't a perfect house by any means, but starter houses rarely are, and we knew that going in. We spoke frankly with our agent about cost and timing. She told us the seller wanted to move quickly. As we would later learn, the seller was the son of the original owners, and he had grown up in the house. He was selling the house for his parents, one of whom had passed away and the other now in a long-term care facility. He had fond memories of the house, but he didn't want the property to linger on the market. We didn't want it to be on the market at all! We were ready to put in a bid then and there. I don't remember which of us put the brakes on our enthusiasm, but one of us did. We needed some time to talk about it to make sure we weren't rushing into this. Besides, the house wasn't on the market yet. We had time.

That night, Katherine and I couldn't talk about anything but our potential house. We didn't come up with any red flags so, the next day, we called our agent and told her to put in our bid. Because the house wasn't on the market yet and our offer was above asking price, we hoped the seller would forgo listing it altogether and agree to our bid. That wasn't meant to be. The seller decided to test the

With Katherine in front of the house we just bought in March 2018.

market and see what other offers he could get. So we sat back and sweated. Once the listing went up the following Monday, we resubmitted our bid. The owner was expected to make his decision over the following weekend, giving us a whole week of waiting and trying (and failing) to distract ourselves. With the prospect of having such a good house, we were too nervous to even contemplate what we'd do if we didn't get it.

Saturday came, and we waited anxiously by the phone. Would the seller make his decision in the morning, or would he get to it in the afternoon? Heaven forbid he wait until Sunday. Saturday afternoon, our agent called. Our offer was accepted! We had bought a house! We were so very excited and so very relieved. At last, Katherine and I found the first house we would own.

On the Newsletter

MY PROFESSIONAL LIFE CONTINUED to flourish as I helped RBR become a voice for robust reform in biomedical research, and my double life leading both organizations remained intact. Katherine's business was more successful than ever. And woven through all of this was the life we continued to build with each other and our daughters. Now that we'd bought a house, packing, renovating, and moving rose to the top of our priorities list. Something had to give, and luckily, that could be Indivisible Montgomery. The organization was established and a prominent part of the resistance community. Our committees didn't need my constant oversight, and Congress had fallen to relative inactivity after Republicans passed their tax cut bill at the end of 2017, despite our efforts. Polling indicated Democrats would likely reclaim the House in November, and Republicans in competitive districts didn't want to take a position on consequential legislation if it would hurt their reelection prospects. This change in pace was welcome, but I still needed to make a change to how the organization operated.

Since the inception of Indivisible Montgomery, I had written at least three newsletters each week, which were sent Monday, Tuesday, and Thursday mornings. I wrote them Sunday, Monday, and Wednesday evenings, respectively. The weekly schedule was intentional because I wanted the opportunities shared in the newsletter to be a constant drumbeat for anyone who signed up. The goal of the newsletter was to communicate what was going on in our resistance and provide our members ways to make a difference. If members weren't already consistently involved, then whenever they got the urge to act, we'd be waiting in their inbox with things to do.

I considered the newsletter as a way for me to show off my leadership skills and focus on the abuses of the administration. Sometimes, something awful happened, like the administration's incompetent response to Hurricane Maria, where our ability to make a difference was limited. In these times, I'd write a message that was pessimistic, angry, or defeatist. Katherine, who often edited the messages before they went out, would tell me, "You can't send this. Do it again." She argued I couldn't rant to the membership. The purpose of the newsletter was to guide people to effective action, not as a space for undirected anger. I didn't always like this restriction. I felt how I felt! Normally, though, getting it out on the page was enough of a release that I could take a different approach before sending, considering what someone who felt as I did needed to hear to keep going. What would turn that person away from pessimism and toward effective action? As time went on, I realized the newsletter was less a space to delve into the details of congressional procedure or electoral expectations and more of an opportunity to write the message *I* needed to hear to keep me going.

The schedule was still a grind. Through the first half of 2017, three newsletters seemed appropriate. So much changed on a daily basis that one action and two update newsletters made sense. Toward the latter half of 2017, Katherine gently suggested cutting the Thursday newsletter. The breaking stories had slowed from a fire hose to whatever is slightly less than a fire hose. And because of the work we'd done educating the members, she argued, the group had a grip on the flow of the news and what we could do about it. "At this point, it's overkill," she said. "Besides, I want to spend more time with you. Between both of us taking a night out of the house, and you taking three nights a week to write a newsletter, that only leaves two nights for us."

I was concerned that without the consistent drumbeat, people would drift away from the work. "Trust the members," Katherine said. "Drop Thursday and see if the open rate on the newsletter changes or anyone complains."

This discussion unfurled over six months until I finally agreed. A short-term benefit of dropping the Thursday newsletter was that it would free up another night to pack and move to our new house. In the middle of March 2018, I told Indivisible Montgomery I was ending the Thursday message.

And Katherine was right. No one said a thing. The sky didn't fall, and our subscriber levels and open rates stayed the same. Everything was fine and I had another night of the week to be with my family instead of thinking about what to tell the members.

Indivisible Montgomery Newsletter: Week 71

May 7, 2018

WELCOME BACK FROM RECESS, everyone! Last week was again awash in news, but the two most consequential stories were about Donald Trump and Michael Cohen and what is likely to take them both down. Too busy to click? It rhymes with schmoney schmaundering.

The highlight of the coming week is that it kicks off a busy part of the primary election season across the country. Twenty-eight states will have primaries over six of the next eight weeks, including Maryland on June 26. The candidates emerging from the primaries in these races will be very important in determining which party will control the U.S. House and Senate come Jan. 2, 2019. The environment favors Democrats come November, but having high quality candidates will make things so much easier.

Each week through the end of June, we'll highlight a few of these races and why they're important for our efforts. Depending on how things shape up in Maryland and across the country, we may find ourselves sending postcards and holding phone banks to support these candidates. Or if they're close enough, we may send folks to canvass!

Primary Season

In between unpacking boxes in our new house and small projects to fix it up, I was writing newsletters about primary elections. Countrywide, primary season started in early May. The Maryland primary was at the end of June. I was jealous that so much more of the country got to vote before we did. I encouraged our members to vote, even if they weren't typical primary voters. Our last voting experience was in 2016, so voting in the primary was a good way to exorcise those demons. Whether your candidate won or lost, I explained, it didn't much matter. Rather, it was important to remember what it felt like to vote in an election where losing didn't imperil American democracy.

The biggest race in the Maryland primary was determining who would face off against Republican incumbent Gov. Larry Hogan. Rushern Baker, former county executive in Prince George's County, was considered the front-runner, but polling in the race was scant and it was difficult to tell if he was really in the lead. Activist and Sen. Bernie Sanders supporter Ben Jealous had racked up several impressive endorsements, and he and state senator Rich Madaleno had the charisma and experience necessary to be an effective governor. There were several other candidates in the race, and everyone was campaigning across the state. We had no idea who might end up with the most votes.

The Democratic nominee had a tough task ahead of them in taking down Republican Governor Hogan. One day, while we visited with Jessica and Craig, our longtime friends who had been a part of Indivisible Montgomery from its inception, I was explaining that we were working to defeat Hogan. One of them asked, "What's so wrong with the guy? Seems like he's been a good governor."

"He's a weasel," I responded. From the looks on their faces, I realized I needed to dive into the weeds a bit for them to understand my position. "Democrats have a veto-proof majority in the General Assembly. So the Dems pass a law, and Hogan sits back and waits to see how it plays out. If it does well, he claims credit. If it doesn't, he attacks Democrats. He's a weasel. We can do better."

Indivisible Montgomery invited the prominent Democratic candidates to speak at our in-person meetings in 2017 and 2018. We got Alec Ross, Ben Jealous, and Rich Madaleno. We were close on Krish Vignarajah, Rushern Baker, and Kevin Kamenetz, but the timing for our meetings didn't match up with their schedules. This wasn't our only exposure to the candidates, though. Indivisible Montgomery was part of a coalition of resistance groups sponsoring gubernatorial forums for the candidates to debate the issues. The forums were well attended—by candidates and voters—but goodness, they were boring. Between RBR and Indivisible Montgomery, I was already knee-deep in governmental policies, but these gubernatorial candidates really sucked the fun out of it. Their policies were all so similar that they had to get deep into the specifics to find any differences. By the time they got there, most attendees were too lost to understand the distinction.

Here's what got me: no one ever threw a rhetorical punch. If you're one of the people expected to get 2% or less of the vote, what is the harm in putting yourself out there and attacking some-one's position? I'm not one for a campaign full of personal attacks, but a good politician needs to be able to explain what they bring to the table and contrast it with their opponents. Sometimes that means inspirational speeches or policy talk, and sometimes that means dragging down your opponent and their record. If you're polling poorly and want to win, why hold back? If you're Jealous or Madaleno and think you have a chance of winning, maybe you don't take shots at Baker. But anyone else should've come in and found a way to make themselves the center of attention. Alas, I was not advising anyone's campaign.

June 26, 2018, was primary day in Maryland and the first time I cast a ballot since November 2016. It felt great. Jealous won the nomination handily. He won every county in the state, except for Prince George's and Calvert Counties, which Baker carried.[3] Jealous won Montgomery County despite it being Madaleno's home turf. Aside from Montgomery, Prince George's, and Calvert Counties, Jealous won nearly every county by about 20 points. I was surprised at how well he did. Maybe that was a reflection of my understanding of the race more than the race itself. None of the news stories on the primary deemed it a surprise so that's on me!

From the perspective of Indivisible Montgomery, we would sup-port the nominee, whoever it was. Now that we knew it was Jealous, we'd be all in through November.

Caged Kids

The launching and building of Indivisible Montgomery were, to me, a huge success. Where there was nothing before Trump's election, now we had an organization of over 1,500 members with an established committee structure and experienced activists. But any sense of accomplishment was swamped by the relentless rush of news from the Trump administration. The headlines in the morning were completely different from those from the night before, and the evening's would be completely different from those of that morning. It never stopped. Any thrill of victory—whether saving Obamacare, winning the Virginia elections, or anything else—was quickly chased away as Trump uttered some new protofascist sentiment or his administration dismantled some other beneficial program. Even with Indivisible Montgomery's systems in place to follow and filter the news, we struggled to keep up. It was too much for a bunch of volunteers to cover everything, and we had to sometimes make tough decisions about what to focus on and what we had to let go. Rather than feeling good about all we had done, I felt like we were failing and falling further behind each day.

As primary season was taking off in May, news broke of a ghastly new Trump administration policy. Federal law enforcement at the US southern border was forcibly separating immigrant families attempting to enter the country.[4] Husbands and wives were separated from each other, and children were separated from parents.

Teenagers, kids, toddlers, and infants were snatched by the Trump administration and kept at locations undisclosed to their parents. Pictures of young children bawling and terrified as they were pulled from their parents were splashed across nearly every news organization's home page. Children in immigration detention were behind chain-link fencing. Stories emerged of some facilities lacking functional plumbing and having other basic structural issues.

This was a tough time for me. I saw two-year-old Hazel in every picture of a bawling toddler reaching for their parents, and I saw five-year-old Nancy in every image of a young child forced to care for their even younger siblings. I couldn't get the pictures of confused or distraught parents being forcibly detained by Customs and Border Patrol out of my head. Every photo I saw, I imagined myself or my family in that position. The thought of Nancy and Hazel being taken from me was heart-wrenching. And to possibly never see them again? Unbearable.

The official line from the Trump administration was that separating families was meant to deter illegal border crossings.[5] Essentially, "If you come to our country, we'll take your kids." If you need an encapsulation of just how morally bankrupt the soulless ghouls of the Trump camp were, this is it. In classic Trump administration fashion, instead of taking the blame for their policy, they falsely claimed the Obama administration did the same thing.[6]

Once the details of this program came to light, Indivisible Montgomery and groups across the country sprang into action. And what we did demonstrated how much the resistance had matured in the past 18 or so months. In January 2017, in response to Trump's Muslim ban, activists swarmed airports in protest, but these actions were not well coordinated and evaporated after a couple of weeks. By contrast, the 2018 protests against the family separation policy were well coordinated, spanned the country, and incorporated more actions than just rallies. Our first response, beyond calling our members of Congress to explain how we felt, was to identify the nonprofit groups helping the people crossing the border. This included groups providing legal aid for asylum and immigration proceedings, those collecting goods for the predominantly poor immigrants, and those helping reunite families. Resistance groups close enough to the camps housing immigrants protested in front of them as often as they could. A few national resistance organizations designated June 1 as the day for nationwide protests against the family separation policy. Katherine, who had stepped back from attending resistance events, wanted to attend. She went to the DC event across from the White House with a large contingent of Indivisible Montgomery members on the hottest day of the year. I promoted an all-of-the-above approach for Indivisible Montgomery, encouraging members to donate money and supplies, attend rallies, and do whatever else they could to pressure the Trump administration to rescind the policy and help those in need.

At the end of June, a federal judge issued an injunction against the enforcement of the family separation policy and ordered the Trump administration to reunite all families within 30 days. And this is where, when we did so much to mobilize to successfully put a stop to family separations, it feels like we failed. The implementation of the family separation policy was so quick that some facilities didn't have accurate files on the people they were holding. Children separated from their parents were sent to foster homes without their parents' knowledge. Due to a lack of accurate records, those children were orphaned by the US government. The immigrant families affected by the policy continued to fight in court, eventually leading to the US government settling the lawsuit with some 5,000 immigrant families affected by the policy in 2023.[7]

Indivisible Montgomery Newsletter: Week 76

June 17, 2018

On this Father's Day, I am finding it difficult to think of my own family without thinking of the families torn apart at the border by the Trump administration. The scale of the program is jaw-dropping. Over the course of six weeks in April and May, nearly 2,000 children were separated from their families due to the administration's ghastly anti-immigration policies. That's nearly 50 children taken from their parents every day. And the government does not appear to have a system to reunite these families.

Our members of Congress are working hard to end these policies, and we will press them to do more. If you haven't already, I hope you will also consider donating to the groups and organizations working on behalf of the families that have fallen victim to Trump administration's vile policies.

An International Disgrace

With the primary behind us and Trump's family separation policy on hold, another potential disaster came into focus. In mid-July, Trump took a trip to Helsinki, Finland, for a summit with Russian president Vladimir Putin. Trump fawned over Putin any chance he got and found every reason to justify his genial approach to Russia. The American intelligence community and much of the rest of the country were deeply concerned about Trump genuflecting before Putin.

From the beginning of his presidential campaign, it was clear Trump wanted to be like Putin. Putin was a run-of-the-mill strongman unremarkable among other strongmen. Instead of seeing Putin as a fraud, Trump wanted to be just like him. Amid the investigation into Russia's actions in the 2016 election and the fiasco of inviting high-level Russian diplomats into the Oval Office after firing the FBI director, Trump tried to cozy up to Putin at G20 summits and the like.[8] For anyone who saw Putin and Trump for who they were, a one-on-one Trump-Putin meeting had catastrophe written all over it. That turned out to be accurate.

As the leader of a group heavily invested in making sure Mueller's investigation of Russian election interference in 2016 was seen through to its rightful conclusion, I made sure all Indivisible Montgomery knew of the impending summit and encouraged everyone to watch any public events stemming from it. There wasn't much else for us to do. We didn't have leverage over foreign policy, and Trump was so gaga for Putin that it wouldn't have made a difference. This was one of those instances where we had to wait to see how bad it would be before we could act.

After a long series of talks, some behind closed doors with only interpreters present, Putin and Trump held a joint press conference. It was bad. Very bad. I listened to the press conference and sat there with my mouth agape. When asked about the US intelligence community's assessment that Russia interfered in the 2016 election, Trump responded, "President Putin just said it's not Russia. I don't see any reason why it would be."[9] I was gobsmacked. He told the world he believed a foreign adversary over the entire US intelligence community. And it continued. Trump was embarrassingly submissive for the entire press conference, and he never asserted American interests if they conflicted with Russia's. He spun it as though we were following Russia's lead. On every question, Trump deferred to Putin. Sen. John McCain said it best: "No prior president has ever abased himself more abjectly before a tyrant."[10]

Indivisible groups across the country jumped into action. Trump's abysmal performance in Helsinki spawned immediate protests at the White House. Democratic members of Congress threatened to subpoena the interpreters so the American people could learn what was said behind closed doors. Two days after the Trump-Putin press conference, nationwide candlelight vigils were held across the country to protest Trump's submission to Putin and demand accountability. One was held at the White House. Our Conflicts of Interest committee, led by Katherine, attended.

Herndon-Reston Indivisible from northern Virginia took control of the White House protests and held events there every night from then through the 2018 election. I encouraged Indivisible Montgomery members to join Herndon-Reston Indivisible if they could. It was the least we could do to make sure everyone remembered what Trump did in Helsinki.

Marching Against Nazis

On August 12, I was sitting on a stone wall, wearing my dark blue Indivisible Montgomery shirt, and baking under the hot summer sun in the middle of downtown DC. It was the first anniversary of the Unite the Right rally in Charlottesville, and the organizers intended to bring their hate show to our town. I sure as hell wasn't going to let these neo-Nazis march through the nation's capital like they owned the place.

I was at a counter-demonstration organized a few blocks from where the Unite the Right sequel was to take place. The plan, as I understood it, was for some speakers to fire up the crowd and then everyone would march to the Nazi rally to peacefully protest. Some resistance groups in Montgomery County told their members to avoid downtown DC this day out of fear there would be violence. I took a different tack, telling Indivisible Montgomery that, if they were comfortable, they should join the crowd to stand up against these far-right goons. My view was, if you have the chance to protest Nazis, you should do it. I wanted to flip off a bunch of them and scream so loud they'd slink back into the hole they climbed out of.

I did have reservations. Going back to the first Women's March, Katherine and I had discussed potential violence at protests and how we would respond. This was the first time people on both the pro- and anti-Nazi sides acknowledged the possibility of violence. I was not looking for a fight though. If fighting started, I'd see myself out. I am not opposed to punching neo-Nazis. In fact, I'm in favor of it. But fights are chaotic and dangerous, and I had responsibilities to my family to not get injured or killed.

Our counter-demonstration was about 100 people strong, scattered across a park that, when packed, probably held 400 people. As I sat in the blazing sun, I wondered if we were even needed. Some members of the far-right groups had booked lodging through Airbnb. Once Airbnb corporate realized what was going on, they threatened to revoke the reservations of rally attendees.[11] It wasn't clear if the organizers had recovered because there hadn't been any social media reports of large groups of neo-Nazis headed to their rally.

It was too hot to sit for long, so I strolled halfway up to the speakers' stage. Fellow counterprotestors were crowding in front of the stage, and it was too hot to be that close to other people. As the program started, whether because of the heat or because they were scanning social media, more than half our group wasn't paying attention. I wasn't interested in what the speakers were saying either, so I walked around until I found some shade. I checked my own social media and noted that antifa gatherings had been spotted in the city. Antifa, short for anti-fascist, is a decentralized movement that operates in opposition to white supremacists and neo-Nazis, sometimes leading to violence.[12] That day, neither we nor antifa had found the Nazi rally, though.

Once the official counter-demonstration program ended, I strolled around the park. One walk around the park and then I'd leave, I told myself. This was the time we were supposed to coun-

I stumbled across Leah Greenberg and Ezra Levin, coauthors of the Indivisible Guide and co-executive directors of Indivisible, at the Unite the Right opposition rally on August 12, 2018.

terprotest, but we had nowhere to go. The neo-Nazis hadn't shown up. In the middle of my walk, while dreaming of the sweet song of the air-conditioned Metro car, I heard someone comment on my Indivisible Montgomery shirt. I looked up and was surprised to see a man and woman I recognized walking toward me. It was Leah Greenberg and Ezra Levin, the original authors of the Indivisible Guide and co-leaders of Indivisible national. They were excited to see a member of an Indivisible group out in the city, and I was excited to meet the people who had launched me on this resistance journey. We shook hands and talked shop. I thanked them for writing the

Guide and inspiring me to get involved. They thanked me for organizing locally. It was fun to meet them in the midst of doing the resistance work.

By the time I got home, I found out that the far-right rally did happen. It consisted of about a half dozen people who were met immediately by about four times as many members of antifa. The Nazis tried to walk down the street, but seriously, there were more cops and media at the rally than neo-Nazis. Idiots. They should have just stayed home.

Let's Have a Picnic

INDIVISIBLE MONTGOMERY WAS IN a good rhythm as the year wore on. By August 2018, the committees had dwindled from twelve to five or six, but the ones that survived had found their niche and consistently produced good work, helping members stay engaged. Our monthly meeting was in a groove: we'd meet on the last Saturday of the month for three months and take the fourth month off. We had done about five dine-around weekends at this point, and we were going to march in the Kensington Labor Day Parade again. I was content writing only two newsletters each week now. The steering committee persisted, albeit with some turnover. Nina Liakos left the steering committee but still led Administration. Carol and Jeff also left the steering committee, part of the fallout from the T-shirt debacle a year ago, but remained part of Indivisible Montgomery. Mollie Ferguson stepped back from resistance altogether. Karen Sultan remained, joined by Steve Pressman, chair of the Elections committee; Susan Zengerle, a longtime member of the Conflicts of Interest committee; and Mike Marceau, a Vietnam War veteran and one of Indivisible Montgomery's earliest members. Much like Katherine and her Communications committee, this was a group of people I could trust to do what was asked and to do it professionally.

That summer, our family trip was to Rehoboth Beach, Delaware. Nancy, at almost five and a half with long wavy blond hair, loved being on the beach and running away from the waves. Hazel, now two, was not that taken with the water and was happy to shovel sand from the beach into her bucket, and some onto her knees, over her shoulders, and into her golden blond hair, all day long. No major news story broke while we were on vacation this year. All in all, if the rest of the year was like 2017, I would've happily coasted to the holidays and into the following year. But this wasn't going to be like 2017.

The 2018 midterm elections gave Democrats a chance to capture at least one house of Congress, a necessary step to hold the Trump administration to account. These elections had the highest stakes of any effort we had been a part of yet. Steve and I were preparing our members for the midterms. At monthly meetings dating back to 2017, I gave a broad overview of how Indivisible Montgomery worked with campaigns: we didn't have the resources for advertising or identifying potential supporters, but we could amplify campaigns' voter contact efforts. Steve would lead sessions discussing the benefits of writing letters and postcards to voters, overcoming fears of phone banking, and why canvassing was awesome. We emphasized the benefits of each voter outreach mechanism to get members to engage in multiple ways. Knocking on someone's door and having a face-to-face conversation tended to be the most effective in turning out voters, but this was time-consuming. Calling or texting voters would get their attention, but it was easy for the recipient to ignore the call or text. Writing letters or postcards was the least effective at turning out voters but could be done on a large scale.

By the end of August, every contested primary race across the country was decided, and campaigns were launching voter contact

The first annual Indivisible Montgomery picnic was a huge success. Several dozen members attended, as well as lieutenant governor candidate Susie Turnbull (*left foreground*), Montgomery County Executive candidate Marc Elrich (*second from right*), Montgomery County School Board candidate Karla Silvestre (*front center, in polka-dot dress*).

operations. This is what we had prepared for. After some long conversations over the summer, Steve and I proposed to the steering committee that Indivisible Montgomery work on eight races: the Maryland governor's race, the race for Maryland's Sixth District in the House, and six House races outside of Maryland. The steering committee approved, and Steve and I started filling our calendar with opportunities for our members to help these campaigns. Postcard- and letter-writing parties occupied our schedules early on, while phone banks and canvasses became more prominent and popular as we approached November.

The end of August was the right time to pivot Indivisible Montgomery's attention from our weekly activism to elections work, and I wanted to do something different from our normal monthly meeting. With the support of the steering committee, I invited Indivisible Montgomery, and our friends and allies at DoTheMostGood, J Walkers, and others, to join us for a picnic at a nearby park. Everyone could bring a lunch, write some postcards, listen to a few candidates speak, and formally launch our get-out-the-vote (GOTV) efforts.

One of the best parts of planning the picnic was the little preparation needed. I rented a pavilion at Wheaton Regional Park, a large county park 10 minutes from our house. Karen Sultan, who often served as our liaison with invited speakers, extended invitations to several local elected officials and candidates to speak and mingle at the picnic. Steve gathered the materials for the postcard writing. And that was it. Far less work than most of our other events.

On the day of the picnic, the weather was perfect—sunny and in the mid-80s with a slight breeze. Our pavilion was a short walk from the parking lot and not too far from a massive playground, which made Nancy and Hazel happy. Just down a slight hill was a carousel that ran throughout the day and a kid's train station. I hung the Indivisible Montgomery banner along our pavilion so attendees could find us. By noon, 75 people had gathered, and I got everyone's attention. "Welcome to the first Indivisible Montgomery picnic and thank you all for coming today!" At that moment, the kid's carousel started up, and I was distracted with its 1920s-era county fair music. I raised my voice a bit. "I always wanted to have background music while I spoke. I just thought it would have been a little more dramatic. And current."

After the laughter, I thanked our partner organizations for coming out, discussed our brief agenda, and indicated where people could sign up to canvass and phone bank. Steve then explained the postcard-writing exercise. Everyone was enthusiastic, and the open format allowed us to mingle in a way we didn't often get to at our meetings. Susie Turnbull, candidate for lieutenant governor and Ben Jealous's running mate, attended and charmed everyone she spoke with. Montgomery County Executive candidate, and eventual winner, Marc Elrich also showed up, and we had several school board and county council candidates present as well. This was great news, because while we invited Turnbull and Elrich, the other candidates came only because they saw our advertisements.

On reflection, this was one of the most fulfilling events Indivisible Montgomery sponsored. The setup was low stress, the weather was beautiful, and attendees engaged with our activities. And because my official duties were minimal, I could handle one or both girls while Katherine spoke to friends and wrote postcards. We finally found an event where we could balance family and resistance work. The event went off without a hitch, and it was a lot of fun. The picnic was so successful and well attended it became an annual event that persisted even after my tenure as Indivisible Montgomery director ended.

Indivisible Montgomery Newsletter: Week 88

SEPTEMBER 3, 2018

THE HOUSE RETURNS FROM recess tomorrow and will likely be in session for only two weeks; the pressure of the building blue wave will cause House leadership to adjourn the chamber until after the election. These two weeks will be intense, as several hot-topic issues, like funding the federal government and President Trump's border wall, must be completed by mid-September.

The Senate could stay in session longer than the House, possibly to try to confirm Brett Kavanaugh to the Supreme Court, but their time in DC is likely short as well.

Not to be outdone, our resistance effort is kicking into high gear. Indivisible Montgomery is marching in the Kensington Labor Day parade, cosponsoring the Blue Wave Kickoff Rally on Sep. 15, and holding an in-person meeting on Sep. 29. Our resistance partners have special events throughout the month as well. And woven through all of this are nearly daily opportunities to knock on doors and make calls to get people engaged in the November election.

The Blue Wave Rally

Two weeks after our picnic, Katherine, Nancy, Hazel, and I put on our jackets and traveled to Rockville High School on an unusually brisk September day. We were headed to the Maryland Blue Wave Rally to energize our members to work hard throughout the midterm election season. Since the early spring, we group leaders in Montgomery County discussed how to best work together for the midterms, including holding a rally to generate enthusiasm for our GOTV efforts. This led to the founding of the Maryland Blue Wave Coalition—a group of resistance organizations working together to elect Democrats in the midterms. With us were our longtime allies J Walkers Action Group and DoTheMostGood, as well as Progressive Action Montgomery County and the Women's Democratic Club of Montgomery County.

We intended the rally to be similar in scale and importance to the town hall we organized in February 2017. We wanted people to get excited about the work ahead and to sign up for canvassing, phone banking, and texting. Prominent elected officials and candidates were invited to speak, and we interspersed group leaders among these officials to specifically advertise voter-engagement opportunities and encourage attendees to get involved. Compared to the town hall 19 months earlier, scheduling the elected officials for the rally was without drama. We had months to plan, and these people knew who we were and had attended at least one of our prior events. Nearly everyone invited agreed to attend. We had Representatives Jamie Raskin and John Sarbanes, Delegate Hala Ayala of Virginia, and the Democratic nominee for governor, Ben Jealous. David Trone, candidate for Maryland's Sixth District, couldn't join us as he was recovering from surgery, but his daughter Michelle spoke in his stead.

In addition to his roles on the steering and Elections committees, Steve Pressman was the Indivisible Montgomery liaison to the Blue Wave Coalition. I checked in with Steve regularly to learn about developments and to see how I could best support him. As soon as we had a date picked, I placed reminders about the rally in messages to the membership. I mentioned it several times at the picnic, a week later when we marched at the Kensington Labor Day Parade, and any other time I was around other Indivisible Montgomery members. The members of the Elections committee either volunteered to work the Blue Wave Rally or kept the committee humming along while Steve and others contributed to the event. Indivisible Montgomery didn't skip a beat.

As the leader of Indivisible Montgomery and one of the founding members of the Maryland Blue Wave Coalition, I was given a speaking slot in the program. I had a brief discussion with Steve to offer him the speaking slot—he had put a lot of effort into the event, and I thought he may have wanted the opportunity. He immediately rejected the idea. That made me happy because I wanted to speak. It was only a two-minute slot, but I was determined to make the most of it. I wanted to shed the steady, reassuring tone I adopted for the newsletter and the focused, relaxed effort of the monthly meeting to try something uplifting and motivational. I wanted to impart the

Indivisible Montgomery at the 2018 Kensington Labor Day Parade.

immediacy of the moment and get people cheering. Without telling her about my goals for the speech, I showed Katherine my first draft, and she immediately picked up on what I was trying to do. She made some great edits and, a couple of drafts later, I was ready.

As we walked from the parking lot, about 100 people crowded the entryway and the path to the Rockville High School auditorium. Once we entered the building, our regular ritual began. Various resistance activists from across the county would shake hands with me and Katherine, coo over the kids, and make chitchat, all while Katherine and I did our best to maneuver us to avoid the cranks. We wove through the crowd and made it into the auditorium. The place was filling in fast. After finding a place to sit, I went to find the greenroom and the last-minute information about where to go and when. My speaking slot was in the middle of the program, so I could hang out with my family for the first third and take some pressure off Katherine watching the girls. Nancy was five and a half and could sit still for about 30 minutes. Hazel was two and could not.

The lights dimmed and the program began. I paid little attention to the first few speakers. If I wasn't helping my kids, I was going over my speech in my head. At this point, it wasn't the words I was concerned about—I had it memorized and a printout in case I forgot anything—but I considered what to emphasize, when to pause, and when to push through. At the appointed time, I gave Katherine a kiss and the girls a hug and headed back to the speakers' area.

I entered the backstage space and immediately spotted half a dozen people I knew from other activist events, including Steve Pressman. While not interested in being a speaker in the program, he seemed more than happy to MC the event. When Steve's mic was off, we chatted and I shook hands with the others directing the backstage traffic. I was scheduled to speak immediately after Michelle Trone. When she went on, I was directed to a position just offstage to wait my turn. I didn't hear much of what Michelle said; I was focusing on my own words. Once she stepped off the stage, Steve's deep, disembodied voice announced me and the applause started. I walked across the stage in my Indivisible Montgomery T-shirt and slacks, waving. I set my notes down on the lectern, looked up to wait for the applause to finish, and nearly panicked. The stage lights blinded me. I could see my notes or I could look to my left at the first two or three rows. Everywhere else was bright light. I gripped the lectern, took a deep breath, allowed my vision to come back, and began to speak:

Hello, Blue Wave! Friends, my name is Chris Pickett and I'm the director of Indivisible Montgomery.

Indivisible Montgomery has been working for more than 20 months to resist the Trump administration and its GOP enablers.

We have marched and protested, called to protect our health care and preserve the Mueller investigation, and we've worked on special elections, attended meetings, and grown our resistance community.

Friends, history will surely judge Donald Trump. But make no mistake, history will also judge we the people. Will history books record that in 2018 Americans kept Republicans in charge because things were going well?

Or will those history books record that Americans stood up and said that it is unacceptable for our government to ban Muslims from entering our country?

That it is unacceptable for politicians to try and take away our health care?

That it is unacceptable for our government to rip children away from their parents after crossing our border?

And that it is absolutely unacceptable that our president would try to erase the lives of nearly 3,000 American citizens that died in Puerto Rico?

This is the crossroads we are at, and it's your work over the next seven weeks that is going to be the most important factor in making the Blue Wave a reality.

As you saw on your way in, we are asking people to sign up to do this work. Of course, we need you to vote and to remind others to vote. Starting this coming Thursday evening and every Thursday evening through the election, Indivisible Montgomery will be hanging signs off of highway overpasses to remind people to vote.

You can join us as we register voters all over the county to get them involved in our democratic process and so we can block the GOP's voter suppression agenda.

You can join us and our partners as we canvass. Knocking on doors and having conversations is the most effective way to turn people out. You can talk to people about Ben Jealous. And be ready, you'll come across people who will say that Larry Hogan has been a fine governor. You tell them that fine isn't good enough for Maryland! We need progressive leaders with a bold vision for moving our state forward and those leaders are Ben Jealous and Susie Turnbull!

And tell them that Larry Hogan has undercut the work of the wonderful Brian Frosh, who we need to return to the attorney general's office.

Join us in phone banks, text banks, and postcard parties so that we can tell people why we need to elect David Trone and reelect Ben Cardin and Jamie Raskin and John Sarbanes and the rest of the Maryland Democrats.

And we're even working on races across the country in Pennsylvania, Virginia, Illinois, Texas, and other places because, while our representatives are great, they need help from the inspiring new crop of Democrats popping up across the country.

And come to our meeting on Sep. 29 at the Kensington Park Library where we'll hear from Susie Turnbull. You can find out more about our events by going to indivisiblemontgomery.org and signing up for our newsletter.

And if you don't join up with us, please, join up with another group here. They're all doing excellent work and we all have the same goal.

Finally, please sign up to canvass or host a postcard party or phone bank. And if you've already done so, please sign up for one more. Because we need to do all the work necessary to build our Blue Wave so that come November, we sweep the GOP out of Washington, out of Annapolis and out of power across the country! Thank you!

I waved to a round of applause as I walked off the stage. I was all smiles as I shook Steve's hand on my way out, and I still had so much adrenaline coursing through me that I nearly ran down the hall. I had fun. My preparation paid off. I spoke forcefully, and I got applause where I expected it. I got some where I didn't expect it, which was surprising. I didn't rush or flub any of my lines, and I was on time. I've never had a talk go as flawlessly as this one. As I picked my way back to my family, I was astounded to see that the auditorium was standing room only, and the crowd was well over 500—easily the biggest crowd I've ever spoken to.

Once I found Katherine we decided to go outside. The girls needed exercise, and I was too energized to sit down. Katherine was excited for me. She said I was able to connect with the crowd, which not everyone had done that day. And even though they were not my target audience, the girls said they liked what I said, and I appreciated their support.

We were the only ones outside as Hazel and Nancy ran around, so Katherine and I noticed when two gentlemen exited the high school, spotted us, and changed direction to come our way. I didn't know what to expect as they got closer. The taller of the two spoke in slightly accented English. "Thank you," he said. "My friend and I are from Puerto Rico, and we are concerned everyone will forget about what happened in the hurricane. You were the only speaker to mention it so thank you for reminding everyone." It was such a warm, unexpected, and heartfelt response to my remarks. I was stunned. Katherine almost cried. We thanked them and chatted a little longer before they went on with their day.

Once I felt ready to sit down and listen to more speakers, we went back in. I hadn't kept track of time, and by then the rally was breaking up. We started the exiting ritual—shaking more hands and receiving compliments on how well-behaved Nancy and Hazel were. The rally served its purpose. Enthusiasm surged and we had phone banks, canvasses, and letter-writing parties all full of new volunteer energy. The Blue Wave Rally was probably the best coalition event Indivisible Montgomery was a part of.

Kavanaugh

AT THE VERY FIRST Indivisible Montgomery meeting in January 2017, I told the attendees that, with complete GOP control of the government, we would lose many of the fights we engaged in. And I was prepared for that. I didn't realize at the time how devastating some of those losses would be.

Supreme Court Justice Anthony Kennedy announced his retirement in June. The Federalist Society, a prominent far-right judicial activist group, had a list of ideologues they found suitable to fill any judicial vacancy, and Trump almost exclusively picked from their list. The administration ran this playbook the previous year with the appointment of Neil Gorsuch, and we knew we would oppose whoever Trump nominated. I'd ask readers to spare me the criticism that the nominee should be judged by their record rather than the nominator. The Federalist Society wouldn't have listed someone who wasn't an archconservative jurist, so there was little mystery as to the nominee's stances on any number of hot-button issues. We soon learned the nominee's name was Brett Kavanaugh.

Kavanaugh's confirmation hearings at the beginning of September were largely pro forma. The expected contentious questions were asked and avoided. Nothing came out that would sink his confirmation. Most of the journalists covering the Senate expected Kavanaugh would get a few Democratic votes and be confirmed without drama. We did what we could to rally opposition to the nomination, but this was flying under the country's radar. It was even under the radar of most members of Indivisible Montgomery. Kavanaugh was barely mentioned at our picnic or at the Blue Wave Rally.

Then the sexual assault allegations against Kavanaugh became public.

Christine Blasey Ford, a woman who knew Kavanaugh when they were teenagers, accused Kavanaugh of assaulting her at a party. She alleged a drunk Kavanaugh and friend lured her to an empty bedroom, where Kavanaugh forced himself on her. He eventually stopped and she ran out of the house and went home.[13]

These allegations focused the entire country on the Kavanaugh hearings. For more than a year, the country had been in the grips of #MeToo, a movement demonstrating how men abused their power to harass and assault women. Prominent men were finally getting their comeuppance and losing their jobs because they were sexual predators. And now #MeToo had come to the Supreme Court nomination process. In-person demonstrations were widespread, easily matching the size and intensity of the protests to save Obamacare a year earlier. The demand from protestors and Democrats was simple—conduct a thorough investigation to prevent appointing a sexual predator to the Supreme Court. Republicans balked. They claimed these allegations were manufactured by Democrats to derail Kavanaugh's nomination.[14]

The most frustrating thing about the entire situation was how much Republicans didn't care about Blasey Ford or the possibility she might be right. They may not have said that, but whenever they were asked about Blasey Ford, they often responded by attacking Democrats for allowing the allegations to become public. They refused to engage with the possibility they might be appointing a sexual predator to the Supreme Court. In this, Republicans demonstrated to the country that any woman's real trauma was secondary to a conservative white man getting a promotion.

The appointment process reached a fever pitch when Blasey Ford testified before the Senate Judiciary Committee. Her testimony was riveting and thorough. She was believable and sympathetic. Typical for Congress, all senators on the Judiciary Committee had a chance to question her. Some Democratic senators took the approach that I thought made the most sense: sympathize with Blasey Ford and all the women who identified with her, remind everyone there was nothing special about Kavanaugh, and tell Republicans to start over. But most Senate Democrats on the committee decided to make speeches without making a point. Whereas the Democrats were, on balance, disappointing, the Republicans were a joke. Republicans, scared they'd make complete asses of themselves, hired Rachel Mitchell, a prosecutor from Arizona, to question Blasey Ford on their behalf.[15]

Kavanaugh had a chance to testify about the accusations. No Republicans had broken ranks saying they'd vote against him, so it seemed like the obvious thing for him to do would be to deny the allegations and focus on his conduct should he be appointed to the Supreme Court. Instead, Kavanaugh came out shouting about how he had been done a grave disservice by having to deal with the accusations against him. He lacked all compassion for Blasey Ford, who had lived most of her life as a survivor of sexual assault, and only focused on how he had been wronged. Committee Republicans, in all their spittle-hurling dreadfulness, joined Kavanaugh in attacking Democrats.

Indivisible Montgomery's work at this time was straightforward. I directed people to the nearest protest. This wasn't hard because, like Obamacare repeal the year before, you couldn't go outside without running into an anti-Kavanaugh protest. What was difficult was everything outside of that. Women were vocally and publicly reliving their rapes, assaults, and the countless harassments they faced. It was tough for me to listen to the stories that women told on TV, on social media, and in person, but not nearly as difficult as for the women who were reliving their assaults because of this national news story.

Kavanaugh was eventually confirmed by the Senate by a narrow vote. The odds of derailing Kavanaugh's nomination were not in our favor. But some fights need to be fought. This was the right fight. But the loss still hurts.

Indivisible Montgomery Newsletter: Week 93

THIS PAST WEEKEND WAS difficult. I, like many, found myself cycling between despair and rage at the confirmation of Brett Kavanaugh.

The raw emotions on display were a stark reminder of the election of Donald Trump. Trump's election made it crystal clear just how much the GOP trades on white grievance, privilege, and nationalism. The Kavanaugh confirmation reminded us just how strong this affinity is, and it brightly illustrated the roadblocks the GOP is setting up to maintain power. It is incredibly frustrating and enraging to see our country consumed by people more invested in their own power than their constituents' well-being.

But the remedy to this is the remedy we've had at our disposal all along: The power of We The People to make the government look and act as we deem it should. If you're looking to shake yourself out of despair, realize the power to change the government is in your hands. If you're looking for a place to put your anger, we have opportunities for fruitful work between now and the election. But know that the only way to block to the GOP's brazen power grab is to vote them all out!

Indivisible Montgomery is committed to inclusiveness, fairness, and transparency in our government, which made the Kavanaugh nomination exactly the kind of fight we should engage in. We may have lost that battle, but the struggle remains. Let's get to work.

The Cruelty

It was impossible to do the work of the resistance for long without trying to understand the motivation behind the Trump administration. What was the throughline that connected the administration's conduct around the Kavanaugh nomination with that of the family separation policy? And how did that relate to the Muslim ban and the push to end Obamacare? Countless op-eds blamed racism or rank incompetence, others suggested idiocy, and still others blamed idiotic racism or incompetent idiocy. These theories explained much of the administration's actions, but they couldn't explain everything.

In science, developing a coherent explanation of a phenomenon that incorporates all the data, even the seemingly contradictory results, can reorganize and reorient an entire field. That was why Adam Serwer's "The Cruelty Is the Point" was such a revelation.[16] Serwer brought the actions of the Trump administration into focus and explained the unifying theme in five words. The administration was incompetent, and no one in the administration cared to do their job effectively. They were idiots and didn't care to learn. They were racist and didn't care to hide it. From its treatment of the people of Puerto Rico to family separation to naming "shithole countries" to Kavanaugh to every tweet and executive order and the mountain of other awful actions, intentional cruelty was the unifying theme explaining the actions of the Trump administration.

Serwer gave us a new framework for understanding the administration's actions and what we should expect in the future. It was incredibly accurate. Unfortunately, it did not alleviate the terrible toll this would take on the country.

A Blue Wave

EVER SINCE OUR PICNIC in August, Indivisible Montgomery had been organizing and amplifying get-out-the-vote efforts with campaigns across the country. With his contacts to other groups, Steve had us plugged into phone banks multiple times a week and canvassing in Maryland, Virginia, and Pennsylvania every weekend. Steve and I organized and hosted texting and postcard-writing events at separate pubs every week starting in September through the election. Members hosted phone banks and postcard-writing parties of their own across the county. And I advertised everything through the newsletter. The Monday message gave an overview of the upcoming week and listed a calendar of elections-related activities. The calendar was updated and repeated for the call-your-member-of-Congress Tuesday newsletter. Even with these messages going out regularly, I received multiple emails each week asking what elections events were coming up. So I resurrected the Thursday newsletter to update the calendar. Along with our partners, we had elections-related events nearly every day from September through Election Day on November 6. Even through the Kavanaugh nomination protests, attendance at each of these events was at or near capacity.

The consistently high turnout for our events was in line with polling across the country indicating enthusiastic support for Democrats. Most forecasters predicted the Democrats would take the House and lose seats in the Senate, but they differed over the size of the Democratic House majority. Those forecasting a great night for Democrats projected a 40–50 seat majority in the House, while dour predictions suggested Dems would hold a 5-seat majority. When selecting campaigns to support, Indivisible Montgomery chose Democrats who hadn't garnered national attention and were running in long-shot, but not impossible, races. We reasoned that, if our work made these races more competitive, it would tie up GOP resources in seats they likely considered safe. And we might even flip a couple seats. The downside was that, if Democrats didn't have a great night, we'd constantly second-guess our decision not to work on more winnable races.

I didn't sleep well the night before the election. Would all the organizing and learning and spending translate into a Blue Wave, or were the positive signs over the past two years a mirage? Would Democratic voters turn out for a midterm? They often didn't. Republican turnout tended to be consistent across all election years, whereas Democratic voters often turned out in presidential election years but not the midterms. Could we reverse that trend with our writing, texting, calling, and knocking on doors?

Despite all these concerns, I felt relieved come Election Day. There wasn't much to do but wait. Katherine and I voted early. There were two newsletters to send that day: one reminding people to vote and the second explaining how they could still help get-out-the-vote efforts. I had written those over the weekend, so I only needed to make sure they were sent as scheduled. Schools were closed, and Katherine and I spent much of the day hanging out and entertaining the girls.

Katherine asked if I was going out that evening, Tuesdays being my regular night out of the house. I laughed. There was no way. I couldn't bear the thought of being around people. What if this night was as bad as 2016? After all that I had invested. After all Katherine had done. After everything Indivisible Montgomery did. What if we lost? I couldn't be around people. Along with some of the other resistance leaders, I had been invited to the Montgomery County Democrats' election watch party, but I turned that down. I didn't want to risk ugly crying in public.

Instead, my "night out" meant that, after dinner, I gave everyone a good-night hug and rushed down to the basement. I opened my computer and pulled up several websites to watch the returns. It was 7:00 p.m. and most polls didn't close until 8:00 Eastern, so I wrote some newsletters: one if we won the House, one if we lost, and one if it was too close to call. I didn't write anything about the Maryland governor's race or who controlled the US Senate. Honestly, the importance of those races paled in comparison to the race for the House. It took one house of Congress to put a check on the Trump administration. The House of Representatives was in reach and we needed to win it.

While writing those messages, I kept an eye on some of the early races. None were critical, but they might indicate how the rest of the night would go. The biggest of these was Amy McGrath's race in Kentucky's Sixth District. McGrath had been a viral star who attracted a lot of money in her bid to unseat Rep. Andy Barr. She was clearly a long shot, but because of the national attention her campaign garnered, Indivisible Montgomery didn't work on this race. Many activist groups did though. Could our national movement motivate people to turn out to vote Democrat in bright-red Kentucky? The early returns showed Barr leading but it was close, much closer than any of his previous races. As the updates came in, McGrath wasn't closing the gap. I told myself that this one race, even though it had gained a ton of attention, was always going to be tough to win. Barr was well liked, and Kentucky was a deep-red state. I should have been heartened that the race was so close. It was fine to have a moral victory in Kentucky, but it couldn't be a night of moral victories. Not tonight.

The next two hours were nerve-racking. Polls were closing, but it takes time to properly tally and report the votes. I had MSNBC on one of my browser tabs, but I mostly focused on Twitter. Every news organization and elections expert was on Twitter. As results came in, it was clear Democrats were doing as expected in the seats they were supposed to win and somewhat better than expected in the seats they weren't. It was the toss-ups, though, that we needed information on and that would take a while.

Katherine joined me around 10:00 p.m. "How's it going?" she asked.

Before I could say "we don't know much just yet," the election results went from a trickle to a fire hose. Nearly all the polls had been closed in the Eastern and Central time zones for an hour or two, and some were closing in other parts of the country. Democrats started to notch victories as races that were expected to flip from Republican to Democrat did flip, and several of the Democrats in close races from earlier in the evening pulled ahead. It was tough to keep track, both because so many calls happened quickly and because there were some surprises. The surprises took investigation. I didn't want to get suckered into thinking we were doing better than we were. Did we win the governorship of Kansas and a House seat in the middle of Oklahoma? We did! Indivisible Montgomery hadn't worked on those campaigns so these were bonus wins. Checking in on the candidates Indivisible Montgomery supported, I saw they were winning or running close.

By 11:00 p.m., multiple outlets made the call: Democrats had won the House. The final number of seats gained wouldn't be known for some weeks, but we hit the magic number needed to flip the chamber.[17] We did it! I was elated and relieved. All our work over the past two years to safeguard democracy and hold the Trump administration to account paid off in this resounding electoral victory. Indivisible Montgomery played a pivotal role in changing the course of our country.

In the races we specifically worked on, we helped Abigail Spanberger, Elaine Luria, and Sean Casten flip seats long held by the GOP, and David Trone's victory meant Democrats kept Maryland's Sixth District. We lost the other races we worked on, but we had picked long shots so going four for eight was pretty good. The races we lost were competitive, and I felt good about our investments. The exception was Ben Jealous's run against Governor Hogan. Jealous's inability to raise money and Hogan's political savvy helped him beat Jealous by a wide margin. Democrats also lost seats in the US Senate, but not as many as had been feared.

I couldn't have felt much better. We accomplished our goal of building a Congress that would hold the Trump administration accountable. It's true that an incumbent president's party often loses seats in midterms, but that is never guaranteed. Certainly the scale of the victory—40 seats flipped in the House—was unexpected.

Our primary goal of removing Trump from office, however, remained. We learned how to work on elections in 2017 and we were a force to be reckoned with in 2018. The presidential election was two years away, and I needed to keep the organization sharp for those two years. As I went to bed that night, I was already thinking about how to shift our focus from elections back to what defined Indivisible Montgomery before the midterm season started: community-based activism.

Indivisible Montgomery Newsletter: Week 97

WHAT AN INCREDIBLE NIGHT! While results are still rolling in, it is clear that the Democrats have won the House of Representatives! This means that the Democrats will finally be able to do the things we've been asking Congress to do since President Trump took office—execute effective oversight of Trump, the White House, and the entire administration. We will finally be able to hold this thieving, racist, misogynist administration to account.

Of course, we didn't win every race. Ben Jealous lost to Larry Hogan. Beto O'Rourke, Andrew Gillum and Stacey Abrams lost their bids. And Democrats lost seats in the U.S. Senate.

But this election is a big deal with big implications for our state and country as this piece lays out. And in Maryland:

- We reelected Brian Frosh with 1.3 million votes . . . so that he can continue to protect us from the excesses of the Trump administration.
- We elected Marc Elrich and four new Democratic At-Large County Council members.
- Democrats were elected to the Maryland Senate and Assembly from across our county.
- Maryland voters approved same-day voter registration!

An Award

I WOKE UP ON November 7 feeling the lightest I had since Trump was elected. Two years of hard work and keeping the faith that we had the power to change the course of our country had paid off. Trump was still the president, and his administration continued enacting awful policies. But we could take this day to enjoy ourselves.

I checked my email before breakfast to see several responses to the previous night's newsletter, expressing excitement that we won or relief that we made a difference. One message was out of place, though. A message from Barbara Noveau of DoTheMostGood. I read her email and my jaw dropped. She attended the election watch party with the Montgomery County Democrats the night before. That was the invitation I turned down in case the night didn't go as planned. At the party, Indivisible Montgomery, DoTheMostGood, and the other founding members of the Maryland Blue Wave Coalition were presented the Democracy Summer Leadership Award by Rep. Jamie Raskin for "remarkable and inspiring leadership and activism in the democratic resistance, resurgence, and renewal." I was shocked. Not only did we help Democrats win the House, but my congressman, one of the most progressive defenders of democracy in our country, gave us an award for our work. In my mind, I clearly said, "Katherine, come look at this!" In reality, Katherine came over to see why I was grunting and gurgling as I tried to process the news of Raskin's award.

The Maryland Blue Wave Coalition won an award from Rep. Jamie Raskin's Democracy Summer Leadership program for our work helping elect Democrats in the 2018 midterms. *From left:* The founders of the Coalition—Peter Henderson (Progressive Action Montgomery County), me (Indivisible Montgomery), Barbara Noveau (DoTheMostGood), and Jon Heintz (J Walkers Action Group). A representative from the Women's Democratic Club of Montgomery County was not able to attend.

I needed to get a message out to Indivisible Montgomery telling them about this news. It was the organization's award, and it was due to all the work the members had done over the past several months. I also told Indivisible Montgomery that J Walkers was throwing a party to celebrate the election outcome and was inviting every person who wrote, texted, called, canvassed, and made donations.

The party was a family affair for the Picketts. Katherine and I wanted to celebrate, and we wanted to bring the girls because they were a big part of our experience in the greater resistance. The trouble was the party was scheduled when we normally ate dinner and put Nancy and Hazel to bed. Any parents of a five- and two-year-old will tell you that dinnertime and bedtime are not something to tinker with. But we were the only people with young children in the group, and those planning the party set it for a time that works best for adults. On top of bad timing, the food was suspect. Everyone was asked to bring appetizers or desserts. Katherine and I agreed we would try to make a meal out of the food there to satisfy Nancy and Hazel.

The biggest difference between parties for kids versus adults is when you show up. There is no "fashionably late" for kids' parties. You show up on time. Katherine and I were still in kids' party mode, so we were the first non-organizers to arrive at the election party. The event was held in a Democratic Party office that was unused that evening. The space was as basic as you could get—white walls, gray cubicle dividers, and fluorescent lighting. It did have a large open area, though, which was where we would congregate. Eventually 75 people showed up, including many members of Indivisible Montgomery. Everyone I spoke to was relieved and excited for the 2020 election. In between brief conversations, Katherine and I both worked the girls through the food line, trying to find food that was nutritious, filling, and that they would eat. About an hour in, Jon Heintz of J Walkers got everyone's attention. He first told everyone about the award we won from Representative Raskin. After the applause died down, the group leaders took the opportunity to make remarks and pose with the award. Par for the course, Katherine missed my remarks because she was helping Hazel in the bathroom. I told her she didn't miss much—I congratulated everyone and asked them to not check out between now and when we started working on the 2020 election. The rest of the party was mingling and snacking, though the food wasn't enough for the girls. We made an early exit and finished our celebration at a nearby restaurant.

Planning for a Whole New Life

The final Indivisible Montgomery in-person meeting of the year was the first weekend of December. We were at Gaithersburg Library, the same spot where Sen. Chris Van Hollen had spoken to us a year earlier. The current meeting, though, wouldn't be such a large affair. It was just Indivisible Montgomery as we talked about how to chart the organization's path for the next two years. I was arranging some chairs when Nina Liakos, the chair of our Administration committee, came up to me and timidly said, "Chris, after your opening remarks, can I have some time to speak to the group?"

Nina was incredibly active in Indivisible Montgomery and attended nearly every meeting. She had never asked to speak to the group before though, and my curiosity was piqued. I said, "Of course! What about?"

"I, um, have something to give you."

I looked at Nina suspiciously but didn't press her anymore. "Yep, you can have the mic. Just wave your hand if I start to move into the Q&A without remembering you wanted to speak." Katherine came up and started talking to me, keeping me from dwelling on the interaction with Nina. We had found a babysitter, and I was happy to have Katherine back at the monthly meetings. She attended only a few that year, and I was always glad when she was there. Katherine had good ideas, regardless of the discussion topic, and she wasn't afraid to voice them. Shortly after, it was time to start the meeting. Attendance that day was looking better than expected. I thought everyone would take a break after the election and the celebration party. Instead, 60 people showed up.

I made my introductory remarks and before the Q&A started, Nina raised her hand. I had already forgotten she asked me to speak, but once her hand went up, I passed her the mic. She took it. "Hi everyone, I'm Nina. And today I have the distinct honor of presenting an award to our executive director, Chris Pickett." I was stunned. She continued to say that Jane Barbara (the producer who invited me to the movie screening earlier in the year and was a local Democratic precinct captain) and her husband, Eric, made an award for me celebrating the work Indivisible Montgomery had done. I was touched, surprised, and more than a little emotional. I fumbled through some off-the-cuff remarks and thank-yous: Jane and Eric for the honor; Nina for presenting it and all her work for the organization; Steve Pressman and the tremendous amount of work his Elections committee had done. I had gotten near the end of my list, and I started to choke up. I paused to hold back the tears. Katherine, realizing I was about to end my acknowledgments, called out, "And how about that wife of yours!?" Katherine looked at me, incredulous, as the room erupted with laughter. I laughed, too, trying to avoid catching her "You forgot about me" look. I thanked her, Nancy, and Hazel profusely. She still ribs me about it.

Collecting myself, I moved on to business. I advertised this event as a chance to redefine how Indivisible Montgomery operated. Some of our committees had grown stale, and there were issues we weren't addressing. Here was an opportunity to see what people wanted to work on. I opened the floor to ideas for new committees, and the crowd was eager to participate. Immigration and gun control were perennial suggestions for which no one wanted to lead. Democracy reform—addressing issues such as the filibuster, voting rights, and gerrymandering—was a new one that seemed to have some traction. In the end, we were able to find people to take the lead on gun control and democracy reform. Members left the meeting excited. Having a majority in one of the houses of Congress was something Indivisible Montgomery had never had before. Ours was an energized group looking forward to a new year.

Indivisible Montgomery Newsletter: Week 104

Today is the two-year anniversary of Indivisible Montgomery! Our two years of work resisting the Trump administration and the GOP agenda culminated in a big blue wave that washed across the country in 2018. Thank you for everything you have done for our group, the resistance, and our country!

2019 | THIS IS NOT NORMAL

New Year, New Congress

As we rang in 2019, a new set of opportunities opened for our resistance efforts. The Democrats would formally take control of the House of Representatives, with Nancy Pelosi elected Speaker for the second time in her career. While Democrats controlled only one half of one branch of the government, they would have the power to launch investigations into the conduct of the Trump administration. And Indivisible Montgomery and the rest of the resistance were ready to push Democrats as far as necessary to make sure the administration's brazen corruption was exposed. We were full of veteran activists, but our excitement at the Democratic takeover of the House was grounded in reality and tempered with the lessons of the past two years.

On the first day of the new Congress, members of Indivisible Montgomery, Indivisible MoCo, and other long-standing resistance groups like MoCoWoMen traveled to Capitol Hill to meet with Rep. Jamie Raskin, Sen. Chris Van Hollen, and other members of the Maryland congressional delegation. We delivered to these offices a letter laying out our priorities for the next two years: expand voting rights, protect health care, and hold the Trump administration to account. We understood divided government meant few, if any, prospects of progressive legislation becoming law, but Democrats had power and we demanded they use it.

At the same time, we had a government shutdown to deal with. In the fall, Republicans in Congress passed a continuing resolution to fund the government partway through December. In December, rather than legislate, Republicans shut down the government. In recent history, government shutdowns occurred because of partisan differences on federal funding levels. Never before had the government shut down when all the levers of power were held by the same party. But this batch of Republicans had dumb ideas. Because they couldn't agree on how conservative their federal funding bill should be, they decided to punt funding decisions until Democrats took control of the House in January. The thinking went that, to fund the government, Democrats would have to acquiesce to some Republican demands, including funding Trump's monumentally stupid border wall, and legitimize other absurd Republican positions on government funding.

On January 3, Speaker Pelosi made the Democrats' counteroffer: Nothing.

The Republicans initiated the shutdown over funding of their extremist projects, and Democrats declared they weren't going to bail them out. The Democrats' position was that Republicans should support a reasonable plan to fund the government or pound sand. It was exactly the position the resistance wanted them to take. Republicans realized they had no cards left to play, as they were being pressured by people across the country to end the shutdown. Not that they moved quickly about it. The shutdown went on long enough

In the Hart Senate Office Building atrium protesting the GOP's government shutdown.

that protests were organized on Capitol Hill to urge lawmakers to do their job and fund the government.

By the end of January, the government was funded without the Democrats making any concessions, including no money for Trump's border wall. With a month lost to the shutdown, it was time for us to pressure Democrats into conducting real oversight of the Trump administration.

The National Emergency That Wasn't

THAT OVERSIGHT WAS TO begin immediately. When Democrats didn't give Trump money for his border wall, he issued an executive order declaring a national emergency at the country's southern border and directed money to build the wall. This was a big deal. Article 1 §9 of the US Constitution says, "No Money shall be drawn from the Treasury, but in Consequence of Appropriations made by Law ..." In other words, Congress determines how the US government spends its money, and it is up to the executive branch to spend it. Neither the president nor the rest of the executive branch can reprogram how federal money is spent without the express consent of Congress.

I couldn't believe it. This was a flagrant constitutional violation. I ran and told Katherine about it, gesticulating wildly and at a volume a couple notches higher than normal.

"Um, wow, that sounds bad," she said, not understanding why I was so animated. "Trump did what again?"

"He spent money meant for one program and used it for his stupid wall!"

"Right," she said. "I'm already against the wall."

"Not the wall. The money!"

I pulled up the Constitution on my phone to read her the passage. She still wasn't sold that this was as big of a deal as I was making it.

This encapsulated the problem. Trump was acting counter to the explicit wording of the Constitution. Katherine, and certainly many of the most committed people in the resistance, either wouldn't understand or wouldn't think it was a big deal. But this was legitimate impeachable conduct. I needed to get people fired up about this. How to message it? All I had now was, "The president made budgetary changes to build his racist border wall, and we need to be angry about the budgetary changes part." Not a winner.

What else could I do? A power grab dressed up in parliamentary procedure is still a power grab. So I laid it out over a series of newsletters. Start broad. Tell everyone where I want them to end up—thinking this is a big deal. Then focus in on the travesty of the situation—the Constitution says explicitly that Congress directs the Treasury how to spend its money, and the executive branch is not allowed to move that money around except in extreme emergencies. Which this wasn't.

After a few attempts, I was able to get our folks there. I think. It helped that some groups were already launching flash marches in protest of Trump's fake national emergency. These types of events started being organized around mid-2017 by the Move On organization. Originally, we were concerned that Trump would unilaterally fire Robert Mueller and end the investigation into Russian election interference prematurely, and we needed to be able to march as quickly as possible in response. Organizers would scout locations for a flash march, and people signed up for an email list to be notified when and where their local march would occur. I signed up for

After I spoke against Trump's fake national emergency, we marched.

three at the time—one in Rockville and two in DC. I'd find out later that the DC marches were actually the same event. At this point, though, nearly two years later, we were less concerned about Mueller being fired. Move On rightly recognized the seriousness of the fake national emergency and gave their march leads permission to launch their flash marches. I don't recall the DC march happening, but the Rockville one did. Nina Liakos, who was part of the group organizing that event, invited me to speak at the rally. A chance to speak in front of a crowd and just be angry was something I hadn't done before. It seemed like a good time.

On a mild Saturday in the middle of February, I went to be a firebrand. My family stayed home. It had been a busy time for us, and Katherine and the girls wanted to relax. I was happy for the quiet on the ride over because I hadn't fully figured out what I wanted to say. I had some ideas swirling around—things I had considered saying in other venues but opted not to. When I arrived, I had mashed those stray bits into a coherent speech. I normally worked from notes, but I decided against that this time. It would be my first time freestyling an activist speech.

As I walked to the rally spot, an odd and unfamiliar feeling came over me. I realized I did not want to be there. It was the feeling you get in your stomach when you show up to the house of a family member who you kind of despise, but it was their turn to host the holiday meal so you went anyway. I enjoy speaking in front of people and had not expected this. There wasn't anything my family had planned that I was missing. I just didn't want to be there. In fact, I would have rather been anywhere else. I had committed, though, and I joined the organizers in the park.

The rally was held at a small park in Rockville, and about 50 people gathered around the only monument in the park, an ornate, circular concrete bench. The breeze had died down and we got perfect weather for a rally given that it was February. The main organizer spoke first, and she was clearly not an experienced orator. She brought a bullhorn, which was good. She stood on the ground and spoke at a normal volume into the bullhorn, which was bad. No one more than five feet away could make out what she said. Once she handed it over to me, my two-plus years of experience speaking in front of people came into play. I stepped up on the bench so everyone could see me. Then I held the bullhorn to my mouth and projected like I wanted the entire park to hear me. And they did. What was it that I said? I don't quite remember. I do remember some people walking along the edge of the park took an interest in what I was saying and joined us. Beyond that, I recall the crowd liked my speech, and there was a fair amount of cheering.

Once I finished and handed the bullhorn to the next speaker, the urge to be anywhere else returned. This time, though, there was nothing compelling me to stay. I fully believed Trump's actions were an incredibly serious constitutional violation, and we were right to call him out. But I wanted to leave. I realized the marching route would take me near my car so I stayed for the beginning of the march. As we approached my car, I told the few people who needed to know that I had to leave.

It wouldn't be until much later that I realized these feelings were signs of burnout. At the time, all I knew was that I wanted to be anywhere but there. So I left.

The Website

"I WON'T BE RUNNING the website anymore."

Directing a volunteer organization is as much about setting a vision and mission as it is about managing conflicting personalities and trying to find people to take responsibility for specific tasks. Some people leave and it hurts. Some people leave and it's a relief. On this occasion, it was a mixed bag. On the downside, I hate building and running a website. On the upside, well ...

I sat in my living room on a warmer-than-normal March evening settling into my Indivisible Montgomery work when I saw an email I had been expecting. Earlier in the day, Carol McShea stormed out of the organization. The email this evening was from her husband, Jeff. "I won't be running the website anymore," he wrote. He was leaving in solidarity with his wife.

Since the T-shirt debacle at the 2017 Kensington Labor Day Parade, Katherine and I knew this split was coming. The trigger was a political interaction between Carol and Katherine on Facebook. Posts were made, comments deleted, and angry emails written. Our relationship became strained over the course of 2018 as Carol perceived honest mistakes as slights. My apologies moved us past the drama of the moment, but her bitterness increased with each successive disagreement. For Carol, her argument with Katherine on Facebook was the final straw. Carol resigned from her Indivisible Montgomery positions immediately. Jeff let me know the next day he would no longer be our webmaster. Because he was the only person managing the website, his absence meant I became the Indivisible Montgomery webmaster. Despite the additional responsibilities, I was relieved. Carol and Jeff's exit from Indivisible Montgomery significantly lowered the amount of drama I dealt with on a regular basis.

Departure

As I fixed up the new Indivisible Montgomery website one April evening, I stopped to check my email. In my inbox was an invitation to a remembrance service for Catherine Schupp. My brow furrowed and I sat down in the kitchen. A remembrance service? I must have read the message incorrectly. I reread it but still didn't believe what I was seeing. Katherine came into the kitchen and found me sitting there, stunned.

"What is it?"

"I think Catherine Schupp died." I showed her the message, and Katherine was shocked. We didn't have any details. We searched for an obituary, but none had been published. All we knew was there would be a service. Six weeks ago, Catherine was helping us organize the latest iteration of dine-arounds.

Catherine was an Indivisible Montgomery fixture. She was one of the founding leaders of the National Engagement committee, and she helped Katherine organize dine-arounds. Catherine showed up to our meetings, she opened her home to dine-around events and Indivisible Montgomery leadership meetings, she hosted postcard-writing parties, and she attended marches, rallies, and other events. She was always thoughtful and generous with her time. She was a consistent donor. A year ago, Catherine convinced her husband to help Katherine and me brainstorm ways to remodel the basement of our new home. She was an important part of Indivisible Montgomery, and she was important to my family.

As Katherine and I drove to the memorial, I thought deeper about the people I interacted with through Indivisible Montgomery. I knew only the activist dimension of the members' lives. The rest was hidden, partly by design. I worked hard to keep my work and family separate from my activism. The more they intertwined, the less I was able to maintain a healthy balance in my life. It worked the other way, too. Most of those in the group didn't know much about me other than what I said at meetings. I came to learn that in these decisions to separate was also a decision to not understand. To not engage with the parts of the lives that had brought these people to activism and to Indivisible Montgomery and to work together for a better country. Those parts that joined us together should have been a source of enjoyment for everyone.

The service was in an Episcopal church across the street from our neighborhood. We drove by the church countless times during our nearly seven years in Silver Spring; this was the first day we went in. We were thankful the service was in the middle of a weekday when the girls were at school. Katherine and I made our way through an ornate hallway into the chapel. I was taken with the deep-red carpets and oak-paneled walls. The soft lights gave the room a welcoming glow. Spaced evenly along the ten rows of pews were brochures with the readings and a page-length bio of Catherine.

The readings were thoughtful, the songs solemn. The eulogies, given by her two children, were moving. Catherine was a wonderful friend, a loving mother, and an amazing wife. The priest leading the service explained it was time for anyone who wanted to approach and receive the sacrament of Holy Communion. I wasn't going to receive the sacrament, so I took the small break to read Catherine's biography in the brochure. I stopped two-thirds of the way to the bottom. While listing the wonderful things Catherine had done with her life, her family included her role as one of the leaders of the Indivisible Montgomery National Engagement committee. I stared at that line. Catherine's work with Indivisible Montgomery was such an important part of what she did and of who she was that her family included it in a one-page story of her life.

I was burned out on resistance work. A day without thinking about Trump or Indivisible Montgomery sounded blissful right about then. Getting lost in the day-to-day grind, though, was an easy way to lose touch with what Indivisible Montgomery and our work meant to people. I set up Indivisible Montgomery so citizens could come to us to engage with the political process and make a difference in the community. To stand against every awful thing the Trump administration said and did on behalf of human decency and American democracy. I wanted our members to make activism a steady, dependable part of their lives, but I never considered what our work would mean to them. Aside from Katherine and myself, I never considered that some of our members would be so proud of the difference they made with Indivisible Montgomery that they would include it in the story of their lives.

I sat in that pew, reading Catherine's biography and staring at the evidence of how important Indivisible Montgomery was to her.

I was not ready to cope with that. I still haven't fully coped with it.

A Whimper

But as with many things in these times, I didn't have the personal time to cope with such things because the Trump administration was always doing something that required our attention. Democrats were slowly launching investigations and holding hearings into the actions of the Trump administration, and activists were encouraging them to go faster. We got sidetracked in mid-March by rumors that the Mueller investigation would soon end. During the investigation, former FBI director Mueller brought charges against Paul Manafort, Trump's onetime campaign manager and a key player in potential Russian involvement, and convicted him.[1] Mueller also brought charges against a prominent Russian international hacking group for their role in hacking the Democratic National Committee in 2016.[2] The end of the investigation meant we'd finally be able to see everything Mueller had found. This was also confusing, because the end of the investigation meant there would likely be no further indictments, despite what appeared to everyone outside the investigation to be crimes. We prepared ourselves for disappointment.

The first indication the public got of what was in the Mueller report was a short letter issued by newly installed Attorney General William Barr. I was at work on a phone call with Shirley Tilghman and the Rescuing Biomedical Research leadership when the *Washington Post* news alert hit my inbox. Our call was wrapping up, so I

On a rare date with Katherine in May 2019.

did my best to ignore the message until we were done. Once we hung up, I went to the story and read Barr's letter indicating the Mueller report cleared Trump, his family, and his campaign of any wrongdoing regarding Russian support for his campaign during the 2016 presidential election.[3] Barr buried Mueller's main takeaway, which was that "while this report does not conclude that the President committed a crime, it also does not exonerate him."[4] With only the Barr letter in hand, news outlets could have published headlines like "Mueller Refuses to Exonerate Trump." Instead, many propagated Barr's framing indicating Trump had done no wrong.

I sat back in my chair, deflated. I was never part of the "Mueller will save us!" crowd that believed the investigation would reveal some silver bullet to rapidly remove Trump from the White House. On the other hand, I thought the public reporting on how deeply corrupt the Trump campaign was meant that surely the Mueller investigation would turn over more indictments. I never thought

Trump would be indicted—standing Department of Justice policy was that presidents could not be indicted. That policy, though, led Mueller to not even consider whether Trump should be indicted for his campaign's interactions with Russia or his 10—10!—separate acts of obstruction of justice documented in the report. This was a terrible misreading of the political environment Mueller was operating in. And with House Democrats reticent to launch formal impeachment proceedings based on the Mueller report, the investigation ended with a whimper.

Indivisible Montgomery Newsletter: Week 117

March 28, 2019

This has been a difficult week for our resistance. The release of Attorney General William Barr's summary of the Mueller investigation stating no charges would be filed regarding conspiracy or obstruction of justice was simply stunning. Setting aside the serious problems in Barr's summary, the lack of any further action by Mueller made the end of the investigation confusing, anticlimactic, and disheartening.

The evidence in the public sphere indicating the Trump campaign coordinated with Russians and that Trump obstructed justice is overwhelming. The reporting on this is solid and has not been refuted. This is why we need public disclosure of the full Mueller report. But it is also important to take a breath.

Resisting is physically, mentally, and emotionally exhausting. We have been doing this for more than two years, and we have yet to find the bottom of the depths of corruption of the Trump administration. Coming back week after week in the face of such awfulness is difficult. I completely understand those who turn away from the news, unsubscribe from email lists, and focus on their personal lives.

And I also understand those who keep coming back to this work. Our people and our country are better than how we're being represented by Trump and the GOP. There is still so much worth fighting for, and so many people who need our help.

Because we no longer have to be on call to march to protect Mueller's job, and because the 2020 presidential race is in such an early phase, this is a good time to take a break for some self-care. If the events of this past week, month, or years have left you drained, take the time necessary to do what you need to recenter yourself. But please come back. The 2020 election is critical to rescue our country from the path it is on, and we are going to need everyone's work to win.

On the other hand, if the events of the past week have revved you up, then keep calling your members of Congress and tell them to move faster in putting a check on this administration.

And me? I'm going to take my own advice and take a breather. Aside from some reminder messages, and barring emergency actions, the Indivisible Montgomery newsletter is taking a break for most of April. I'll still be at the dine-arounds and working with Indivisible Montgomery leadership to make sure we're in the best position to resist effectively. But the updates and weekly actions will be on hiatus. The next edition of this newsletter will be in your inbox on Apr. 29.

Resistfully yours,

Chris Pickett

Let's Talk Impeachment

Back in April 2017, I stood on my porch talking on the phone as the sun set. Spring had taken hold and House Republicans had pulled their Obamacare repeal bill from the floor a few weeks before. I was feeling good. I was talking to my contact at national Indivisible as she checked in to see if we needed anything. We didn't, but I appreciated the check-in. She pivoted somewhat abruptly: "In the office, we're thinking it's time to start talking publicly about impeaching Trump." I was astonished. I wanted Trump out as much as the next person, and if there were a way to evict him sooner than January 2021, I'd be on board. But impeachment? At this point? The House would need evidence of serious misdeeds by Trump to start impeachment investigations, and the Republican Congress had shown no interest so far in the mountain of evidence that Trump was breathtakingly corrupt. Besides, I had been beating the drum for months that Indivisible Montgomery was going to work on the opportunities in front of us and not burn out on long shots, like an impeachment push in the first 100 days of an administration.

"I want to keep my folks focused on achievable victories and figuring out if Obamacare repeal is coming back," I responded. "If I take impeachment to my members now, it will tear down everything we've built." And I never heard anything more about it from national Indivisible.

But in 2019? The Mueller report detailed the interactions of the Trump campaign with Russians to subvert the 2016 election and 10 instances of Trump obstructing justice by trying to derail the investigation. The more I read of the stories, digging into the Mueller report and Trump's actions, the more I became convinced that a reasonable person would agree that Trump had abused the powers of his office. Should House Democrats impeach Trump based on the facts in the Mueller report? I thought so. But then the case would move to the Senate, where they would hold a trial and vote whether to convict or acquit Trump. In an evenly divided Senate, and Republicans showing no inkling of splitting with Trump, Trump would be acquitted. What was the point of impeachment if we knew the eventual outcome?

Nevertheless, I read a variety of articles discussing the benefits and pitfalls of the Democratic House launching an impeachment investigation. I became convinced to support impeachment when I realized that conviction in the Senate was not the only outcome of the process. The actions of the House in investigating wrongdoing by the president are important in and of themselves. Publicly airing everything Trump did to abuse his office would make it widely known. His corruption needed to be made plain—we could not simply assume all Americans knew of Trump's deep corruption. The investigations were the mechanism to increase support for Trump's impeachment. If he was impeached, the trial in the Senate was an additional forum to describe Trump's criminality to the American people.

Once I was in favor of impeachment, I needed to see if I could bring others along. I had many conversations with Katherine and the steering committee to convince them to support impeachment. The sticking points were whether the investigation was necessary and the anticipated acquittal in the Senate. I slowly won over Katherine and the steering committee. With my core sources of support in favor of impeachment, I turned my attention to the wider membership. I used the newsletter to advertise the next in-person meeting and made it clear we would be talking impeachment. We had been getting about 80 people at our monthly meetings, but that day in Gaithersburg Library, we had over 100. I guess impeachment piqued everyone's interest.

I led the meeting with some brief announcements, then got straight to the point. "The main topic for today's discussion is impeachment. After some intense discussions, the leadership of Indivisible Montgomery is in favor of supporting an impeachment inquiry into Trump's actions as outlined in the Mueller report. But we need the membership to buy in, which is why we're talking about it today.

"I want to make clear what we are saying. We are calling on the House to launch open, public impeachment proceedings. This means the House Judiciary Committee would hold a series of public hearings to question witnesses and present evidence of Trump's corruption and criminality. Beyond the corruption of the Trump campaign, there were also 10 instances Trump may have obstructed justice." I held up 10 fingers. Or I tried to as I was also holding a mic in one hand and my notes in the other. Call it six and a half fingers. "After these hearings, the committee would vote on individual articles of impeachment. Articles affirmed by at least half the committee would be forwarded for a vote by the full House. Should the House approve at least one article of impeachment, the Senate would then hold a trial."

A hand shot up. "Is an impeachment investigation necessary? Can't Democrats have their hearings without this formality?"

"Good question. I can think of two benefits. First, we can assume Democrats will call members of the Trump administration as witnesses, and they'll be reluctant to testify. The formal inquiry will provide a strong legal footing for Democrats to require witnesses to appear and for the White House to turn over documents. Second, the formal inquiry will focus the media and the public on the hearings. What better way to lay out Trump's criminality for all to see?"

Another hand. "The Senate won't convict, right? So what's the point?"

"Right. I don't think we should let the Senate dictate what the House does. The House should stand up against corruption and for the rule of law, investigate Trump, and, if warranted, impeach him. Whether or not the Senate will soil itself on this issue is immaterial to whether the House should stand up for what is right." There was some vigorous nodding, and that ended the discussion.

The following week, I led the Indivisible Montgomery steering committee to Capitol Hill to meet with the House members who represented Montgomery County—John Sarbanes, David Trone, and Jamie Raskin. It was a busy day in the House offices that day, and I wasn't sure if we'd be able to speak with the members or with their staff. Our first meeting was with Trone. I had met with Trone as part of a group of resistance leaders a few weeks before, and we had a vigorous discussion about impeachment. Trone said he supported impeachment, but, as a new member, he was cautious not to get on the bad side of Speaker Nancy Pelosi, who was still publicly opposed to it. However, that day with the Indivisible Montgomery steering committee, Trone seemed much more open to impeachment. I'd like to think our meeting from a few weeks prior had an effect, but it probably had to do more with Pelosi announcing that her fellow Democrats could speak their mind on impeachment without crossing her. The number of House Democrats publicly supporting impeachment was growing, which gave Trone room to say what he really thought. He gave us indications he was close to publicly endorsing impeachment.

When we got to Raskin's office, we learned he'd been called away and couldn't meet with us. That was too bad, but there was no suspense with this meeting. Raskin was one of the first Democrats to publicly support impeachment.

The most frustrating meeting was with Sarbanes. He, along with a couple of his aides, met with us. We made our argument for impeachment, and Sarbanes's counterargument was that the Republican Senate would never convict him, so why try. We made the same arguments to him that had won over the Indivisible Montgomery membership, but Sarbanes was too loyal to Pelosi to go against her. When it was clear no minds would be changed, I underscored the importance of our request for him to support impeachment. "I understand your position," I said. "You should also know that if House Democrats don't conduct aggressive oversight of this administration, I can't guarantee our members will work as vigorously in 2020 as we did in 2018."

Sarbanes locked in on me and turned his shoulders to face me fully. In his most reassuring tone, "We understand what you and groups like yours did in 2018. And we will do all that is reasonable and fruitful to hold this administration to account." The meeting ended shortly thereafter. After a brief set of goodbyes, members of the steering committee each set out to make our way home.

I was proud of myself for being so forceful in calling out Sarbanes and drawing a hard line, in a respectful way, as to what we expected from him. I never would have done this prior to launching Indivisible Montgomery. The change came from experience and realizing I didn't care what the members of Congress thought of me. I wasn't using these meetings to hone my skills, and I wasn't trying to get a job. I used these meetings to get my point across, and I had too many other things going on to shy away from clear and direct language.

Did it work? Well, Raskin was already in favor of impeachment before we went to Capitol Hill. Trone supported impeachment a couple of weeks after our visit.[5] Sarbanes never did. But I think we played a role in moving Trone, and I'm glad we did it.

The Double Life Continues

I HAD SET A path to keep my activist life leading Indivisible Montgomery separate from my professional life leading Rescuing Biomedical Research. No one in RBR knew I was leading this double life. That doesn't mean there weren't close calls.

Every year, RBR would convene in DC for a two-day meeting to discuss our progress and goals for the coming year. We invited federal officials to discuss matters pertinent to biomedical research and how we could work together to solve pressing problems. This was a point of anxiety for me. I kept RBR and Indivisible Montgomery separate, but I didn't go out of my way to hide my positions. If a federal official googled the employees of RBR before accepting our invitation, I was sunk. Searching the internet for "Chris Pickett RBR" brought up a couple of RBR hits and then Indivisible Montgomery ones. My picture was with both, so there was no hiding.

As these meetings approached, my mind would spin out scenarios. Does the Trump administration official meet with RBR if he knows a resistance leader is in the room? Is it more contentious because I'm there? If he declines the meeting, does he explain he won't meet with us because of my role with Indivisible Montgomery? What do Shirley and the rest of RBR do with that information? The way out of this anxiety spiral was to remind myself that, from the view of a Trump official, I was not the only red flag in RBR. Nearly all RBR members were Democratic donors. Shirley had been on the Commission on Presidential Debates, which Trump despised. Harold Varmus was appointed director of the National Institutes of Health by President Clinton and director of the National Cancer Institute by President Obama. I could go on. Instead of doing anything rash, I stayed quiet about my double life and let the situation play out.

The first time I went through this was 2017. The Trump administration was newly installed, and RBR was working to find anyone in a White House office who might give us insight into the administration's views on science policy. Shirley had a connection to Reed Cordish, assistant to the president for intragovernmental and technology initiatives. Cordish was a friend of Jared Kushner, Trump's son-in-law, who took a position in the Trump administration when they were having difficulty hiring competent people. Cordish accepted our invitation, and I was on pins and needles until he arrived. For the entire meeting, I was sweating, waiting for him to unmask me. It never happened. Cordish spoke to us and left without fanfare. The meeting was a waste of time—he had no science policy insights—but my secret remained.

This happened again in 2019. We invited Kelvin Droegemeier, the newly appointed director of the White House Office of Science and Technology Policy. OSTP coordinates science policy across the government, and the office included several people responsible for biomedical research policies. I was certain someone in OSTP would be savvy enough to look up the members of RBR. Apparently not. Aside from some Trump-esque comments from Droegemeier about immigrants, this meeting was also a waste. He admitted he was powerless on any issue of real importance.

Would my double life last through 2020 as well? There was no use in worrying about that now. RBR's funding, and my job, would end at the close of 2020 if we didn't secure a new grant. By the time we ensured new funding, we would hopefully have elected a new president and the double life wouldn't be necessary anymore.

Impeachment for Real

MUCH OF THE LATE spring and early summer was spent urging Democrats in Congress to support impeachment proceedings. It was slow going, but we felt good that more than half of the Democratic caucus signaled their support to open proceedings, including Representatives Raskin and Trone. While we worked on the Dems, the calendar kept flipping. It was the end of August, Indivisible Montgomery was preparing for our third march in the Kensington Labor Day Parade, and Katherine and I were preparing Nancy for first grade and Hazel for preschool. The girls had a good summer and enjoyed their day camps, but they were excited to be heading back to school, seeing their friends, and having a more regular schedule.

While we focused on the girls and on converting Democrats into impeachment supporters, rumors were swirling that a whistleblower from the US intelligence community was trying to catch the ear of members of Congress. A few weeks later, an incredible story broke that the whistleblower complaint dealt with Trump's conversations with a foreign leader.[6] A week later, the administration was tired of badgering from the press and attempted to defuse the situation by releasing the transcript of a call, which had been with Ukrainian president Volodymyr Zelenskyy.[7] And holy shit, whoever thought releasing the transcript would solve anything was very, very wrong. All hell broke loose. On the call, when Zelenskyy indicated his

Indivisible Montgomery at the 2019 Kensington Labor Day Parade.

country was ready to purchase US-made weapons, Trump brushed him aside and said, "I would like you to do us a favor." Trump went on to indicate the sale of the weapons would depend on whether Zelenskyy publicly announced a Ukrainian investigation of former vice president, and candidate for the 2020 Democratic presidential nomination, Joe Biden.

Trump plainly conditioned a formal US government response on a foreign leader helping his personal presidential campaign.

Grade-A, Mafia-level corruption from the president of the United States. Astounding.

The fallout was swift. Where it had taken us months to get Democrats on board with impeachment after the release of the Mueller report, these politicians consolidated behind an impeachment push over the call with Zelenskyy in a matter of weeks, including Pelosi.[8] It happened so fast that Indivisible Montgomery didn't have time to call our representatives to tell them to support impeachment. Representatives Raskin and Trone voiced their continued support for impeachment, and once Pelosi publicly supported impeachment, Representative Sarbanes did too.

The process moved quickly. Dismayed with how the Judiciary Committee handled its hearing with Robert Mueller over the summer, Pelosi turned the impeachment process over to the House Permanent Select Committee on Intelligence, led by Rep. Adam Schiff. Over the course of October and November, HPSCI held hearings to interview several witnesses. A firsthand witness from the White House testified to the veracity of the transcript. There were multiple Americans in Ukraine who testified the same and provided other damning background on their end of the call. Trump's ambassador to the European Union testified that there was, in fact, a quid pro quo in which Trump would release aid to Ukraine in exchange for the announcement of a Biden investigation.[9] There were so many smoking guns we were tripping over them.

Republicans rallied to Trump's side. It seemed like every member of the GOP found their own reason to excuse Trump's use of the powers of the presidency for personal political gain. It was telling that they had no real defense, because even the people closest to Trump couldn't agree on the best cover story. Just rank leader worship. It would have been embarrassing if it weren't so awful.

A Blue Streak

Elections? Again? The 2019 elections were a low-key affair. The contests that drew our attention were for the governor's mansions in Kentucky and Louisiana. Much of Indivisible Montgomery's membership had checked out for the 2019 election season, since it was an off year for Maryland, but we still advertised phone banks for those interested in doing elections work. It worked. Both Kentucky and Louisiana elected Democratic governors. Our streak of winning elections in the Trump era continued.

The most notable thing about the 2019 election season was that the end of it marked the beginning of the 2020 election season. This was the ultimate chance to get Trump out of the White House. It didn't matter who the Democratic nominee for president would be, we were all in. I made it clear that Indivisible Montgomery would support the Democratic nominee, regardless of who it was, but that didn't stop members from emailing me and telling me who they thought should be the nominee. Members supporting former vice president Joe Biden or Mayor Pete Buttigieg told me we needed to pick a moderate Democrat to woo independent voters. Those supporting Sen. Bernie Sanders or Sen. Elizabeth Warren told me we needed a bold progressive to energize the grass roots and turn out the base of the party. Among the 10 major candidates for the nomination, I got emails from members supporting almost all of them.

The whole family attended the December 2019 Indivisible Montgomery meeting as we kicked off our 2020 election work. Katherine and Hazel are sitting at the table and Nancy is on the floor looking through a book.

Even national Indivisible was getting in on the act. I received multiple messages from the organization saying that national Indivisible wanted to endorse a candidate in the Democratic primary, and they wanted to know how best to include the Indivisible chapters in that process. I responded as forcefully as possible, saying that national Indivisible endorsing someone would be a grievous mistake. I knew Indivisible Montgomery didn't depend on the national group and that communication between us was minimal. But most rank-and-file members didn't know that. An endorsement from national Indivisible would be misconstrued as an endorsement by Indivisible Montgomery, and that would fracture our membership. I was doing my best to hold Indivisible Montgomery together through the nomination contest, and an endorsement would undo all that work. Luckily, many other group leaders felt as I did and gave similar feedback. National Indivisible never made an endorsement in the 2020 Democratic nomination contest.

With regard to doing the work to get Trump out of office, Indivisible Montgomery wasn't going to wait until primary voting started in January. I advertised to the membership that the final in-person meeting of 2019 would be the first in our nearly 11-month-long campaign with Vote Forward to write letters encouraging voters to turn out for the 2020 election. With Vote Forward's system, we addressed form letters and personalized them by writing a few sentences explaining why voting was so important. The rest of the letter, prepared by Vote Forward, had information on where the recipient could vote. Eighty-five people showed up for our final meeting, and we wrote several hundred letters that day.

We would put the finished letters in envelopes, address and stamp them, and hold on to them until the final send date in mid-October. We didn't want money to be a big hurdle for writing letters, so Indivisible Montgomery committed to paying for stamps. To keep that promise, I set our end-of-year fundraising goal at $6,000, double any of our previous goals. We surpassed it in three weeks.

Indivisible Montgomery was ready.

A Firebrand

After the November 2019 election, the efforts to impeach Trump for extorting the Ukrainian president moved into a new phase. The House Permanent Select Committee on Intelligence had conducted all the necessary hearings and referred its findings to the Judiciary Committee for a formal series of hearings and votes on whether to refer Trump to the full House for a vote on impeachment. The Judiciary Committee approved the articles of impeachment in the beginning of December, and the full House was slated to vote on December 18.

In the lead-up to this momentous event, Move On, Indivisible, and several other groups organized impeachment rallies across the country for the night of December 17, save one slated for the Capitol complex on the morning of December 18. Nina Liakos invited me to speak at the Rockville protest on December 17, and I accepted immediately. Katherine wanted to go as well, so we packed a picnic dinner and brought the girls to make this another family resistance outing. On a frigid December night, we pulled into a parking lot near the rally point and ate our sandwiches and chips. In between bites, the girls chattered about how excited they were that I'd be speaking. The family hadn't been to a resistance event, not even an in-person meeting, for more than a year. Although we hadn't explained the intricacies of impeachment, even Hazel and Nancy knew this was an important time in our fight against Trump.

Nancy and me at the Rockville rally to impeach Trump, December 17, 2019.

As the time grew near, we left the warmth of our car. I separated from Katherine and the girls to stand with the other speakers. When it was my turn, I held the bullhorn high and put the mic to my mouth.

Hello Montgomery County! I am Chris Pickett, and I am the director of Indivisible Montgomery. Welcome to this celebration of American democracy!

We are here to bear witness to an incredible moment in American history. Tomorrow, President Donald Trump WILL. BE. IMPEACHED.

This should have been done long ago. But it's being done now and the reason is because of YOU.

Trump is no fan of American democracy. It is clear he has tried to undermine the power that each and every one of us holds. The founders realized the power of this country lies in each and every one of us. Not the elected politicians, but us. And when Trump asked Ukraine to interfere in the 2020 election, he was trying to rob us of our power! The power we have to choose our leaders!

Is that what democracy looks like?

Because you keep showing up and speaking out, Trump and the GOP have no choice but to try to take away our power. This whole affair proved it.

The only way we lose our power is if we sit down, check out and choose not to get involved. All of the lies, all of the deception, all of the gaslighting. None of it is meant to make a persuasive case. It's to make us disengage. It's meant to make us give up our power.

They're scared. They're scared of the power that we have. And they're scared that we use it. Because we've beaten them before.

We beat them in 2018 with our Blue Wave.

We beat them in 2017 when we saved Obamacare.

We beat them in 2016 when Hillary Clinton won by 3 million votes.

And we're going to beat them tomorrow when Trump is impeached, and we'll beat them in 2020 at the ballot box.

Keeping showing up! Keep speaking out! Keep using your power! Let's keep working!

Cheers! Applause! Warmth! Well, maybe not warmth, but I forgot how cold I was for a couple of minutes, and I think everyone else did, too. After I finished, I found my family and gave them hugs. Katherine was excited about my speech and said the crowd was excited, too. Shortly after, the cold became too much. Katherine and Hazel went back to the car to warm up. Nancy and I stayed to listen to more speakers. No one seemed to learn from me and how I held the bullhorn, so it was hard to hear anyone. Five minutes later, Nancy and I joined Katherine and Hazel to warm up and drive home.

Impeached

The next morning, I dropped off Hazel at daycare and then hopped on the train to go to the impeachment rally in DC. I walked to the Capitol area where the rally would be taking place. I was impressed. They went all out getting a stage and a professional sound system. Good crowd, too. Maybe 500 people? And the lineup of speakers was fantastic: some big names from big organizations. After the enthusiasm of last night's rally, I was excited to be at this event! It didn't hurt that it was also significantly warmer than last night.

Too bad it sucked.

Every speaker remarked on how impeachment was a solemn occasion and how we should be reflective at this moment. I don't know if the speakers truly thought that or if Democratic leadership sent a message this shouldn't be a party. Fuck that. Trump tried to extort a foreign leader into launching a bogus investigation of his political rival to mislead the American people and corrupt the 2020 election. He was undermining the power of our votes, and we needed to celebrate him getting his comeuppance. We should have chanted "Ding dong, the witch is dead" while cartwheeling on the Capitol and sipping champagne. The founders of this country explicitly put impeachment in the Constitution, and the fact that we exercised this muscle didn't make it a solemn occasion. It was a celebration of their foresight that our country might be saddled with some jackbooted thug in the Oval Office, and we needed to get rid of him.

It was boring. I should've just gone to work.

Trump was impeached on December 18.[10] Maybe Democratic leadership didn't like it, but I was celebrating.

Indivisible Montgomery Newsletter: Week 155

December 18, 2019

The House of Representatives just passed two articles of impeachment against President Trump for his abuse of power and obstruction of Congress.

The founders of the United States vested the power of the country in We The People by enabling us to choose our leaders. When Trump called the president of Ukraine and asked him for help with his reelection, he committed a crime against all Americans by attempting to undermine the 2020 election and rob us of our power to choose our leaders.

That is antithetical to American democracy.

Hundreds of thousands of Americans rallied last night and this morning calling for Trump's impeachment. And while most politicians want to say this impeachment is a solemn event, using our power as American citizens is also a celebration of our democracy.

Every time we send a postcard or write a letter to a prospective voter, we celebrate our democracy. When we call our members of Congress to give them a piece of our mind, we are using our power as citizens. And when we use the tools entrusted to us by the founders of this country, like pushing for the impeachment of a lawless president acting in his own self-interest, we are celebrating American democracy.

Trump and the GOP are scared of our power because they know that, if we wield it effectively, we are a formidable force. The only way we lose our power is if we don't use it. This is why they constantly lie and gaslight the American people. They are trying to make us disengage, check out and give up our power.

The way to counteract this is to keep turning out. Keep speaking up. Keep working and keep using our power.

Thank you for everything you have done and all the times you have used your power. Because of you, we saved Obamacare in 2017. Because of you, we created a Blue Wave in 2018. Because of you, we held President Trump to account in 2019. I am so thankful you are with us as we get to work to win at the ballot box in 2020.

From my family to yours, I wish you a safe and happy holiday season.

Clarity

With impeachment behind us, the holidays coming up, and the Senate trial far off, I looked forward to relaxing and taking some quiet time with my family before launching into 2020. One night a few days before Christmas, Nancy and Hazel were asleep while Katherine was out with her friends. I was doing the dishes and trying to figure out what was wrong with me. Whenever someone thanked me for my Indivisible Montgomery work, I felt incredibly uncomfortable and changed the subject as quickly as possible. I wore my Indivisible Montgomery T-shirt when I led meetings, but I couldn't stand to be in the shirt once the meeting was over. It wasn't about others seeing me in the shirt. Even if I was driving straight home after the meeting, I would bring a shirt to change into for the drive. It would be a year after I left Indivisible Montgomery before I realized these were all signs of burnout. What I was feeling at a visceral level was that, for all the work we did, we were living through a terrible time in our country's history. We couldn't stop Trump from withdrawing the US from the Paris Climate Agreement or the Iran nuclear deal.[11] We couldn't stop Trump from creating a far-right Supreme Court whose decisions were bound to reshape our lives for decades, and not for the better. And for the issues we did have a positive influence on—Obamacare repeal, the family separation policy, the extortion of the Ukrainian president, and others—we were able to mitigate the damage done by the Trump administration but not avoid damage altogether. Rather than feeling like we had real successes, every day I went to bed thinking, "Well, it could have been worse." What a terrible way to live for four years. But I wouldn't figure this all out until later. That night, I was washing dishes.

In the middle of scraping some melted cheese off a pot, a random thought popped into my head: "What if something awful happens to Katherine on her way home?" I wasn't actually worried about her, but running through what-if scenarios was a way to pass the time without dwelling on politics. So what would I do if I suddenly found myself to be a single parent? This wasn't the first time I had run this scenario or something similarly catastrophic. As I began ticking through what I would do, I realized something: of late, my first response to these hypothetical personal catastrophes was the same—quit Indivisible Montgomery. Not wind down my time, not take a break. But send Steve Pressman all the passwords, turn over the banking information, unsubscribe, and never log in again. Quit.

In the early years of Indivisible Montgomery, I would have felt guilty for abandoning the organization. But three years in, I felt little remorse at the thought of leaving. I had launched the organization, and there was a thread of me in everything the group did. The needs of Indivisible Montgomery were tangled up with my life. I had seen the organization through difficult times. But something had changed. This work had worn me down to the point that I wasn't sad to consider stepping away. We were in the thick of the presidential primary—first votes were a little over a month away—and I was almost upbeat at the thought of quitting.

I launched Indivisible Montgomery to be a force for change in the 2020 election, and I wanted to see it through. But it was also time to acknowledge the emotions that accompanied the prospect of no longer leading the group—freedom, relief, rest.

I finished the dishes and wiped off my hands. Time for a reality check. How would I feel if Trump won in 2020? Could I step away if the country remained under his bootheel? Another realization hit me: the outcome of the election didn't matter. If we failed to evict Trump from the White House in 2020, then our resistance efforts had failed. I could not, in good conscience, remain the leader of this organization after failing to reach our overarching goal. If we succeeded and a Democrat won the presidency, Indivisible Montgomery would have to retool how it operated and would require a new vision. In either outcome, Indivisible Montgomery would need to take a dramatically new direction, and a new direction is often best implemented with new leadership.

So I ended 2019 with clarity and a decision. After the 2020 election, I would step down. I had given enough of myself to this effort. It had taken enough from me. Enough was enough.

2020 | Nevertheless, We Persist

New Year, New Trials

2020. Finally. The year we oust Donald Trump. It didn't matter we still had 10-plus months to go. It felt good just to flip the calendar to the new year.

Before I had even sent out the first 2020 newsletter, the year was looking like it would rival 2017 in terms of how busy we would be. We had our monthly Indivisible Montgomery meetings, our annual picnic in August, another Blue Wave Rally at the end of the summer, more house parties, dine-arounds, phone banks, letter-writing parties, canvassing, and on and on. The Indivisible Montgomery steering committee brainstormed more ways to amplify campaign voter outreach efforts and engage our own members. We had over $6,000 on hand, and I wanted to put as much of it as possible into our elections efforts.

Before we got there though, we had an impeachment trial.

After the House impeached Trump, the volume of emails from Indivisible Montgomery members increased significantly. They were concerned about the Senate trial: What could we do to make sure Senate Majority Leader Mitch McConnell wouldn't immediately dismiss the charges? What could we do to make sure the rules of the trial were fair and allowed the truth to come out?

I was overjoyed that people were looking for actions rather than simply voicing worries. This was a testament to the action-oriented structure of Indivisible Montgomery. But unfortunately, there wasn't much we could do. The trial would be held entirely within the Senate and according to Senate rules, which had been adopted when the new Congress started a year ago. With Republicans in control, they would likely slant the rules to favor Trump. We weren't sure how much they could do, though. Our best option was to call our senators and let them know how we thought the trial should be run.

When the trial opened, Rep. Adam Schiff led an impressive and compelling case against Trump. Trump's lawyers dissembled, played what-if games, and generally tried to create a smoke-screen. As his sycophants in the House demonstrated, there was no coherent defense of Trump's actions. Trump used the power of his office to extort an ally for his personal political gain. It's a textbook definition of an abuse of power.

As the trial progressed, the Democrats prosecuting the case pressed the Senate to call witnesses. They intended to call Republican stalwarts like former national security adviser John Bolton to testify. Bolton tacitly admitted Trump was guilty in media interviews. He refused to testify before the House, but he indicated he would respond to a summons from the Senate. Coward. If Republicans gave a damn about the proper execution of the powers of the presidency on behalf of the American people, they would have come forward with what they knew immediately. Instead, they hid behind the Senate and hoped they wouldn't call witnesses. Democratic impeachment managers requested a vote to call witnesses. Republican advisers admitting under oath that Trump abused his office would make it quite difficult for Republican senators to acquit. The vote failed mostly along party lines.[1] Even the Republicans who were retiring, who had nothing to lose by going against Trump, voted against witnesses. Again, cowards.

Seven days later, the Senate acquitted Trump.

Indivisible Montgomery Newsletter: Week 161

JANUARY 31, 2020

BARRING A DRAMATIC REVERSAL, the Senate GOP will soon be complicit in covering up President Trump's crimes against the American people. By voting against allowing witness testimony, the Senate GOP will deprive the public of the full accounting of Trump's actions and place themselves squarely in opposition to nearly 75% of Americans.

When I heard so many GOP senators coming out against witnesses, I found myself surprised. And I was surprised that I was surprised. With everything we've seen and been through over the past three years, how could I possibly be surprised by this? I mean, we always say the GOP will not save us. And they continue to prove us right.

And I realized that my surprise actually sprang from a shred of hope. A hope for a different outcome. A hope that Republicans would value the power of the institutions of our democracy over their own partisan power. And that hope is stubbornly persistent, so when Senate Republicans cravenly betrayed that hope, I was surprised.

In these demoralizing times, it can be tough to remember that we are harboring hope. Everything we do in our resistance, from checking the news to knocking doors and writing letters, is driven by a sense of hope. You may not even realize it's there. But it is. And I know that I'm not going to let mine go by giving into cynicism or despair. Hope, even a little bit, is motivating. And we need that motivation because there is much to be done.

Spreading the Word

As we moved past impeachment, the 2020 election came into full focus. The organization was committed to taking every opportunity to get Trump out of office, and the election was our next best chance. I was working on a dual track, though. I needed to orchestrate a graceful exit from Indivisible Montgomery while making sure the organization was its most effective when it needed to be. I decided that beginning early was the best way to ease any shocks at my leaving. February would be when I set the plans in motion for my exit from Indivisible Montgomery.

The first to tell was Katherine. I decided to step away from Indivisible Montgomery in December, but I sat on that decision to make sure I didn't change my mind. I did not want to tell Katherine only to go back on that decision. She was having a tough time with the schedule I kept with Indivisible Montgomery and how short I was on patience. "When this election is over, I want my husband back," she told one of our neighbors. Five weeks after making the decision to step down, I hadn't changed my mind. And I hadn't come up with any scenario that would make me stay. Shortly after Katherine came downstairs from putting the girls to bed one night in early February, I said, "Kath, I have some big news," barely suppressing a grin. "After the election, I'm resigning from Indivisible Montgomery."

She was stunned. "What?"

"I'm going to leave Indivisible Montgomery after the election," I said. "There are only two options. One, Trump wins. That would mean all the work Indivisible Montgomery has done wasn't enough, and the organization would need a new direction. Two, the Democrat wins and Indivisible Montgomery, if it keeps going, will need to change its advocacy strategy. Either way, the best way to start a new direction is with a new leader."

Silence. Katherine appeared happy with the news but unsure. She had wanted me to step down for some time but she knew how committed I was. Now that I told her it was going to happen, she wasn't sure what to think. "Are you sure? Have you told anyone yet?"

"Yes, I'm sure. No, I haven't told anyone else yet. I wanted to tell you first."

"What if no one steps in to take your place? What if Indivisible Montgomery ends?"

I sighed. "Yeah, I sat with that for a while," I said. "I don't want to do this anymore. If no one steps up, then Indivisible Montgomery disappears. And I'm at peace with that."

Katherine took a moment. "I'll believe it when I see it," she said. We talked for a while longer, but she remained skeptical. Having launched her own editing business in 2006, she knew what it was like to found and lead something for a long time and how hard it would be to let go. "There's just so much that could happen between now and the election," she said. "Something might change your mind."

I hadn't yet fully grasped how burned out I was on leading the organization, so it was difficult to convey how certain I was. But I knew my mind. I chuckled. "I'm not changing my mind," I said.

A week later, I told the Indivisible Montgomery steering committee. I wanted to let them know well before the end of the year so they could decide whether to shutter Indivisible Montgomery or find a new leader. Steve, Karen, Susan, and Mike—the steering committee I had had for nearly two years—said they were sad I planned to step down, but they understood how draining this was for me. I laid out a few options for how we could proceed in finding a new leader. The rest of the committee thought we should wait until after the election to announce the search for a new leader. They felt it best to decide the fate of the organization once we knew more about the fate of our country. Toward the end of the conversation, Steve said, "I bet Katherine is glad you'll be stepping down."

I laughed. "She doesn't believe I'll actually do it."

Shortly after making the decision in December to step down, I also decided to tell Shirley about the whole thing. Rather than waiting for a Trump administration official to unmask me, I wanted to come clean on my terms. I planned to be more vocal about activism on social media, and I was tired of keeping it from her. RBR didn't have an in-person meeting scheduled in 2020, so I led with it on our next phone call.

"I wanted to say something before we get started. Do you know about the Indivisible Project?" She didn't, so I explained the overall effort. "And at the end of 2016, I founded and have been leading Indivisible Montgomery, one of the groups in this larger effort to resist the Trump administration."

"Oh." There was a pause as she digested the information. "That's fantastic! I totally support you doing that." Another pause. "I understand why you kept it from us."

That was all I needed. I didn't have to explain about the potential conflict between the two organizations because Shirley connected the dots as quickly as I had four years ago. She also didn't say whether she agreed that it was a conflict or what she might have done differently. There was no need. I gave a few more details about the work we were doing—monthly meetings, newsletters, amplifying voter outreach efforts, and the like. Then we moved on to RBR-specific work.

In these few conversations with my wife, my steering committee, and my boss, I relieved so much stress. I felt buoyant, like I could make it through the rest of 2020.

We Have a Nominee

THE MAIN INDIVISIBLE MONTGOMERY event of February was our last set of dine-arounds. Katherine and I mapped out the likely election-related activities for the rest of the year, and the calendar was full. We agreed these would be the last dine-arounds before the big vote. To encourage members to attend, each of the dine-arounds doubled as Vote Forward letter-writing activities. I attended several events, as I had for every dine-around weekend since 2017. Normally, each group had its own discussion, and attendees would take their time starting the work we had set up for them. This weekend was different. All the discussions were the same—speculation over who would win the Democratic nomination—and we got to the business of writing letters much faster than in years past. We were nine months away and the members didn't want to waste one moment.

On February 29, one week after the dine-arounds, we held the February Indivisible Montgomery meeting. I started the meeting talking about COVID-19. Everyone was cognizant and wary of the spreading disease, but no one knew how dangerous COVID was, and we weren't sure how it spread. I shake my head in retrospect thinking about cramming 80 people into the tiny library meeting room that day. I encouraged our members to follow the guidance of the career federal employees at the Centers for Disease Control and

Prevention (CDC) and the National Institutes of Health rather than Trump's political appointees. Extensive testing was the best way to understand the epidemiology of the disease and to craft public policy to keep people safe. The Trump administration barked about its ability to generate COVID tests, but no one believed they would follow through. At that time, only three cases had been documented in Montgomery County.

Next, we discussed our efforts to support the eventual Democratic nominee. The best thing we could do at this time was write and bank Vote Forward letters, which were generic get-out-the-vote letters and didn't require us to know who the presidential nominee would be. As a group, we had already written several hundred, and our letter-writing parties were moving into full gear. Right before the meeting, Steve informed me that we and our partners had such parties scheduled for every evening in March and in the first two weeks of April. I advertised these to the attendees and encouraged them to sign up for as many as they could. I saw encouraging their attendance as a two-for-one deal. First, we would get people to parties to write letters, which would drive voter turnout. Second, getting comfortable with others at these events would make it easier to convert these folks to text banking, phone banking, and canvassing later in the year. If you are invited to do something you haven't done before, like text or phone banking, you're more likely to agree to join if it's with someone you're comfortable and friendly with. But that was getting ahead of ourselves. We had more immediate questions to address.

Specifically, who was going to win the Democratic primary? Mayor Pete Buttigieg and Sen. Bernie Sanders had been neck and neck coming out of Iowa and New Hampshire, and Sanders took the lead with a decisive win in Nevada.[2] The strength of Sanders's Nevada win made people on the right giddy that a self-proclaimed socialist might be the Democratic nominee. Nevada also prompted several notable opinion pieces from left-leaning writers who accepted that Sanders would be the eventual Democratic nominee and urged liberals to come to grips with his nomination. There is no greater job than beating Donald Trump in November, they argued, regardless of who is on the top of the ticket. This had been Indivisible Montgomery's posture since 2017. But that didn't mean a Sanders nomination was an easy sell.

Sanders's ascension rattled the Indivisible Montgomery meeting. Montgomery County is super blue, but it's more an old-timey, mom-and-pop liberalism rather than a bastion of modern progressivism. The difference is that the old-timers wanted a candidate who they thought would appease centrists, while progressives wanted someone unabashedly pushing progressive policies. The contrast was clear in the abundance of second-guessing in our group. Everyone wanted to put on their political strategist hat and pretend they knew how to win an election. My inbox was riddled with people telling me how candidates X, Y, and Z could never win over the independents and moderates, so we needed to nominate A, B, or C. This frustrated me because it betrayed a lack of faith in the work we did. The nominee would be the one who excited the most voters in the Democratic primary. I tried and tried (and tried!) to impress on our members that they should stop playing pundit and simply support who they wanted to win. It was our job, as it had been since our inception, to turn out the people who weren't the base of the Demo-

Rep. Jamie Raskin (*right*) addresses Indivisible Montgomery at the end of February, only a couple of weeks before COVID-19 shut down the country.

cratic Party and get them to vote. If the nominee got more of the base involved, that meant less work for us.

My first task that day in February was to quiet the jitters. Because I was 20-plus years younger than the average Indivisible Montgomery member, and Sanders had a large following among young people, many assumed I was a Bernie supporter. I started with the usual spiel: vote for who you want to be president. Then I confronted the issue head-on. "Bernie Sanders is doing well and that may not sit well with some people. I'll admit he's not my first choice to win this contest. He's also not my second, third, or fourth choice to win." A lot of eyebrows went up around the room in surprise. "But if he does win the nomination, then he's our best chance to oust Donald Trump and, dammit, I will do everything I can to get him elected." I reminded everyone we hadn't worked for over three years to fall apart because of our guesses about how voters in swing states would react to the Democratic nominee. I reminded them that our coalition was far more formidable than Trump's, regardless of who was at the top of the ticket. A lot of the nervous energy dissipated, and we had a healthy discussion about the rest of the primary. Helpfully, Rep. Jamie Raskin, our featured speaker that day, delivered the same message about supporting the eventual nominee. And I reminded everyone that we were still at the beginning of the primary—only three states had voted and we hadn't even reached Super Tuesday. Anything could happen.

Jesus. Talk about prophetic.

South Carolina Democrats were voting while we were holding our meeting. Former vice president Joe Biden was expected to carry South Carolina, but most pundits thought Sanders's recent surge would help him close the gap on Biden in the state. They were hilariously wrong. Biden beat Sanders by 30 points and Buttigieg by 40.[3] Biden's win was so convincing that, in the three days between the South Carolina primary and Super Tuesday, Buttigieg, Sen. Amy Klobuchar, and most of the other serious Democratic contenders dropped out and endorsed Biden.[4] In a handful of days, Biden went from an embarrassing also-ran to a juggernaut who couldn't possibly lose. Even Sanders and Sen. Elizabeth Warren, who stayed in the race longer than the others, admitted Biden was likely to capture the nomination after he won 10 of 14 contests on Super Tuesday.

Just like that, the worried emails stopped. Biden, the centrist candidate who all our armchair pundits thought was our best chance at beating Trump, was cruising to the nomination. There were some Bernie diehards, but even those who didn't quite like Biden realized he could unify Democrats around a coherent message. I wasn't thrilled with a Biden candidacy. His proposed policies weren't as far-reaching as I believed the country needed. And could we please stop putting ancient white men in power? Part of me was glad the nomination was decided because it meant I wouldn't have to spend my time calming the nerves of our members. Now we could do our work to get Biden elected.

The Pandemic Hits

WITH THE PRIMARY ESSENTIALLY decided, my attention was captured by COVID. The country still didn't have a sense of how serious this disease was, how fast it moved, or how dangerous it could be. But cases were rising everywhere, and community transmission was a given in any place of significant population, including Montgomery County. The prevailing wisdom was that COVID spread on surfaces—touching surfaces with the COVID virus on it and then touching our faces. COVID is very rarely transmitted on surfaces, but we didn't know that at the time. To slow the spread, we were supposed to stop touching our faces and wash our hands more often and for at least 20 seconds. Nancy's and Hazel's schools sent home information about how they were increasing hand-washing opportunities to make sure our kids stayed healthy, and how every sniffle and headache was cause for kids to stay home. Hazel came home from preschool with an activity where she had cut out squares with the hand-washing steps and pasted them in order as a helpful reminder. We taped it to our bathroom wall. To encourage everyone to wash their hands, someone created a website where you could type in any song, and it would give you the first 20 seconds of lyrics so you could sing your favorite song while washing your hands.[5] It was a nice distraction that kept us from dwelling on how much COVID might upend our lives. Upon reflection, it was wholly inadequate to the problem at hand.

Steve Pressman and I set a coffee-shop meeting for the morning of March 6 to discuss Indivisible Montgomery's elections activities. We were supposed to talk about the full schedule of letter-writing parties and begin sketching out our GOTV activities for the summer and fall. I arrived first, maskless, to a coffee shop that was a third full, which was normal for this shop at 10:00 a.m. during the workweek. Steve arrived shortly after I did, also maskless, and slid into the seat across from me. We were only six days past our in-person meeting, but we were tense. Everyone was tense. COVID cases were increasing rapidly across Montgomery County, and we had few ideas on how to stop the spread. Should we be sitting at the same table? Should we even be in this coffee shop at all? Wise or not, Steve and I set aside our concerns and the chitchat and got right to talking about the letter-writing parties. These events were the centerpiece of our GOTV efforts and the perfect setup for our GOTV activities closer to the election. But now that COVID was a threat, we had to factor that into our planning. Could we maintain our members' high enthusiasm for letter writing while keeping everyone safe from this new illness? This seems like it might have required a long conversation, but it was just the opposite. We didn't know how COVID spread so we didn't know how to keep people safe. Steve and I agreed it would be reckless to continue to hold letter-writing parties if cases continued to climb. On March 10, COVID showed no signs of relenting, and we canceled the letter-writing parties through March 17.

The stress and fear of the emerging pandemic increased daily. In December, Katherine was invited to speak at a National Press Club event on March 13, and while some events were canceled or postponed, the organizers of Katherine's event decided to move ahead. I wasn't sure she should go, but we didn't know enough about the risks for her to cancel. Having been out in the world and around people in close spaces, I insisted she find a seat on the Metro by herself and keep her hands in her pockets as much as possible. Katherine worked from home and hadn't been out in public as much as I had. She took the suggestion in stride, but it was clear she thought I might be overreacting. When she returned, her shoulders were bunched up next to her ears, and it wasn't because it was cold outside. "Oh my god. I do not want to ride the Metro again."

Then the world stopped. The American public had a sense the Trump administration was bumbling the pandemic, but it wasn't clear just how badly until stories leaked about the administration's frustrating incompetence.[6] In the complete absence of national leadership, every organization and person fended for themselves. The National Basketball Association and the National Hockey League suspended the rest of their 2020 seasons on March 11 and 12, respectively.[7] Stock indexes tumbled as people stayed home and stopped spending money.[8] Montgomery County Public Schools—the school system that governed Nancy and Hazel's schooling—closed for two weeks starting March 16 to prevent the spread of COVID.[9] That Friday was the last day Hazel would be in preschool until September and the last day Nancy would enter her school for an entire year. Steve and I canceled the Indivisible Montgomery letter-writing parties for the rest of the month. A week later, Governor Hogan closed all nonessential businesses across Maryland.[10]

Four weeks ago, we had 15 people in our house for a dine-around. Two weeks ago, 80 people gathered in a small room for the last in-person Indivisible Montgomery meeting. A week before, I was working in coffee shops and meeting with Indivisible Montgomery leaders. Now, we weren't supposed to go anywhere. Large gatherings were restricted. Businesses were closing. School was shut down. Even some government operations were being shut. The message was clear: Stay home. Don't go out. Don't get sick. Stay safe.

COVID in the House

On Sunday, two days after MCPS shut down, we were eating lunch when Hazel said she was too tired to keep eating. Then she got up from the table, ambled over to the couch, lay down, and said in her three-year-old squeak of a voice, "I ready for nap." Like most kids, Hazel always ate her lunch and resisted taking a nap. This was weird.

Kids contract viruses on the regular, and they don't merit much mention. However, given that everything had just shut down because of an uncontrolled, global pandemic, Katherine and I immediately suspected COVID. We were still learning about the disease, and this was months before at-home tests would become plentiful. We knew the sickness often started with a fever and fatigue and was followed a couple days later by a cough. "Let's take your temperature before you fall asleep, Hazel," said Katherine. I picked Hazel up from the couch, took her to the bathroom, and fished out our thermometer. She didn't feel hot, but my mind spun for those three minutes as Hazel held the thermometer under her tongue. What would we do if this was COVID? How could we isolate our nearly four-year-old daughter? Would Katherine or I isolate with her? Would whoever was with her catch it? How could we take care of our kids if Katherine or I had COVID? What if both of us had to check into the hospital?

My timer went off: 98.6°F. I felt the tension leave my shoulders, and Katherine was clearly relieved. I walked Hazel into her room and helped her to bed for a nap. She was still tired that evening, but her temperature was again normal. By Monday morning, she was her old self, and Katherine and I moved on.

Only for a day. Tuesday was Nancy's turn. She didn't finish her lunch and was clearly exhausted. We took her temperature that afternoon, and it was 100°F. Well, shit. Katherine called the pediatrician, and they said if the fever got over 101°F or if she developed a cough, then we should call them back. Nancy, now nearly seven, then took a nap, which hadn't happened for three years. Like we did with Hazel, Katherine took Nancy's temperature right before bed—102°F. Damn. I pulled out my phone to call the pediatrician. Katherine said, "Wait. It's eight o'clock, and they're not going to see her tonight."

"Right," I said. "I guess they could send us to the emergency room."

"I really don't want to spend my night at the ER," said Katherine. "And the ER is full of COVID patients. If we don't have COVID now, we'll certainly have it after sitting in there."

I agreed. "Let's see how she's doing in the morning."

We woke up nervous on Wednesday and took Nancy's temperature first thing—99.5°F. She didn't have any other symptoms, and we were relieved the fever had broken. By lunchtime, her temperature was under 99°F. Katherine and I were happy to think this was probably some bug the girls got as a parting gift right before schools shut down.

Did our kids have COVID? We'll never know for sure, but I think they probably did, although I can't explain how neither Katherine nor I picked it up. It would have been great to have been able to test for it, but our government had abandoned us. Two weeks earlier, Trump said, "Anybody who wants a test gets a test," contradicting nearly every other administration official, including Vice President Mike Pence, who said the administration couldn't keep up with testing demand.[11] Trump blatantly lied to cover up his incompetence and inability to lead. Even at a time when basic leadership qualities were needed to protect the lives of American citizens, Trump couldn't be bothered to do anything but deny and deflect.

On Our Own

EVERYTHING CHANGED IN THOSE first two weeks of COVID lockdown. Trips to restaurants, coffee shops, stores, and the like weren't possible because everything was closed. Nancy and Hazel were home with us full time. The next weeks and months all blended together and were like nothing we had ever gone through.

I told Shirley at RBR that I would monitor my messages and work on a few of our low-key projects when time permitted, but I needed space to work with Katherine to find a rhythm that merged our new home-all-the-time reality. I received no pushback. Shirley and the others needed to make their own pandemic adjustments, and since RBR was volunteer work for them, they were happy to put it on the back burner. Thankfully, the pandemic didn't threaten my paycheck, at least not yet. RBR would run out of money by the end of 2020, and I needed to either find RBR a new grant or find myself a new job. I didn't relish the idea of looking for a job during a pandemic, and I hoped we could convince a new organization to fund our work. But that was an issue for the future.

Katherine's job was the more immediate concern. The editorial and production side of bookmaking was all done on computer, and this industry was accustomed to freelancers and employees working from home. Katherine's clients indicated they didn't expect to cancel any of their book projects, but they did delay some of their deadlines to accommodate the lockdown upheaval. This was understandable, but freelancers don't get paid if they don't work. We felt fortunate that none of Katherine's projects were canceled, but what would happen when these projects ended? Within two weeks of nationwide lockdowns, 10 million Americans lost their jobs and the unemployment rate skyrocketed.[12] No one could forecast how far the layoffs would spread or what industries would be hit the hardest. Would publishing work become concentrated with in-house employees rather than freelancers like Katherine? Would the people who hired Katherine have their own jobs in a few weeks? Would those clients be able to pay Katherine for her work? Would they still exist?

So on top of the "is this the end of American democracy" existential dread and the "death by COVID" existential dread, we now had to contend with the "will we have jobs" existential dread. Still, we had to move past this paralysis and find a way to live our daily lives. The only way out was through. Work, grocery runs, and activities for the kids couldn't be avoided. Katherine and I did what made sense to us and set up a daily schedule. We traded half days of work Monday and Tuesday, Katherine worked all day Wednesday and Friday, and I worked all day Thursday, and Saturday morning if necessary. To minimize our COVID risk, only I went to the grocery store, and we tried to make shopping lists that would last us more than a week. I became an expert at self-checkout and an early adherent to the unidirectional grocery aisles.

Nancy and Hazel were our heroes. They were scared about COVID, but we did our best to let them know we were doing everything necessary to keep them and our family safe. We explained all their friends were taking similar precautions, and we hoped they'd

A few days into our lockdown, the girls wanted class photos for their new school situation. Who was I to say no? Hazel (*top left*), Nancy (*top right*), and me. Katherine was working and didn't get her class photo.

see them soon. We set their "school day" in 30-minute blocks of reading, math, art, and science, with playtime strategically thrown in. We weren't set up for long-term education at home, but we did what we could. We put all the games and activities we had in the house to good use. Hazel even had the idea to take class photos one day. Despite everything going on, we had fun.

We looked forward to our walks around the neighborhood. Spring had sprung, we needed to get out of our house, and our dog Jerry needed exercise. Jerry, forever the pack dog, was the only one who thoroughly enjoyed having everyone home during the pandemic. We explained to the girls we needed to be COVID-conscious on our walks and we would keep our distance from others. Nearly four-year-old Hazel took the point a little too well. The moment we saw anyone on our walk, from any distance, she was on the verge of tears and pleading with us to cross the street. Nancy, soon to be seven, was calmer than her little sister, but not by much. It took a month of Katherine and me ratcheting down the anxiety and explaining that we had to be very close to people to catch COVID, so if we didn't panic and gave people space, we could make it through our pandemic world.

Everything moved slowly during those days. The calendar flipped, but it felt like we were living the same day over and over again. I was working one afternoon in early April when, from completely out of the blue, my mother called. Aside from exchanging perfunctory texts on birthdays and other holidays, we hadn't spoken since the beginning of 2017. Most recently, I had sent her and everyone else I knew a message that Nancy's and Hazel's schools closed because of the pandemic. Now, two weeks later, my mom was calling me. Did she have COVID? Did her husband? Maybe she reevaluated what was important considering the pandemic and was calling to start on the road to reconciliation.

"Hello?"

"Uh ..." She sounded confused that I picked up. What did that mean? Who was sick? "Can I talk to Nancy?"

I paused. This wasn't my mom telling me someone was sick. "Um. Yeah ..." I walked out of the office to find Nancy reading a book and handed her the phone. I was confused. What did Nancy have to do with anything? Was she going to tell Nancy someone was sick and then have Nancy tell me? This didn't make any sense. As I listened to Nancy's side of the conversation, I realized my mom called to wish her a happy birthday. Katherine and I had done our best to give Nancy a nice day, but in my certainty that my mother was calling with bad news, I had forgotten all about that. I paced as they spoke, and I found myself getting angry. My mom called me at the beginning of a pandemic where people were dying and my kids' schools had shut down and we couldn't even go to the grocery store without freaking out, and she didn't even think to ask how we were doing? She couldn't ask if we were all healthy? Judging from Nancy's side of the conversation, my mom didn't ask Nancy if she was healthy or recognize she hadn't been in school for two weeks. We were in a pandemic, something none of us had ever been in, and the only thing she could talk to my daughter about was the presents she received and avoiding any mention of the reason she couldn't see her friends or have a birthday party? If she cared, not saying anything about it was a weird way to go.

That same week, the CDC and director of the National Institute of Allergy and Infectious Diseases Tony Fauci started encouraging masking to prevent the spread of COVID, and ordinances went into effect across the country. With no help coming from the government, we scrambled for masks. Every outlet that might have a mask worthy of protecting someone from COVID was sold out and had no information on when they would receive more. Katherine remembered that she had a single N95 mask with her house-painting materials. It fit Katherine and me well, and it was fine when I went grocery shopping. But COVID was going to be with us for a while and

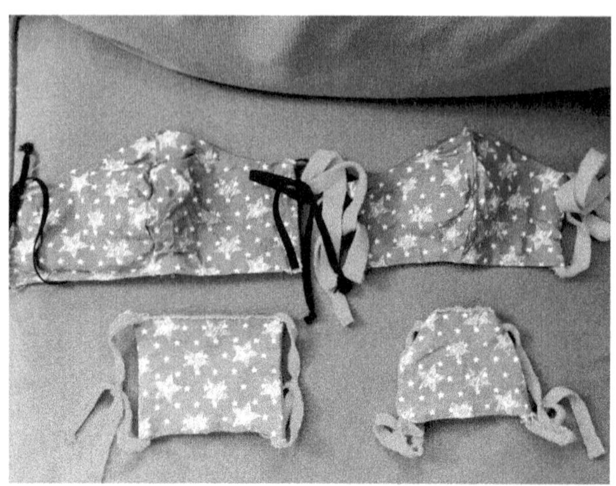

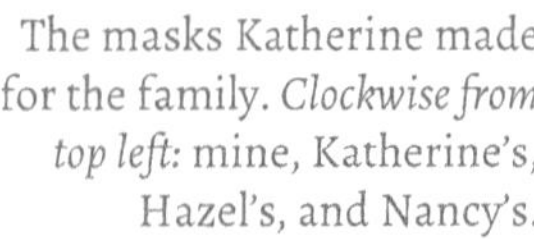

The masks Katherine made for the family. *Clockwise from top left:* mine, Katherine's, Hazel's, and Nancy's.

we needed functional masks for everyone. Like many other people, we made our own. Or, I should say, Katherine made ours. Katherine found a mask pattern online that she liked, and she made masks for the four of us.

The shift to having everyone at home nearly all the time instead of at their places of work and school led to some unexpected complications. Like grocery store shelves were bare in odd places. One time, there were no Grape-Nuts. Another time, no pepperoncinis. The most enduring scarcity was toilet paper. Multiple outlets indicated there was no toilet paper shortage, but that didn't keep people from hoarding it. At least twice while walking through the store, I said out loud, "How can you people use so much toilet paper!?" One day I found an eight-pack of toilet paper stashed among the black olives. I looked up and down the aisle, assuming this was some kind of trick. Toilet paper? In the wild? We were low, so I didn't care where I found it. I took it. The broader scarcity did ratchet up my anxiety. If I couldn't get what was on my list, was there a substitute? If they were stocked on something we often used but didn't need that week, should I get it? What if they're not here next week? Every grocery run for the first two months felt like a failure. I never got everything we needed. Sometimes I got most of what we needed, sometimes less than half.

For matters outside our family well-being, we were lost and alone. The Trump administration had little interest in developing a working COVID-19 test or controlling the spread of the disease. Reasonable governments would have allowed senior scientists to direct the public health response, encouraged everyone to wear a mask, invoked the Defense Production Act to direct companies to manufacture the materials to combat COVID, and provided comfort during this unpredictable and unprecedented time. Trump didn't do that. The Trump administration could have expedited test production, but it didn't. The Trump administration could have sent masks to everyone in the country, but it didn't. The Trump administration could have helped implement lockdowns across the country to save American lives, but it didn't. At the end of March, Trump told the country everything should be back to normal by Easter.[13]

The Trump administration betrayed the American people, and the GOP shoved it in our faces. Even the people imbibing everything spewed by Fox News knew COVID wouldn't be gone by Easter. This was the insidiousness of it all. It wasn't just that Trump did nothing to save people's lives. That would have been bad enough. Instead, he purposefully painted a picture of the future that everyone knew would cost lives. We were on our own.

Virtual Activism

THE PANDEMIC WAS A mixed bag when it came to leading Indivisible Montgomery. On one hand, I had an excuse to spend less time on the resistance because I had more important things to consider, like survival. On the other hand, the pandemic required activism—the Trump administration was sabotaging efforts to protect the populace from COVID, and we still had an election to win. I couldn't get out of the house, so what else was I going to do? In the end, I worked on Indivisible Montgomery issues about the same as I had before, just in a bit of a different cadence given our lockdown reality. Every so often I would count the months or the weeks until I planned to step down from Indivisible Montgomery. The pandemic hadn't changed those plans, and I found myself getting excited as the numbers ticked down.

I built Indivisible Montgomery as an organization that was constant and steady in its activism and engagement. Maintaining the newsletter schedule and pointing people to ways they could still make a difference was how I injected some normalcy into my life and hopefully the members' lives as well. Besides, it was one of the few ways I could hold on to the pre-COVID era. I also built Indivisible Montgomery as a community for those opposed to Donald Trump. Coming together in person was now out of the question. We canceled our letter-writing parties and in-person monthly meetings. I still wanted to have Indivisible Montgomery come together.

Our next scheduled meeting was at the end of May, which gave me nearly two months to investigate Zoom and prepare to run a virtual meeting.

Regarding our GOTV activities, the pandemic didn't really slow us down. Steve Pressman and I emailed daily discussing how to adjust our activities. On the Indivisible Montgomery election calendar, this time was slated entirely for writing and banking Vote Forward letters. With in-person events canceled, our members transitioned to virtual letter-writing parties. These parties proved popular, and I was happy to advertise them through the newsletter.

While letters were being written, the pandemic scrambled Indivisible Montgomery's approach to encouraging letter writing. After the fundraiser at the end of 2019, Indivisible Montgomery had over $6,000 to spend on election activities. This was double any other year's fundraising effort, and I intended to spend almost all that money printing letters and buying envelopes and stamps so that no one in our group had a financial reason not to participate. Steve and I went over it several times, but with the pandemic forcing us to limit physical interactions, we had no real way to print and distribute letters and envelopes to the members. Stamps, on the other hand, were something we could deal with. Buying stamps was easily the biggest expense in writing these letters. Steve and I put our heads together and came up with a plan.

At the end of May, Indivisible Montgomery convened for its first virtual meeting. I expected attendance to be around 60 people—a little less than what we would normally get for an in-person meeting. Somehow the lesson from 2017 to stop guessing how many people would show up hadn't stuck. One hundred twenty people joined the call, eager to hear what Indivisible Montgomery was doing and to see the people they had come to know and work with over these many years. It was heartwarming to see so many familiar faces again. In addition to talking about politics and staying safe from COVID, we discussed how Indivisible Montgomery would support Vote Forward letter writing. The organization had money for stamps, but social distancing meant we had to get creative about getting stamps on the envelopes. With hundreds of letter writers scattered across the county, we set up four drop boxes across the county: Katherine's and my house in Silver Spring, Steve's in Rockville, Nina Liakos's in Gaithersburg, and Laurie Pfeiffer's in Kensington. We each set a box outside our house with a clearly labeled sign for Indivisible Montgomery letters. Whenever they wanted, members could drive over and drop their unstamped letters in the box. Steve, Nina, Laurie, and I would each clean out the boxes on a regular basis and store and stamp the letters. Folks could even drop off letters they had stamped themselves, and we would put all of them in the mail in October.

The members were enthusiastic about our letter-writing plan and the virtual meeting was much more fun than I expected. I was happy to see that the members of Indivisible Montgomery weren't going to let something like a global pandemic get in the way of liberating our country from Donald Trump.

Black Lives Matter

A FEW DAYS AFTER Indivisible Montgomery's first virtual meeting, George Floyd, a Black man, was murdered by a white Minneapolis police officer. The officer knelt on Floyd's neck for nearly 10 minutes, slowly suffocating him despite his pleas and those of others around them to let Floyd breathe. The whole encounter was recorded and immediately went viral.[14] Two other high-profile killings of Black people happened near the same time: Breonna Taylor was killed by Louisville police in a botched raid,[15] and Ahmaud Arbery was killed by white vigilantes for jogging while Black in the "wrong" neighborhood.[16]

Black lives matter. American history is littered with examples of white people disagreeing with that fact, and those examples either start or end with murdered Black people. The sheer brutality of these murders, combined with the previous years of widespread activist organizing and the frustration of COVID quarantines, launched immediate protests across the country. Millions of people poured into the streets to protest police brutality and proclaim that Black lives matter. In many places, the cops attacked and brutalized protestors, demonstrating exactly why change was necessary. Like the first Women's March, people marched in small cities and towns as well as large ones. Floyd's murder even sparked protests in Europe and elsewhere around the world. Millions of people rallied against these injustices.

These protests helped me and countless people see past the immediate dread of COVID. For the past two months or so, COVID was the most imminent threat facing a lot of people in the country. The killings of Floyd, Arbery, and Taylor reminded everyone that the threats to the Black, immigrant, gay, Jewish, and other communities did not magically go away because of a pandemic. Black people were still being shot by police. Immigrants were still being rounded up and deported. We couldn't ignore this. We needed to respond. Indivisible Montgomery firmly stood committed to our mission of protecting the people in our community from any threats, especially those from agents of the state. I listed opportunities for our members to join protests, but within a couple of days that information became moot. Protests were everywhere; you simply needed to walk or drive around to find one to join. My whole family walked from our house to the local high school for an hour-long protest attended by Rep. Jamie Raskin. A few days later, we went into downtown Silver Spring and joined a protest and march through the heart of the city.

The response in many communities was long and sustained. I saw Black Lives Matter signs all over our neighborhood and beyond. Most were clearly bought from the Black Lives Matter organization, but others were beautifully handcrafted. Our neighborhood had a brilliant chalk artist who chalked most sidewalks with "Black Lives Matter" and other slogans. Nancy and Hazel asked questions about the chalk and the signs, and we were up-front with them. This wasn't our first Black Lives Matter discussion, and they were as eager as Katherine and I were to make their voices heard in protest.

We turned out to multiple Black Lives Matter protests in June 2020, while being thoughtful about keeping safe from COVID.

In downtown Washington, DC, protestors held nearly daily events and marches toward the White House. The Trump administration and Republicans were scared. Extra barricades and fencing went up around the White House. Sen. Tom Cotton wrote an op-ed calling for the deployment of the 82nd Airborne Division to quell the protests.[17] Alarmingly, armed federal officers appeared on the streets of Washington without insignia or indication of what agency they came from.[18] How often did we have to say that things like this don't happen in a normal, functioning democracy before people grasped that, with Trump in the White House, we were not a normal, functioning democracy? As I had for every major protest event since I launched the organization, I was encouraging Indivisible Montgomery members to march and make their voices heard, if they were comfortable going out in the pandemic. But the unidentified federal officers gave me pause. Police officers with identification at least gave the appearance that they could be disciplined for mistreating protestors. But people with no identification acting on behalf of the state? We were in new territory.

Several days after the start of the protests, Trump was tired of hiding in the White House and decided he wanted a show of force, a way to show he was in control while pretending he was a tough guy. Lafayette Park, just across the street from the White House, was the site of one of the longest-running protests. On June 1, Trump decided to walk through Lafayette Park to the church a short block away from the White House. Trump, forever afraid of people who disagree with him, directed federal agents and DC police to sweep Lafayette Park, in essence blessing the brutal beatings meted out by police against peaceful protestors and members of the media who couldn't get out of the way.[19] The zeal with which some cops took to it was shocking. Then, in one of the most bizarre spectacles in a presidency of bizarre spectacles, Trump stood in front of the church, held up a Bible upside down while media snapped photos, and said something in his typical word salad.

Just a straight-up wannabe-dictator.

Indivisible Montgomery Newsletter: Week 180

June 8, 2020

Thousands turned out for Black Lives Matter protests last week in all 50 states, from major metropolitan areas to small, Midwestern townships. Other countries across the world have also seen massive protests in opposition to police brutality and systemic oppression.

If you have protested, made donations, or took part in another way, thank you! There were large rallies in Bethesda, Rockville, and elsewhere this past week, and more are still to come. Check out the list of upcoming rallies for Maryland here, and for Montgomery County here.

So many people are rising up to protest against systemic racism and to press for justice. The outpouring of support from cities small and large and across the world is simply inspiring.

But this can't be the end of it! We can't overcome systemic racism without putting in the work …

Our Pandemic Summer

TRUMP'S WALK ACROSS LAFAYETTE Park backfired spectacularly. The media were all over the brutal police assaults, hounding Trump for months over his coercing the highest members of the American military to walk him through the park. Despite Trump's show of force, robust peaceful protests over George Floyd's murder continued through June. None of the protests turned out to be superspreader events, despite the large number of people taking part, but COVID ruled the summer.

Indivisible Montgomery was moving along. After initially scrambling to figure out how to continue our activism amid social distancing, the organization had hit its stride. Our weekly actions continued, our monthly meetings were virtual, and our letter-writing campaign was going well. We had already had several batches of unstamped letters dropped in the box in front of our house, as did our other collectors. Because I held the Indivisible Montgomery debit card, I bought the stamps we needed for these efforts. Mid-June was the first time I made a loop to Steve's, Nina's, and Laurie's houses to deliver rolls of stamps for their letters. Only Nina was home, and she came out of her house so we could chat at a distance. This was the first time I had seen an Indivisible Montgomery member in three dimensions in three months, when Steve and I met at a coffee shop right before the lockdowns went into effect. It felt like years.

Our COVID summer. When not sticking to our schedule so Katherine and I could work, we got outside. *Top:* The girls in the inflatable pool we bought that summer. *Bottom:* The family on a hike at Seneca Creek State Park.

One thing COVID hadn't scrambled was my intention to step down from leading Indivisible Montgomery once the election was over. In fact, the pandemic made me even more determined to step away. Lockdowns forced me to spend more time with my kids, and even though I would get bored or lose patience with them on a nearly daily basis, I was also having a lot of fun.

At the end of May, school was officially canceled for the rest of the school year. I applauded the teachers for doing what they could after being thrown into online instruction in mid-March. Nancy's first-grade teacher scheduled a weekly hour-long video call to read her students a book and check in with them. Hazel's virtual calls with her preschool teachers were less frequent, and they often were scheduled shortly after she got up from a nap, so there wasn't much benefit. Even though the school year was over, Katherine and I kept our schedule of working and being with the girls. We had found a rhythm over the past two months, and we didn't see a reason to change now.

This was a time of contradiction. We were constantly in a state of fear and concern for the health and well-being of our family and everyone around us. But we also cherished this time because we got to spend so much of it with our seven- and four-year-old girls. We found ways to enjoy the outdoors and each other while being COVID-conscious for our family and those around us. We took several extended day trips to local parks, where we hiked, picnicked, and enjoyed being outside. Earlier in the year, we had planned to go to Rehoboth Beach for a summer vacation. The pandemic scratched that plan, and we spent a bit of money on an inflatable backyard pool that was large enough for all four of us to get in if we wanted. Nancy and Hazel were in it almost every day splashing and trying to swim. The pool sprung a leak at the end of the season, but it was awesome while we had it. The pandemic also meant we couldn't invite our friends over for a summer party, but Katherine suggested we have a party ourselves where we make party foods and pretend like we were all strangers meeting for the first time. We all dressed up, filled our paper plates with snacks, and balanced them awkwardly on our laps while pretending not to know one another. We introduced ourselves, and we all wondered whose dog this was that kept walking around to everyone to sniff their food. It was a blast. These weren't the parties, the cross-country trips to see family and friends, or trips to the beach to enjoy the sun that we were accustomed to, but it was what we had in 2020. And we enjoyed it.

Madam Vice President

ON A TUESDAY AFTERNOON in August, I was sitting on our back porch rereading Agatha Christie's *Murder on the Orient Express* while Nancy and Hazel played in the pool when I got a text from my friend Steve Moore. All he said was, "It's Harris." I knew immediately that he meant Joe Biden had selected Sen. Kamala Harris as his running mate.[20] I was excited. If we did our job, the US would have its first female vice president, its first Black vice president, and its first vice president of South Asian descent.

I let the girls know I'd be right back, and I ran inside to tell Katherine and get my laptop. I took it back out to the porch, sat down, and logged into Mailchimp so I could send a newsletter to Indivisible Montgomery with the news. Members regularly emailed me to proclaim who they thought the best VP pick would be. I knew Harris wouldn't knock everyone's socks off, and I balanced my message saying Harris was a great pick while also acknowledging some people thought another running mate would give Biden a better chance. As with every discussion on this issue since the primary contest started, I reminded everyone we needed to get past any uncomfortable feelings and go all in to get Trump out of office.

Once I sent that message, it was time to get the girls out of the pool. I helped them towel off and got them ready for a bath. I checked email on my phone to make sure the newsletter had gone out, and I saw I already had several responses to my message. Most were some variation of "YES!" or "So exciting! Let's get to work!" I was happy to see the excitement. Then I got to the final response. One guy thought I wasn't excited enough by the news that Harris would be running for vice president, and he chastised me for a lack of enthusiasm in my message. I was so angry because this guy clearly didn't understand what I was trying to do with the Indivisible Montgomery newsletter. I desperately wanted to respond with my true feelings: I don't care what you think makes a good email. Start your own organization that sends multiple emails a week. Spend time away from your family and friends so you can direct strangers into fighting the greatest threat to our country in the past 80 years. Find a way to walk a line that satisfies 1,700 people all the time. Try to do that and then come talk to me about what's wrong with my messages.

Instead, I ran the girls' bath, and right before they got in, I sent my critic a short message using my most professional manner to remind him that everyone in Indivisible Montgomery might not be as excited as he and I were about the selection of Harris, and it was my job to bring everyone along, even those who felt Harris was a lackluster choice.

By the end of Nancy and Hazel's bath, I was still irked, but calmer than before. Not so calm that I could stop myself from checking to see if my critic had responded. He had. And he doubled down, saying simply that everyone needs to get on board with Harris. My guy. My message was about getting everyone on board! I deleted the exchange and tried to move on. After nearly four years running Indivisible Montgomery, I knew someone would argue every single point.

She Didn't Have Us

THE END OF AUGUST also meant the start of the new school year. On the first day of school, we got the girls ready, we took beginning-of-the-year pictures, and then we took them to school. I packed Hazel into the car, and we spoke the whole way about what preschool would look like this year. She would need to wear her mask all day long except to eat and drink, her friends and teachers would be in masks as well, and there would be fewer of them in class to reduce the chance of anyone catching COVID. Katherine and I were confident the school had taken all possible precautions to keep everyone safe.

Hazel was in a private preschool, but Nancy was in the public school system. Taking her to school meant going back inside the house so she could start virtual second grade. We were lucky to have a kid-sized desk and the space for Nancy to work. The county lent all students Chromebooks for virtual instruction. Katherine and I still worked from home, so Nancy had live-in tech support. No one in our house loved this setup, but it was our best option.

The end of August heralded the Democratic and then the Republican conventions. Barack and Michelle Obama boosted Biden and excoriated Trump and his demonstrated incompetence and inadequacy as president. Trump threw away over 200 years of tradition and used the White House as the site of the Republican convention, appropriating the symbols of American democracy for his campaign.

The end of the conventions meant the campaign season had begun in earnest. We had been writing letters to voters for over 10 months, but now all GOTV activities were available: phone banking, text banking, and even canvassing for those interested. Steve Pressman and I spoke often and were impressed at the level of enthusiasm our members showed for all these events, even during the pandemic.

Trump was attempting to establish a narrative that the election was rigged and speaking out against the use of mail-in ballots. Why bash mail-in ballots? Most voting in American history was done in person, but, in the middle of a pandemic, voting in person might mean exposing yourself to COVID. No one wanted that, and we had a reliable alternative: mail-in ballots. Since the lockdowns of March and April, voting-rights activists pushed states to expand access to mail-in ballots, and we did all we could to support this effort. Republicans traditionally voted by mail more often than Democrats, but the risk of COVID exposure at polling places led many to assume that Democrats might vote by mail in far higher numbers in 2020 than in the past. Always looking to corrupt the 2020 election, Trump decided to claim mail-in votes were illegitimate. The Trump campaign launched preemptive lawsuits to block the expansion of mail-in voting in many states.

Trump's attacks on mail-in voting fed into the panic of the conspiracy-minded who saw Trump and his pliant subordinates as maneuvering to steal the 2020 election in case of a legitimate Joe Biden victory. I received emails from worried members telling me about potential doomsday scenarios they found on Facebook and asking how we could mobilize to defeat them. I often pointed out the most obvious logical fallacy in the conspiracy theory and encouraged our members, if they were concerned, to put that energy into phone banking or writing more letters. One line that I had begun to bring up regularly in newsletters and Indivisible Montgomery meetings was "She didn't have us." As in "We're all scared that Trump will win this election, but when we think back to what happened to Hillary Clinton and the US in 2016, you have to remember one very important thing—she didn't have us. Clinton didn't have this resistance movement conducting this massive GOTV effort on her behalf. She didn't have us writing letters and knocking on doors and making phone calls. Biden does. And we are making a difference." I couldn't guarantee we weren't walking into a devastating election loss as we did in 2016, but it was important to remember that we were in a very different, and in my opinion better, situation than we had been four years prior.

RBG

On September 18, Supreme Court Justice Ruth Bader Ginsburg died.[21] Ginsburg was incredibly influential in progressive politics, having been one of the legal architects of the push for expanding women's rights in the 1970s and beyond. Her health had been failing for some time. On a closely divided Court, we hoped she would live to see Joe Biden elected so he could name her replacement. That didn't happen. Ginsburg's death meant that Donald Trump would get to name his third justice to the Supreme Court. A 5–4 conservative court would quickly become 6–3, and the possibility of a hyperconservative court blocking all kinds of positive actions from a potential Biden administration became a reality. And the cases that established the precedents affirming a woman's right to an abortion, for LGBTQ people to marry whom they want, for access to birth control, and many others were now under threat of being overturned by a far-right Court.

As I did each time major news struck, I wrote a newsletter. If Twitter were any indication, our members would be upset to the point of tears. This was a crushing loss, but we were so close to this election that I didn't want this tragedy to discourage people from the work we were doing. Katherine came downstairs after putting the girls to bed, and I broke the news to her about Ginsburg's death. She was devastated. We talked about it for a while. During a break, I said I wanted to finish the newsletter I was working on. This did not sit well with Katherine. It was a Friday night and we had plans to watch a movie.

"Do you really need to say anything? Do you have anything to add?"

The directness of the confrontation surprised me. "From the few emails I've already received, folks are talking about the end of our country. This isn't the end, and I don't want people trailing off or throwing in the towel. Not this close to the election."

She wasn't convinced. "Calling our senators won't do anything because McConnell and those bastards won't listen. So we're effed. There's nothing we can do."

I was burned out on lifting everyone up in these dark times, and I dropped my usual comforting demeanor. "Look, getting Biden into office is the only chance we have to stop this. If we hold the House, and win the Senate and White House, we can expand the Supreme Court, reform it, or some other option to repair this damage. But if everyone throws in the towel now then, you're right, we truly are fucked."

Katherine was surprised. I don't think she expected quite as succinct or straightforward an answer, much less the passion I brought with it. Winning the election was the only real way to fix the Supreme Court. I wasn't going to give up. Not after what we'd been through.

An hour after the newsletter went out, Katherine received a text from a friend saying my message was exactly what she needed to hear in that moment. Katherine told me later she didn't like sharing her husband with the resistance, but this experience drove home for her how valuable this work was for our community.

Indivisible Montgomery Newsletter: Week 194

SEPTEMBER 18, 2020

AS YOU MAY HAVE heard, Supreme Court Justice Ruth Bader Ginsburg passed away this evening from complications with metastatic pancreatic cancer.

There are an incredible number of thoughtful and heartbreaking obituaries already published about Ginsburg, so I will only say this: Ginsburg earned her place in American history because of who she fought for and how passionately and tirelessly she carried out that fight.

We should all take the space we need to mourn her passing. But push aside the thoughts that conflate her passing with the death of American democracy. The fate of our country rests on the actions that we take until Donald Trump and his enablers are out of office. Regardless of how this plays out in the short term, we have the power to remake and reform our country in the ways necessary to right the wrongs of the Trump presidency.

Let us use the light of RBG's memory as inspiration to keep fighting for this country, and let's do it with as much passion and tireless effort as she did.

Election Day −35

AT THE END OF September, 35 days before Election Day, Biden and Trump met for the first of three presidential debates. Presidential debates are pure theater. From a policy perspective, there is next to nothing of interest discussed. We're gawking to see if someone slips up. But the debates were the only major event planned between the conventions and the election, and they were probably the last best chance to sway any swing voters out there.

That assumes swing voters existed. People usually have opinions that don't perfectly align with parties and candidates. But now? The options were that you opposed what Trump stood for, that you didn't mind his racism, misogyny, outright cruelty, and rank incompetence, or that you supported it. There were no other options. Professional contrarians and cynics still tried to sell "well, both parties are bad." But there was no comparison between one candidate who was impeached for trying to undermine the upcoming election and anyone else. If you hadn't already made up your mind, that meant Trump's proven awfulness wasn't a dealbreaker for you. Anyone voting Republican can go jump in a lake, and, if you're still undecided at this point, you can join them.

Back to the debates. As in 2016, Trump teased he wouldn't show up at all. Please. The man never met a TV camera he didn't like. The debate itself was awful. Trump incessantly interrupted Biden to throw him off his game.[22] An endearing and relatable thing about

Biden was that he stuttered as a kid and has worked his whole life to overcome it. Trump thought being a complete jerk would force Biden to stutter and look feeble. Trump's tactics failed. Instead, during one of Trump's many interruptions, Biden said, "Will you shut up, man?" It was hilarious. Trump deserved it and so much more. Once the debate ended, everyone thought Trump came off looking like the jerk he was trying to be, and Biden's poll numbers went up. Biden eventually apologized for telling Trump to shut up. He shouldn't have. Apologizing to a bully only encourages them to keep bullying. Wait until the bully has changed their ways, then act civil. But apologizing to a bully who is still bullying achieves nothing.

Shortly after the debate, Trump tested positive for COVID.[23] I try not to wish ill on people, but I'll admit I thought it would be poetic justice if COVID killed Trump. What better way for him to go than due to the virus his incompetence let spread unchecked throughout our country? He was rushed to the hospital and received the absolute best care, as you'd expect for the president. He recovered. Alas.

Because of Trump's COVID diagnosis, the second debate was canceled. The final debate took place as planned. It was less of a circus than the first, although it still lacked substance. Once it was over, I was glad. We were only a couple weeks from the election and this would be done soon.

One Line

I T W A S T H E S E C O N D week of October, and I had just dropped Hazel off at preschool. Instead of heading home, I was taking my final trip around the county to deliver stamps to Steve, Nina, and Laurie so they could finish preparing our last batches of letters. We would be mailing them in a little over a week. The pandemic greatly limited opportunities to canvass, so we sponsored virtual text and phone banking parties, but they weren't as well attended as our in-person GOTV events from 2018. This meant the Vote Forward letters were Indivisible Montgomery's largest GOTV effort.

I had just delivered the stamps for Nina, and I was on my way to Steve's. As I drove, the music was on, but I wasn't listening. I was in my own head. The end of our letter-writing campaign was near, and the election was bright on the horizon. That meant my departure from Indivisible Montgomery was not too far away. I started thinking about what life would be like after I stepped down, and I wondered what would happen to Indivisible Montgomery. Would the organization go on? Was it important enough to the members to continue? Had I done anything to truly make a difference?

These questions were invading my thinking more and more these days. I struggled with the doubts. I founded Indivisible Montgomery, but that's just a fancy way of saying I opened a MailChimp account and started a website, right? I wrote so many newsletters, and some people said they helped. But maybe they also drove some people away. And what had Indivisible Montgomery accomplished? All our victories were as part of a larger network. Would they have been accomplished without us? There were so many other groups in the area. Surely our members would have found their own way to be active without Indivisible Montgomery, right? What was the point of my effort over the past four years? Did I drag my family through this just to make a superfluous addition to a larger movement?

While these questions spun faster and faster on my carousel of self-doubt, "I Am Moana" from the movie *Moana* started to play. In this song, Moana is similarly confronting doubts about the difference she has made. In a moment of clarity, she realizes that, regardless of how else her problems may have been solved, she acted. And despite some setbacks, she was the one responsible for delivering her community to the precipice of victory.

I was thunderstruck. That was me. I. Me. Chris Pickett delivered us to where we were. I led Indivisible Montgomery, and everyone who had stuck with us, to this point. I delivered us right here, right now. None of those what-if games mattered. It didn't matter that people *could* have gone to other groups to resist; they came to Indivisible Montgomery and stayed with us. It didn't matter that people *could* have taken different actions; they were taking Indivisible Montgomery's actions. Everything I did since those late days of 2016 with this organization delivered me, Katherine, my girls, and all of Indivisible Montgomery to this moment. At our first meeting, I told the group that we needed to build ourselves into an electoral force for 2020 and we couldn't do that if everyone burned out. In October 2020, three weeks before the election, Indivisible Montgomery was a 1,700-plus-person organization busting our collective asses to evict Trump from the White House. The plan worked. We were doing the work. We were an electoral force. Of the very few things in this world that I could control, I used them to get Indivisible Montgomery to this point.

Resisting Trump was the right and necessary thing to do. I saw a need for like-minded people to form a community and learn how to resist effectively. I did that. Katherine did that. My daughters did that. We did it together, and here we were, with everyone in our resistance, weeks away from the final payoff. What I did was find a group of people who felt like Katherine and I did, and I created an organization to direct our energy into something positive. We created a group where energetic activists could get involved so that Indivisible Montgomery became something not just I built, but our community built. Everything Indivisible Montgomery did was because of our efforts to stand up this group, to set a clear vision, and to execute on it consistently for four years. *Of course* things would have been different if we hadn't done that. People would have found different groups and other ways to use their energy. That was an alternate universe. In this universe, I started this ball rolling and delivered this group of people to this point, and I had to see it through. No more what-ifs. The proof of our efficacy was in the fact that so many of us were still doing this work four years later.

I delivered us to where we were.

Election Day −18

At the start of September, the Indivisible Montgomery bank account balance was perilously low. We had over $6,000 in the bank at the beginning of the year, but Indivisible Montgomery members were writing so many Vote Forward letters that we spent nearly all our money on stamps. I talked to Nina, Steve, and Laurie to estimate the number of unstamped letters we each had on hand, plus how many were still circulating. We went around with the numbers a few times, but we agreed we expected the number of letters we needed to stamp would be double what we had already done and about $7,000 more was needed. We had never raised that much money in one drive, but we had to give it a shot. Our members had written so many letters.

We launched the fundraising drive at the end of September with a goal of $7,000. I never expected to make it, but I thought we'd get close. While Steve and I never said so explicitly, we had both indicated we'd cover any shortfall with our own money. But Indivisible Montgomery never faltered in fundraising. By October 5, we met our $7,000 goal. Indivisible Montgomery members came through in a big way, and we got all the stamps we needed in time.

On October 16, 18 days before Election Day, I took 11 USPS letter boxes and packed them into the hatch and back seat of our Honda CR-V. Steve, Laurie, and Nina were doing the same with their boxes of letters. We all then converged on a USPS warehouse to drop off

The final results of Indivisible Montgomery's letter-writing efforts in October 2020: 64,000 letters written, put in envelopes, stamped, and ready to go.

our boxes of stamped letters. The facility had an outdoor loading dock where we could drop the boxes, which meant we didn't have to go inside the facility and risk catching COVID. I was the first to arrive at the warehouse. Nina and Laurie pulled in shortly after, with their cars packed full like mine. Steve then arrived in his sedan full of letter boxes, followed by his wife in her sedan, also full of letter boxes. I was astonished at just how many letters we collected encouraging voters across the country to turn out and vote on November 3. We pulled our cars up to the loading dock one at a time and worked together to unload them. It took 30 minutes to work through all five cars. As we rested, I did some back-of-the-envelope math. Average number of letters in each box times the number of boxes—that couldn't be right. I probably messed up the multiplication ... no. Did I count the letters wrong? No. I got that right, too.

Indivisible Montgomery Newsletter: Week 199

We did it! The members of Indivisible Montgomery wrote well over 64,000 Vote Forward letters encouraging people to turn out and vote this year. 64,000!!! For all the letters you wrote, money you donated, and emails you sifted through, I applaud you!

But we still have a bunch of work to do! First, phone and text banking is moving into encouraging known Biden/Harris voters to make sure they get out and vote! We have events running every single day between now and Nov. 3. Please sign up now!

Then sign up for the next Indivisible Montgomery meeting this coming SATURDAY, Oct. 24. It is our last meeting before the election season ends. You must RSVP to attend.

We need you to protect the election! Sign up with the Biden campaign to be a poll watcher or staff a voter protection hotline on Election Day. And be ready to mobilize for post-election protests and stay up to date on information to help prevent Trump from stealing this election with our new webpage: A Free and Fair Election.

Election Day –1

I HAD NOTHING LEFT. No ideas. No answers. Nothing.

The two weeks since we sent the GOTV letters had been a blur. I sent newsletters to our members nearly every day. I took the week before the election off work so I could focus on Indivisible Montgomery projects. We phone banked. We sent texts. Some of our members even went to Pennsylvania to help congressional campaigns that decided to canvass. We did everything we possibly could to turn out voters for Joe Biden. I was so drained from four years of preparing for this very moment. I had thrown everything I had into it. Strategically, there wasn't anything we could or should have done differently. We were in the best possible position to evict Trump from office. And if this country still elected that authoritarian charlatan, that vile garbage bag of a human, for another term, I had no response.

I really hoped no one asked.

Election Day

Katherine woke up before the sun came up on November 3, Election Day. The pandemic had set off a scramble across the country to find enough people to staff polling places for in-person voting. Katherine wanted voters who intended to vote on Election Day to have their opportunity. And she also didn't want to sit at home all day waiting for the vote tallies to come in. So, early that morning, Katherine rode her bike to our nearby polling place to help our community vote.

The girls had the day off school, and the three of us hung out all day. The weather was nice so we went to the park and got a snack from Panera. After lunch, while Hazel napped and Nancy was engrossed in her book, my mind turned toward Indivisible Montgomery. I flipped on my computer to make sure the morning's newsletter—"There are still chances to work!"—had gone out, and the evening's message—"Thank you for all your work!"—was ready to send. Once I was satisfied with the newsletter situation, I took a deep breath and opened my election outcome prewrites. Normally, if an outcome of an event was uncertain, I would craft newsletters in my head based on the possible scenarios, but I didn't often write them out like I had today. Once the winner of the election was announced, I knew I'd be too emotional to have the discipline to write a newsletter, regardless of who won.

If Biden won:

WE DID IT! Joe Biden will be the 46th President of the United States! Donald Trump's time destroying our country will come to an end on Jan. 20, 2021.

We were prepared for this to be a long and drawn-out period to count votes. And while some states have not yet reported their final vote totals, Biden's projected wins in XX, XX, and XX are enough to secure the 270 electoral votes needed to be the next president.

And Democrats have won control of the Senate! We secured victories in a slew of states, and while the full number is not yet clear, we have won enough to know that Democrats will control the next Senate.

The future is bright, but we cannot let our guard down just yet. If you haven't already, please sign up with Protect the Results to make sure Trump cannot steal our victory.

I am filled with so many emotions right now, but pride and thankfulness are at the top of my list. I am thankful that we all found each other and came together to form such a formidable electoral force. And I am so damn proud of all the work we put in over the past four years and that it has paid off.

We will be in touch again with future actions. Until then, thank you. Thank you for everything. Have a restful night.

Chris Pickett

And if Trump won:

It is with incredible disappointment and frustration that I write to you this evening. Barring some change of fortune, President Trump has won reelection. While some states are still counting their votes, it is clear Trump will secure an Electoral College victory.

We put in an incredible effort over the past four years to try and safeguard our country from Trump's creeping fascism and authoritarianism. I am proud of what we have done, yet our efforts were not enough.

These are times of great darkness and sorrow for so many. But I do know that the sun will rise tomorrow. And in that day, we will be confronted with a chance to do something. Our task is to make sure we do that thing right, whatever it may be. And after that, we have to take the next step to do the next right thing. Perhaps if we start there and just keep doing the next right thing, we can find our path to light.

In solidarity,

Chris Pickett

It turned my stomach to have to reread the Trump-won newsletter. But it needed to be done ahead of time because I'd be in no mood to write new words should Trump pull out the victory.

The rest of the day was spent with Nancy and Hazel doing chores, playing, and checking in with the news. The girls were in bed by 8:30, and I went downstairs to watch the news and see how the night played out. Katherine unexpectedly got home from the polling station around 9:30 that evening. No one knew what in-person voting would be like because so many mail-in ballots had been cast in Maryland and across the country. A lot of people, like Katherine and me, voted early in person. Would the polling locations be busy? Apparently not. At Katherine's location, there were so few voters that the polling station was overstaffed. Katherine told stories of how the workers were practically falling over each other to help voters. Once the polling stations closed in Maryland, they sent her home.

Katherine stopped in to ask how things were going. I didn't have much to tell her. No notable calls had been made, but things seemed to be trending in our direction. The states that were going to be a far reach for Trump, like Colorado and New Hampshire, were being called early for Biden. The battleground states were too close to call, but strong turnout for Biden across the country suggested a substantial move in his direction relative to Clinton in 2016. But we still couldn't make any definite conclusions. Katherine shrugged and went to take a shower.

The memories of the 2016 election meant the evening was going to be tense, but I wasn't grinding my teeth at the television commentary this time. Everyone from the news anchors to the professionals who knew all about elections was being careful about making judgment calls on which way a state might vote. This was due to Trump's insistence, long before Election Day, that the vote was rigged against him. Because of the villainy of his campaign doggedly working to undermine Americans' faith in the electoral system, no one wanted to make a call on who won in a close state only to have to reverse it. Whether it went from Biden to Trump or the other way, any change would be fodder for the rigged election claim. In response, anchors and their elections desks wanted to be completely sure of the vote before declaring winners. And Twitter was also cracking down on false or premature calls with a rule that anyone making an election call, other than the Associated Press and a few other select outlets, would be immediately suspended from the site.

Katherine came back from her shower, and I told her not much had changed since she left. We were at the point of the night where vote totals in uncalled states would change by fractions of a percent. This was the time four years ago that I began to realize Trump might win the presidency. Remembering that feeling made me dizzy. But I balanced myself by looking at the counts in Michigan, Wisconsin, and Pennsylvania. Those were Clinton's most notable losses in 2016. However, in 2020, we were feeling cautiously optimistic because Biden was either ahead or within striking distance in these states, and most of the vote remaining to be counted was in areas already trending well for Biden. The races in Arizona, Georgia, and North Carolina were too close to call as well. Michigan, Wisconsin, and Pennsylvania would be enough for Biden to win, but having these others would be great.

Around 11:30, Katherine and I started discussing going to bed. The election wasn't going to be called that night, so we might as well get some sleep. I stood up, turned off the TV, and checked Twitter one last time before going upstairs. I quickly sat back down. Katherine noticed the change in my expression. "What? What is it?"

"I can't believe it," I said with a grin. "Fox News just called Arizona for Joe Biden."

My Twitter feed was alive with people talking about the Arizona call. Fox News made a call that no one else had, in a hotly contested state where Biden held a razor-thin lead. I couldn't envision a scenario where Biden won Arizona but lost the election. I tried to keep it under control because no one else had called Arizona. About a half hour later, it was reported that the Trump camp was furious about Fox's Arizona call and had even reached out to get Fox News to recant. The election analysts at Fox who made the call went on the air and stood their ground: "We're not wrong in this particular case."[24]

Calling Arizona was momentous. Not just because the state went to Biden, but because it punctured Trump's narrative. We knew several states would be too close to call on the night of November 3, and it was expected Trump would simply claim victory, then try to use the courts to stop counting any more ballots. If Arizona, a longtime GOP state, went blue before Trump could roll out his plan, then the administration would look even more foolish when they tried to execute it.

We went to sleep soon after that, but we felt more secure than we had four years ago. We just needed the final sets of votes to be counted to lock it up.

Election Day +1

WHEN I WOKE UP on November 4, I immediately went to the kitchen, where my phone was charging. I opened it and checked my email for news alerts from *The Washington Post* that would indicate if the election was called. I exhaled and calmed down when I saw the election was more or less where we left it when Katherine and I went to bed. Ohio, Texas, and Florida moved to the Trump column. These were not surprises. The Associated Press joined Fox in calling Arizona for Biden, which gave us more confidence that Arizona would stay in Biden's column. Biden had 238 Electoral College votes to Trump's 217. The remaining 83 votes in Wisconsin, Michigan, Pennsylvania, Georgia, Nevada, and North Carolina would determine who would get to 270 and win.

I have no idea what I did that day. I felt frail and exhausted from having done so much work with Indivisible Montgomery and a little disappointed that we didn't have a winner yet. But I was also upbeat. At this point four years before, I was coming to grips with the reality of the coming Trump administration. This year, Biden was doing well in the uncalled states. I didn't want to take anything for granted, but the situation seemed better than it had in 2016.

I was on Twitter so much that day, checking to see if any new races had been called. Later that afternoon, the AP called Wisconsin and Michigan for Biden. I nearly jumped out of my chair. These were huge wins! Biden now had 264 electoral votes. He needed to win only one of the remaining uncalled states, and it would be all over.

The wait was excruciating. Biden maintained his lead in Nevada, and he was projected to overtake Trump in Pennsylvania. Georgia and North Carolina were too close to call. We went to bed that night, again not knowing who had won the election.

Election Day +4

TWO MORE DAYS PASSED without any other states called for Biden or Trump. The trends were mostly moving in Biden's direction. Biden's slim lead in Pennsylvania and Nevada was growing, and he was pulling even in Georgia. North Carolina was slipping to Trump. Still, the wait was excruciating.

At just after 11:30 a.m., I saw the email come in. To no one in particular, I said, "Oh my god, they called the race."

Katherine heard my muttering. "What?"

"Biden won! They called Pennsylvania for Biden!"

"WHAT?!"

"WE DID IT!"

All the major news outlets announced that Biden won Pennsylvania. Even with three states left to be called, the 20 electoral votes from Pennsylvania put Biden over the 270 needed to win. Katherine, Nancy, Hazel, and I all hugged and jumped and danced around the living room. Jerry the dog got up, his tail wagging, wanting to be a part of it all. A couple of minutes later, after we had all calmed down some, Katherine looked at me with a smile. "Don't you have a newsletter to send?"

I smiled back and said, "Yes I do." I went downstairs, opened my computer, and sent a modified version of the newsletter I had pre-written for Biden's victory. This was the first time I sent a newsletter with tears in my eyes.

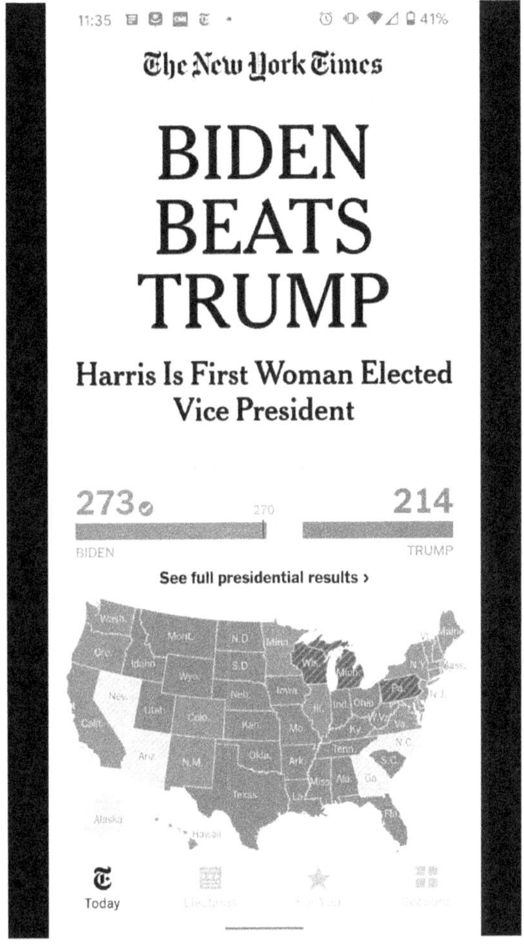

Front page of *The New York Times* on November 7, 2020.

After lunch, we walked Jerry around the neighborhood. On this beautiful fall day, we couldn't get away from signs of celebration. Cars honked their horns. Kids ran around banging on pans. People were outside chatting and laughing. After we finished the walk, Katherine and I put our own celebration into action. Well before Election Day, we decided we'd get ice cream as our celebration for a Biden victory. We hopped in the car and went to Baskin-Robbins, grabbed our ice cream cones, and walked over to the local park. The only hitch was when I got too aggressive with my ice cream, and I pushed it off the cone onto the ground. In true dad form, I jammed the ice cream that hadn't touched the ground back onto my cone and ate it anyway. I wasn't going to let a little dirt ruin our great day.

Indivisible Montgomery Newsletter: Week 201

November 7, 2020

My friends,

Multiple outlets are now saying that Joe Biden and Kamala Harris have secured more than the 270 electoral votes they need to become the next President and Vice President of the United States. We won!

That the vote took so long to count is a testament to the people who run our elections and their commitment to get it right, even if it may have caused a few extra high-stress days for the rest of us.

This is an incredible achievement! We won in the middle of a pandemic against a cheating, incumbent president who ramped up voter suppression to try to win. We elected the first Black and South Asian woman to ever serve as Vice President.

…

I am filled with so many emotions right now, but pride and thankfulness are at the top of my list. I am thankful that we all found each other and came together to form such a formidable electoral force. And I am so damn proud of all the work we put in over the past four years and that it has paid off.

We will be in touch again with future actions. Until then, thank you. Thank you for everything.

Sedition

I WAS ECSTATIC ABOUT the results in the presidential election, and I was mostly pleased with the results of the congressional races. Democrats retained control of the House, albeit with a slimmer majority. Jon Ossoff and Rev. Raphael Warnock also did well enough in their Senate races in Georgia to force a runoff with the Republican incumbents. Several other Senate pickup opportunities were missed, meaning Ossoff and Warnock needed to win their runoffs to get the Senate to a 50–50 split between Democrats and Republicans. This would give Democrats control of the body, as incoming vice president Harris would be on hand to break any tie in favor of Democrats. Had you told me beforehand that Biden won the election with a 7-million-vote edge in the popular vote, I would have assumed Democratic control of the Senate was a lock. That wasn't to be.

Meanwhile, Trump and his campaign, arguing that the election was rigged and stolen, took their arguments to court after court. I paid close attention to news of the first few trials. Trump's attorneys were trying to argue there were deficiencies in the electoral process, or miscounted votes, or some other random thing they found on the internet. None of it held up. Over the course of the six weeks between the election and voting in the Electoral College, the Trump campaign lost 61 court cases and won only one.[25]

A sitting president trying to overturn an election he lost is no laughing matter. Except when his lawyer, Rudy Giuliani, made a complete mess of things. The day Biden won the election, Trump tweeted that Giuliani would be holding a press conference at the Four Seasons in Philadelphia. Whoever booked the press conference, though, apparently didn't know what they were doing and booked an area outside of Four Seasons Total Landscaping, a small landscaping outfit in downtown Philadelphia. Instead of looking like a professional operation with a press conference in a fancy hotel ballroom, Giuliani complained about a supposedly stolen election while standing at a lectern in the landscaping company's back parking lot in front of a closed metal garage door, bare scaffolding, faded green paint, and a couple of trash bins.[26] A week later, Giuliani somehow topped that spectacle when he held a bizarre press conference spinning wackadoo conspiracy theories while his hair dye ran down the sides of his face.[27]

Aside from Giuliani's comic relief, I mostly tuned out from Trump's attempts to use the courts to overturn the election. There was no evidence that anything went wrong on a scale large enough to overturn the election. And by December 14, it didn't matter. The Electoral College met that day and cast their votes supporting Joe Biden to be the 46th president. Any litigation the Trump campaign could have waged was now moot. There was no legal recourse to reverse or alter the results of the Electoral College votes.

Despite Biden's Electoral College victory and the lack of any shred of evidence of fraud in the 2020 election, the Texas attorney general filed a case directly to the Supreme Court to bar the electoral votes from several Biden states from being counted.[28] This was a stupid case built on the lies that the Trump campaign used in its 61 failed attempts to convince any judge that something had gone wrong in the election. That didn't stop 126 congressional Republicans from signing on to support Texas's position. These people were trying to overturn the results of a democratic election. This was no less than sedition. We called our members of Congress, encouraging them to bar any Republican supporting this court case from being seated in the next Congress. If they want to overturn a free and fair election, then they don't belong in the government of the United States.

Signing Off

ON THE SATURDAY AFTER Thanksgiving, I announced my resignation as the executive director of Indivisible Montgomery. I made it. The Trump years would be coming to an end, Indivisible Montgomery achieved the goals I set for it nearly four years before, and I could go out with my head high. Rather than scheduling this newsletter as I had with most pre-planned messages, I made sure to press send on this manually. I sat in our living room and reread the message I had crafted over the past week. Once I decided it was good, I didn't hesitate. I had no qualms. I pressed send. And I was happy.

Soon enough, the responses started coming in. The vast majority of them were congratulatory and wishing me well once I stepped away. The fellow group leaders who received my message, like Barbara Noveau of DoTheMostGood, were the most understanding and sent their well-wishes. Some members said they were disappointed I was stepping away but expressed they understood this was an incredible strain. And then there were the few who seemed put out. Maybe passively angry. Curt responses from people who were never curt. I was surprised, but I wasn't going to get caught up in it. I did this for myself and my family. No one else knew what this job was like, and I felt zero regrets about leaving.

Not until she saw my resignation in her own inbox did Katherine believe that I would step down from Indivisible Montgomery. She always thought I'd find some reason to stick around. Many of the things we fought against remained, and much of what we fought for was yet to be achieved. The country needed a full-fledged activist campaign to ensure the Biden administration would right the ship. That wasn't my fight. Not as the leader of Indivisible Montgomery. After four years, I would step down after Joe Biden was inaugurated on January 20.

The question of who would lead Indivisible Montgomery into the future was answered two weeks later as Steve Pressman volunteered to take over. All that was left was to show Steve the ropes and skate out the door.

Indivisible Montgomery Newsletter: Week 204

After much consideration, I have decided to resign as the Executive Director of Indivisible Montgomery. There are many reasons for this decision, but they can all be summed up by simply saying that it's time for me to move on. The past four years have been exhilarating, but also quite a grind. I look forward to putting that time and energy toward my family and exploring new venues to make our community, country, and world a better place.

I can't fully express how much each and every one of you have meant to me. Every big and little thing you did helped move us from one hurdle to the next. Each hurdle we cleared meant we were that much closer to beating Trump. And we did it. We beat Trump! But the work doesn't end. Now we must work to reverse the damage his administration wrought and build a better future for everyone.

Indivisible Montgomery will continue beyond my time leading it, but it will look quite different. This group was founded as an anti-Trump organization. With President Trump on the way out, Indivisible Montgomery will need to find a new purpose. So I encourage you to join us one week from today, Dec. 5, for the town-hall style

Indivisible Montgomery meeting where we will talk about this new direction. RSVP here!

My final day as the Executive Director of Indivisible Montgomery will be Jan. 20, 2021. Once Joe Biden is inaugurated, I will step down. It seems fitting that this organization will transition to new leadership as our country transitions to a new government and a new set of challenges. Until then, Indivisible Montgomery will run as it always has with weekly updates and actions, except for holiday breaks.

Thank you for everything. I look forward to seeing you in one week, and I hope you enjoy the rest of this holiday weekend!

2021 | From Dark to Bright

New Year, New Future

We made it. 2021. I became increasingly emotional as the calendar flipped to the new year. I was nearing the end of my time with Indivisible Montgomery, and our country was nearing the end of our COVID paralysis. In the middle of December, the Food and Drug Administration approved two vaccines that showed remarkable levels of protection from COVID.[1] The first vaccines would be administered only a few weeks later. Katherine and I wouldn't get our first doses until April, but even in January I was overjoyed that the end of our COVID life was close. I was overwhelmed with so many emotions that I nearly wrote a Christmas / New Year's newsletter riffing on John Lennon's "Happy Xmas." As I sat down to write the message, I realized I was maybe being a bit melodramatic. I closed the computer and went back to my family.

When we pinned the new calendar to the wall on January 1, I said, "20 days." Twenty days until Joe Biden and Kamala Harris were inaugurated as president and vice president. Just 20 more days of leading Indivisible Montgomery. I loved everything we had done, but I was ready to be finished with it. I just needed to write a few newsletters, and I'd be done. Right?

January 4

T HE FIRST MONDAY OF the year was the first school day of the year, and it was also my first day of true unemployment. We weren't able to renew the grant for Rescuing Biomedical Research so I was officially looking for a new job. In the meantime, I took Hazel to preschool. She had been in person since September, and the school had done well keeping everyone healthy. A few of her classmates missed time due to COVID, but the school didn't turn into a vector for the disease, and they were open the whole time. Nancy was still at school-by-Zoom. The county school system was considering an option for some students to return to in-person schooling for part of the year while others would remain virtual. We leaned toward in-person because of our good experience with Hazel's school. Nancy was doing well with her work, but she missed being around her friends. Didn't we all.

After dropping off Hazel, I came home to figure out what it meant to no longer have a job. I went to our family room, flipped on my computer, and finished up some paperwork to ensure the family still had health and dental insurance. I did some investigating into how to file for unemployment. I wasn't looking too closely, though, because my networking over the previous months gave me some solid job leads. Because I didn't have any calls coming up that day, my attention drifted to Indivisible Montgomery. To get Steve Pressman ready to take over the group, I was putting together documents on how I ran everything, along with a few how-to documents specifically for running fundraising campaigns, using Mailchimp, and so on. Steve and I had several phone calls set up over the next two weeks to go through everything I didn't have time to write down.

My attention also drifted to social media to see what people were talking about. Today, Twitter was abuzz with the fallout from the bombshell story that Trump was taped on a phone call pressuring the Georgia secretary of state to corruptly reverse the state's vote total.[2] "I just want to find 11,780 votes," said Trump to Georgia Secretary of State Brad Raffensperger. Georgia had been through multiple recounts, all of which confirmed that Joe Biden won the state by nearly 12,000 votes. Nearly nine weeks after the election and three weeks after the Electoral College cast its votes, this guy was still trying to find a corrupt official who could help reverse his loss. This wasn't the first story indicating Trump was in touch with officials in states he lost, but it was the first indication of just how blunt he was being in these efforts. Raffensperger's tape of the phone call exposed one part of Trump's plot, but the rest wouldn't come out for at least 18 months.

Having states declare something amiss in their presidential results wouldn't amount to much at this phase of the process. The electoral votes had been cast, and the only thing left for Congress to do was count them. There could be challenges to whether a state should have their votes counted, but rejecting the votes required a majority of both houses. Democrats controlled the House of Representatives, so actually rejecting the votes was a long shot.

That said, Trump was telling people in the Department of Justice, "Just say that the election was corrupt [and] leave the rest to me" and Republican members of Congress.[3] The Trump team's play became clear: get enough states to say their presidential vote was corrupt and their electoral votes shouldn't be counted. With neither Biden nor Trump receiving enough votes to win the presidency, the House would select the president. In this scenario, each state gets one vote, and all the representatives of the state convene and determine which candidate to vote for. Because Republicans were in the majority with 26 state delegations, they could have delivered the election to Trump. His comments to Raffensperger confirmed he was colluding with Republican members of Congress to precipitate this very situation.

The extent of Trump's plan wasn't widely known at this point, but the fact that he continued his efforts to overturn the election was incredibly concerning. The country was saved from being plunged into an electoral crisis by a handful of Republican officials who decided they were going to do their job instead of bend to Trump's whims. All that was standing in front of Biden becoming president was the ceremonial counting of electoral votes on January 6, and if Trump couldn't corrupt any GOP officials into helping him stay in power, what else could he do?

January 5

JANUARY 5 WAS THE first election of 2021 and the day we would find out who would control the Senate for the next two years. If Rev. Raphael Warnock and Jon Ossoff won their runoff elections in Georgia, Democrats would control the chamber, along with the House and the White House. It was a bit of a miracle we were even here. Joe Biden surprisingly won Georgia, and no candidate in the state's two Senate races reached 50% of the vote. By Georgia's rules, the top two vote recipients enter a runoff to determine the outcome. Indivisible Montgomery's involvement in the Georgia runoffs was far less intense than our actions leading up to November 3. We wanted to win these races and thus the Senate, but the entire nationwide resistance was focused on these two elections in this one state. Rather than revving up our members to engage, I went with the soft sell, telling them that there was so much activist attention focused on Georgia that each person should decide how much energy they wanted to pour into the runoffs. I gave the members links to get engaged with the campaigns and left it at that.

The Indivisible Montgomery message on January 5 was twofold. First, there was the standard Election Day message indicating how members could play a role. The second was the script for our call to Congress. It was Tuesday, after all, and just because we won the election in 2020 didn't mean we were letting up with our activism. Because dozens of Republican members of Congress indicated publicly they were going to vote against certifying the electors from multiple states on January 6, we called on our members of Congress to speak out about the GOP's blatantly anti-democratic actions.[4]

Later that morning, Trump was holding yet another rally selling his lie that the 2020 election was stolen.[5] This wasn't the first rally Trump held spouting conspiracy theories about a stolen election, and it wasn't even the first in DC. They had happened enough that they merged into background noise. Another Trump rally where people whine about losing? Is it a day ending in *y*? Whatever. There was literally nothing they could do to influence what would happen when Congress convened to count the electoral votes. January 6 was a ceremonial event.

I ignored the rally and went about my business. I had had a good phone call on a job lead that day, and I was feeling quite happy. My unemployment would be short, Katherine had several high-paying projects this month and next so we likely wouldn't need to dip into our savings because I didn't have a job, and we still had health insurance. That evening, the election results started coming in. Early returns indicated red areas would stay red and blue areas would stay blue. But turnout was substantially stronger for the Democrats in several bellwether precincts. As the night went on, the returns only solidified the Democrats' strength, and Warnock and Ossoff were projected to win their races. The Democrats would control the Senate.[6] As Biden took the helm, so much was now open to him for repairing the grievous wrongs committed by the Trump administration. From appointing judges to passing life-changing legislation, all of it was now possible. Things were looking up.

January 6

January 6 was a Wednesday. It started out as a day like any other, but it would turn into an indelible event, like 9/11.

Hazel and I bundled up against the January cold, and I took her to preschool, while Nancy went to virtual school and Katherine got to work. Once I returned home, I relaxed during the morning, checking on social media and talking to friends over text. Trump held his umpteenth rally that morning for no real reason except to make himself feel good. The counting of electoral votes was a ceremonial process, and there was no way Trump could twist this process to stay in power. Any rally falsely whining over a stolen election was an exercise to make Trump's supporters angry over something that couldn't be changed.

Around noon, Katherine, Nancy, and I had lunch and took Jerry for a walk. Afterward, they went back to work and school, and I went downstairs. Congress was to convene at 1:00 p.m. to count the electoral votes and certify the presidential election won by Joe Biden. I wasn't planning to watch it, but I would check in from time to time on Twitter to see what shenanigans Republican members of Congress might be pulling. I logged on and found that Vice President Pence had just released a statement. Trump was pressuring him to cast aside electoral votes from select states and install Trump as president for another four years. Pence's statement said he refused.[7] Of course Pence refused. Neither the Constitution nor any law gave him the authority to exclude any set of electors during the electoral vote count. Trump's pressure campaign was a fantasy.

At 1:00 p.m., the counting of electoral votes began. At the same time, attendees from Trump's event at the Ellipse in Washington, DC, marched toward the Capitol. Some people on social media voiced concerns that they would try to enter the Capitol. I wasn't concerned. I've been on Capitol Hill for work, and it only takes a couple of glances at the Capitol building before you notice the guards at the top of the steps, at least two per stairwell, in bulletproof vests carrying automatic rifles across their chest. If you go more than one or two steps up, you get yelled at by those guards to get off the steps and move along. When something important is going on at the Capitol that might draw a larger than normal crowd, I've seen guys on top of the building with a gun longer than a standard assault rifle. When I heard Trump's supporters were approaching the building, I thought the weaponry of the Capitol Police would be on full display to deter anyone from trying anything stupid. They'd stop at the barriers, yell, and eventually go home.

That was not what happened.

As Trump's rioters arrived at the building, the scene immediately became chaotic. Capitol Police in yellow vests were standing behind metal bike racks, attempting to keep the crowd from breaking through. The rioters eventually pulled the racks away and beat the police until they broke through their lines and moved closer to the Capitol. Rioters began climbing on and tearing down the scaffolding for the presidential inauguration, now two weeks away. Surely the officers with the automatic rifles would soon arrive to put an end to this, right? While this went on outside, inside the

House chamber, Republicans objected to the electors from Arizona, and the House and Senate went to their own chambers for concurrent two-hour sessions to debate whether Arizona's electoral votes should be counted.

Shortly after Congress broke up, the mob broke in.

I was glued to my seat in the family room watching these disturbing scenes play out all over Twitter. Rioters fought Capitol Police, beating them with whatever implements they brought with them. In front of the Capitol were Trump flags, Confederate flags, Blue Lives Matter flags, American flags, and more as rioters smashed their way into the Capitol itself. As I watched videos of Trump supporters stream through the Capitol, I said out loud, "Where are the people with the guns? Shoot them!" These rioters were using force to try to install a leader who had lost the election. It was a full-blown insurrection. Protecting the nation and the Constitution required more than bike racks and riot shields.

The pictures from that day were stunning. Rioters scaling the Capitol building. A man carrying a Confederate flag inside the Capitol. Armed guards pointing guns through the door of the House chamber. A noose. Once I could tear myself away, I texted Steve Moore with something as insightful as "JFC." His response: "???" He hadn't been watching. I told him Trump's rioters breached the Capitol and he needed to turn on the news. I walked upstairs past Nancy, still at school, to make sure Katherine knew. As I turned into her office, the look on her face and the tears in her eyes told me she already did.

AROUND 3:30 P.M., ONCE I could focus on something other than the ongoing insurrection in DC, I had the urge to pick up Hazel from school. We were far from downtown DC, but events spiraling out of control was a real possibility. To be safe, I wanted to have the whole family under one roof, and that meant getting Hazel early.

Shortly after I got home with Hazel, Biden went on national television with an address to the nation, chiding the insurrectionists in the Capitol and their supporters that political violence was never appropriate, and it was time to leave.[8] What was amazing was that Biden's statement came out before anything from Trump—the actual president at the time and the supposed leader of the country. But Trump didn't want to be shown up by Biden, and he finally posted a video on social media addressing the siege. He told the rioters they were completely right to be upset, they did nothing wrong in storming the Capitol, and he loved them, but it was time to go home.[9] There was a collective WTF gasp from all corners of the internet once this came out. He loved them? Seriously? After years and years of letting him get away with his doublespeak and incitement to violence, Twitter and Facebook quickly took down Trump's video.

A little before dinnertime, the rioters started to leave the Capitol. The withdrawal of the insurrectionists from the Capitol was chaotic, and I don't remember the full order of how I witnessed the events. Insurrectionists in the Senate chamber. A gallows erected outside the Capitol: "Hang Mike Pence!"[10] I recall the Capitol Police letting insurrectionists walk right out of the building. Seriously? *This is clearly a bunch of crimes! Arrest them!*

I couldn't keep watching—the strain was too much, and I had kids who needed their father to be present. Incalculable damage had been done to our country and to our government. We did not have a peaceful transfer of power—one of the hallmarks of American governance. How do we grapple with the severity of what happened? How do we move forward? There were so many pieces to pick up. What I was grappling with was trying to understand what I saw happen in real time without fully believing what I had seen.

January 7

I WAS FURIOUS. FURIOUS at what happened and what didn't happen. Congress reconvened in the middle of the night to certify the 2020 election. Joe Biden would be president in two weeks. Once that finished, I thought Speaker Nancy Pelosi should have immediately moved to a vote on articles of impeachment for Trump. He incited a violent attempt to cling to power, and he was a danger to the country every minute he was left in office. That wasn't what happened. Instead, Pelosi adjourned the House. Pelosi is one of the best Speakers we've ever had, but, to me, not immediately holding Trump to account for sending his murderous supporters to the Capitol was her biggest failure.

I was also furious I had to put more effort into Indivisible Montgomery this close to the finish line.

I was done. *I was fucking done!* I was supposed to be able to skate for two weeks, but Trump's fascist bullshit meant that wouldn't be the case, and I was so angry. This was the first time in American history we didn't have a peaceful transfer of power between two administrations. Trump's insurrection was a direct attack on the United States, and we couldn't let that go unanswered. There needed to be repercussions. Repercussions for Trump, his abettors, and his supporters who stormed the Capitol building. They all needed to be in jail for what they did. I didn't have the power to put them in jail, so I did what I could: I rallied Indivisible Montgomery.

I called on Indivisible Montgomery members to light up the phones of our members of Congress and express how they felt. Whether anger, frustration, despair, or anything else they might be feeling, they needed to use these feelings to communicate that Trump needed to impeached and immediately removed. Two more weeks in office was two more weeks full of opportunities for Trump to destroy American democracy. We also called on our members to support Rep. Cori Bush's bill to censure all the Republicans who voted against certification of the election, even after Trump's violent insurrection had been put down.

That's right. Even after Trump's rioters invaded the Capitol and threatened the lives of everyone therein, violently attacked Capitol Police, and contributed to the deaths of multiple people, well over 100 Republicans voted against certifying Biden's victory. They should all be launched into the sun. Short of that, they should be expelled from Congress and never allowed to hold public office again.

Indivisible Montgomery Newsletter: Week 210

January 7, 2021

My friends,

No words can express the quaking rage and profound sorrow with which I watched President Trump's insurrectionist mobs storm the U.S. Capitol yesterday afternoon. But one thing I did not feel was surprise. Over the past four years of watching Trump stoke the fires of hatred and after repeatedly calling on our members of Congress to hold Trump and his cronies to account, we knew this could happen.

We have worked tirelessly over the past four years to limit the damage Trump could do to our country, and, when appropriate, try to have Trump removed from office. After Joe Biden won the Nov. 3 election, we had assumed that Jan. 20 would be soon enough for Trump to leave. Now, Jan. 20 is too far away. Every minute Trump remains in office is another minute he has to incite a new insurrection to overthrow our government.

That is why we I am asking all of Indivisible Montgomery to call their members of Congress today.

For inciting yesterday's insurrectionist mobs, we will call on our members of Congress to support new impeachment proceedings against Trump and bar him from ever again holding office.

Similarly, we will expect our members of Congress to publicly speak out demanding Vice President Pence invoke the 25th Amendment to remove Trump from power. While impeachment and the 25th Amendment would achieve similar ends, it is not clear which would be the faster mechanism at this point and we will pursue both.

Additionally, newly elected Rep. Cori Bush will introduce a resolution calling for the expulsion of all members of Congress who took part in the stunt to object to certification of states' electors. They played a critical role in what happened yesterday, and they should have to answer for their actions attempting to subvert democracy. This effort is currently only happening in the House.

After the awfulness of what happened yesterday, there must be a reckoning. We must demonstrate that there are real consequences for this kind of lying for political gain. Because if we don't, it will surely happen again.

Impeached Again

In my mind, Democrats impeached Trump in the wee hours of January 7, shortly after voting to certify the election. Or at least within 24 hours of the insurrection. Instead, Speaker Pelosi and Democrats issued an ultimatum addressed to Vice President Pence: he had one week to remove Trump using the 25th Amendment or the House would impeach Trump for his actions on January 6.[11] Pence quickly responded by saying he'd do no such thing. Trump's supporters went to the Capitol, broke in, chanted "Hang Mike Pence!," got people killed, and delayed the certification of the election, but Pence couldn't be bothered to use his power to remove a clear and present danger to our country.

On January 13, Trump was impeached a second time.[12] All Democrats and 10 Republicans voted to impeach. It would've been more than 10 had they moved the impeachment resolution to right after the insurrection. Senators and representatives were pissed, but the right-wing media complex went to work on the GOP members of Congress and got them to change their mind. Senate Leader Mitch McConnell sent the Senate into recess rather than immediately receiving the articles of impeachment and trying Trump. Despite everything Trump did to destroy our country, Republicans still largely fell in line.

A Service Award

FIVE DAYS AFTER TRUMP'S second impeachment, I led my final Indivisible Montgomery meeting. It was the Sunday before Inauguration Day. After I announced my resignation, Montgomery County Councilmember Evan Glass contacted me, saying he'd like to give me a citation on behalf of the county council in appreciation for my work with Indivisible Montgomery. I was honored and humbled. Two hours before the meeting, Glass came to our house to give me the award. Still COVID-conscious, we posed for a picture outside the house.

Montgomery County Councilmember Evan Glass presented me with a commendation for leading Indivisible Montgomery and my service to the local community.

Just before the meeting started, I took my computer into Katherine's office to lead our virtual gathering from a quiet space. Katherine wanted to see my last meeting, though, so she and the girls watched from the family room. Around 80 people showed up. I ran the meeting as I always did. I covered the issues for the first half hour. People were interested in talking about how Democrats would run the country now that we delivered them full control of the government. After that, we took time for Glass to virtually present the award to me in front of the members. I accepted it graciously and thanked everyone I could possibly think of. I didn't come close to forgetting Katherine this time! I was also able to pull off a remark that I had been playing around with in my head. In accepting the award, I thanked all the members for being a part of Indivisible Montgomery. "The only reason we met was because Trump won the 2016 election. And to this day, I wish I had never met any of you." The group laughed. "But Trump won, and we did find each other, and for that, I am eternally grateful."

Steve took over the meeting from there. I grinned and chimed in when necessary, but I had checked out mentally. It was time to go.

Final Tally

Four years.

49 months.

212 weeks.

Over 600 newsletters sent.

Over 200 weekly actions taken.

Over $30,000 raised.

36 monthly meetings.

Three August picnics.

Three Kensington Labor Day Parade marches.

10 dine-around weekends.

Over two dozen marches and rallies.

1,700 members.

Four elections won.

One day to go.

Inauguration Day

FINALLY. THE DAY I had so looked forward to since November 9, 2016. I held a lingering fear that Trump's supporters might try to disrupt Joe Biden's inauguration. But there was no indication of any large gathering of Trump supporters near Washington, DC. Trump himself had declared a few days earlier that he wouldn't be attending the ceremony. Good riddance.

Biden's inauguration ceremony will probably appear mundane in retrospect, even weird given the COVID precautions. I thought it was wonderful. I tuned in early to watch various dignitaries take their seats and to listen to the unnecessary banter of the television hosts. The speeches, songs, and poems were uplifting and inspirational. And I breathed a tremendous sigh of relief when Biden officially took the oath making him the 46th president of the United States.

Once the inauguration ended, Katherine, Nancy, and I had lunch. At 2:00 p.m., my final message went out to Indivisible Montgomery, officially marking the end of my term leading the organization I had founded so long ago. I was turning the whole operation over to my good friend Steve Pressman. I knew he'd do a stellar job.

Then I went for a walk.

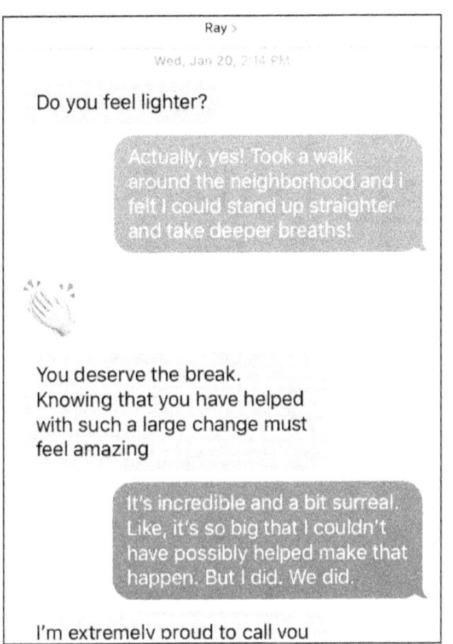

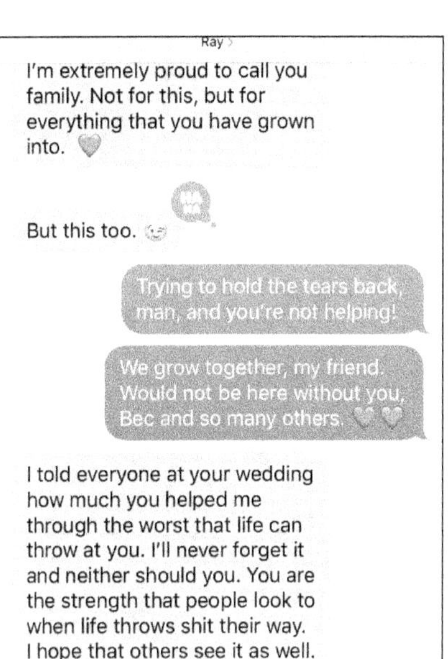

Text messages between me and my friend Ray the day Biden was sworn into office and right after I stepped down from leading Indivisible Montgomery.

Indivisible Montgomery Newsletter: Week 212

January 20, 2021

My friends,

Today, Joe Biden and Kamala Harris were inaugurated as President and Vice President of the United States. The presidency of Donald Trump has ended. The past four years will undoubtedly go down as some of the most tumultuous and momentous in American history. The near destruction of our country at the hands of the president is something no American should ever forget.

The Biden-Harris inauguration is the culmination of four long years of work on our part to protect and preserve our country from the Trump administration. While most news stories omit the work we put in, you should have no doubt that it was us, Indivisible Montgomery, and our friends and colleagues across this country that formed the backbone of the resistance to Trump. We rejected attempts to normalize Trump and his awful policies. We propelled Democrats to victory. Our country would not be where it is today without us. This is a day we should celebrate.

And we should also take a moment to remember those who are not here to celebrate with us. So many people started down this path with us, and, for myriad reasons, they aren't here with us today. Today's celebration is as much theirs as it is ours.

And with the advent of the Biden presidency, so ends my time as the Executive Director of Indivisible Montgomery. I am incredibly proud of everything we accomplished over the past four years. Thank you for all that you have done. I feel incredibly lucky that we all found each other, united in a common purpose, and put in the work necessary to achieve our goals. By no means were the past four years easy. But they were made manageable because of our camaraderie and willingness to do what needed to be done.

Yet our work is not finished. I am completely confident my good friend Steve Pressman, who will succeed me as Executive Director, will continue to decisively guide Indivisible Montgomery to make real, concrete differences to the members of our community and country.

And truly I could not have led this group without the seemingly infinite patience, wisdom, and love of my wife Katherine and our daughters. I look forward to building a better country and a better world with them and for them.

I wish you health, safety, and all the very best.

Thank you,

Chris Pickett

Epilogue

DECEMBER 19, 2024

THIS IS NOT THE ending I wanted to write.

I finished this book in 2023 and have written six epilogues since, each quite different from the other. Some were written when I was in a bad mood, processing my feelings about the first Trump term. Others were written when I was in a good mood and optimistic about the future. One even had an overly saccharine level of hope and good cheer. It took Trump defeating Vice President Kamala Harris in the 2024 election to crystallize my overall sense of our country during Trump's first term in office.

Trump's reelection made many, me included, throw up our hands and ask what our work had been for. Why did we work so hard during Trump's first term only to have the American public return him to the White House? One day, while I was struggling with this, I vented to one of my longtime friends over text. He had read an earlier version of this book and said, "Maybe you should read your own book. You could use the reminder." I scoffed. What was he talking about? I didn't need to compound my current sense of dread with memories of an earlier dread. Nevertheless, the next day, I did as he suggested and flipped through the chapters of this book, daring myself to find something that, knowing what I know now, I wouldn't have done. Where was the wasted effort that I could have avoided? I made it through the 2016 section without finding anything. That time was just a reaction to Trump's first election, but surely there would be something from 2017. I found things I would have done differently, but nothing I would have cut out altogether. So I plowed into 2018. And 2019. And 2020. And 2021. I never found anything I would take back. Everything I did was for the benefit of Indivisible Montgomery and its members. Everything Indivisible Montgomery did directly or indirectly benefited others in our group, the greater community, or our country. Everything.

And I finally understood what my friend was getting at. We did so much, and everything we did made a difference. Every phone call, every letter and postcard, every canvass, every difficult conversation, every donation, every protest, and every march mattered. Some had big effects and some had small, but they all had an effect. Each action was a pebble placed on the ground. By Joe Biden's inauguration, Americans across the country had piled up four years' worth of pebbles and made a mountain of difference. *And that mountain is still there!* Nothing about the 2024 election erases or invalidates that work. Because we fought to prevent Obamacare repeal, people received the care they needed and are alive today. Because we fought against the family separation policy, most separated families were reunited and further separations were greatly reduced. Because we care about our communities, we listened to public health experts, stayed home during the pandemic, reduced the disease burden on our health care system, and saved countless lives. All of that matters. None of it is taken away by Trump's reelection.

What we did mattered, and what we do in the coming years will matter, too. As I told Indivisible Montgomery at our first meeting in 2017, Republicans control all the levers of power in government, and it's possible we will lose many of the upcoming fights. But we must fight, because we can't win if we simply give up. The history of Trump's first term teaches us our successes will come from unexpected places. The rhetoric of the 2024 Trump campaign and its boasting of plans to tear down our communities and turn our government over to billionaires must meet the reality of the federal bureaucracy, the US legal system, and the American public come Inauguration Day. These are each formidable forces that can give space for opposing Trump's authoritarianism, and in this space is the opportunity for action. For resistance. But only if people are willing to add their pebble and make a difference.

If Trump had won in 2020, I would have sent a message imploring people to get up in the morning, find something to do, and do it right. That advice holds now. Do something that will protect yourself, improve your community, or support American democracy. And the sun will rise the next day. And in that day, find the next right thing to do, big or small, and do that. And the sun will rise the day after that. And the day after that. And if we do the next right thing often enough, we will wake up one day to find ourselves living in a much better community having made a mountain of difference.

Acknowledgments

First and foremost, none of this happens without Katherine—not Indivisible Montgomery and not this book. I took so many words to tell the story of this organization and only touched on a small fraction of all that you did. You mean so much more to me than I can fully express. I'm lucky to have you. Thank you. For everything.

Thanks to my daughters, Nancy and Hazel. You grew up as your parents grew into activism. Every time I was away doing resistance work, I couldn't wait to get back to be with you. Thank you for being with us along the way and for being your amazing, awesome selves.

The friends I had before launching Indivisible Montgomery formed an amazing foundation I relied on far more than I expected. Thanks to Kevin Breen, John Goshorn, Steve Moore, Jessica and Craig Flint, Mary Nelson, Coco Strong, and especially Ray, Rebecca, and Kaelen Woodruff. And an additional thanks to Ray, John, Coco, and Jessica for reading earlier versions of this manuscript. They helped me smooth out some rough spots and work through some tough memories.

A grassroots activist organization is, by definition, a community effort, and I have a community of people to thank. From the 30 people who called into the first Indivisible Montgomery phone call to the 1,700 who were with us on Election Day in 2020, thank you to everyone who put their faith in me to lead this organization. Steve

Pressman masterfully ran our Elections committee; we ran so much of the organization together, and he became a great friend and confidant along the way. I am grateful he led the organization once I stepped down. I am thankful for the friendship of Angela Hvitved and Damian Dalle Nogare, who also consistently did so much for Indivisible Montgomery. Teri Blandon ran our Twitter account and was often the friend giving me the virtual kick I needed to break out of a doom spiral. Nina Liakos kept all our meetings organized and running smoothly, and she was a constant source of strength and support. Of all the other people who contributed so much, I also want to single out Mollie Ferguson, Carol and Jeff McShea, Lois Hampton, Mike Marceau, Karen Sultan, and Susan Zengerle for being a part of the Indivisible Montgomery steering committee at various times, among other critical contributions; Lauren Petersen, Dawn Leaf, Catherine Schupp, and Martin Trocki, longtime committee leaders who organized some of our most successful efforts; and ever-present volunteers Suzanne Baktash, Valerie Barr, Claire Robertson, Tamara Prince and Alan Crane, Betty Dooley, Jennifer Thompson, Rose Crandall, David Kameras, Lynn Litterine, and Laurie Pfeiffer, among so many others who consistently supported this organization. And special thanks to Dee Clarkin, who continues to lead Indivisible Montgomery through these arguably more difficult times.

Indivisible Montgomery did not exist in a vacuum, and we had the amazing luck to have so many committed people in our county. Our most consistent partner was DoTheMostGood, led by Barbara Noveau, and we worked together on nearly every event either group put together. Working with veteran get-out-the-vote experts like

Nancy Walker and Jon Heintz, of J Walkers Action Group, and Laura and Peter Henderson, of Progressive Action Montgomery County, was invaluable to Indivisible Montgomery's election efforts. And a special thanks to other resistance groups in Montgomery County, such as Indivisible MoCo, MoCoWoMen, Rockville Resistance, Takoma Park Mobilization, and the Women's Democratic Club of Montgomery County. I thank Rep. Jamie Raskin for giving so much of his time to Indivisible Montgomery, and the larger resistance effort, and for being a constant light for liberty and justice in our country. I also thank the rest of the Democratic Maryland congressional delegation for their hard work on behalf of the people of this great state.

Finally, thank you to everyone who showed up to fight for American democracy. Whether in the first Trump term, the second, or both, if you donated to pro-democracy candidates, worked to turn out voters, stood up to this administration, or ran for office, you made a difference. And I hope you'll join me in continuing to make a difference long into the future.

Notes

2016

1. David Remnick, "An American Tragedy," *New Yorker*, Nov. 9, 2016, https://www.newyorker.com/news/news-desk/an-american-tragedy-remnick-trump-wins-presidency-2016.

2017

1. Heidi M. Przybyla and Fredreka Schouten, "At 2.6 Million Strong, Women's Marches Crush Expectations," *USA Today*, Jan. 21, 2017 (updated Jan. 22, 2017), https://www.usatoday.com/story/news/politics/2017/01/21/womens-march-aims-start-movement-trump-inauguration/96864158/; Erica Chenoweth and Jeremy Pressman, "This is what we learned by counting the women's marches," *Washington Post*, Feb. 7, 2017, https://www.washingtonpost.com/news/monkey-cage/wp/2017/02/07/this-is-what-we-learned-by-counting-the-womens-marches/.

2. "Find Your Group," *Indivisible*, accessed Mar. 21, 2024, https://indivisible.org/groups.

3. Michael Crowley and Tyler Pager, "Trump Urges Russia to Hack Clinton's Email," *Politico*, July 27, 2016, https://www.politico.com/story/2016/07/trump-putin-no-relationship-226282.

4. Ellen Nakashima, "Russian Government Hackers Penetrated DNC, Stole Opposition Research on Trump," *Washington Post*, June 14, 2016, https://www.washingtonpost.com/world/national-security/russian-government-hackers-penetrated-dnc-stole-opposition-research-on-trump/2016/06/14/cf006cb4-316e-11e6-8ff7-7b6c1998b7a0_story.html.

5. Gregory Krieg, "Hillary Clinton: Donald Trump Would Be Putin's 'Puppet,'" *CBS News*, Oct. 19, 2016, https://www.cbsnews.com/philadelphia/news/hillary-clinton-donald-trump-would-be-putins-puppet/.

6. MJ Lee and Eric Bradner, "Anger Erupts at Republican Town Halls," *CNN Politics*, updated Feb. 10, 2017, https://www.cnn.com/2017/02/10/politics/republican-town-halls-obamacare/index.html.

7. Andrew Metcalf, "Democrats Fire Up Base at Town Hall Meeting in Silver

Spring," *MoCo360*, Feb. 27, 2017, https://bethesdamagazine.com/2017/02/27/democrats-fire-up-base-at-town-hall-meeting-in-silver-spring/.

8. Stephen Collinson, Dana Bash, Phil Mattingly, Deirdre Walsh, Lauren Fox, and MJ Lee, "House Republicans Pull Health Care Bill," *CNN Politics*, updated Mar. 25, 2017, https://www.cnn.com/2017/03/24/politics/house-health-care-vote/index.html.

9. Matt Apuzzo, Adam Goldman, and Nicholas Fandos, "Code Name Crossfire Hurricane: The Secret Origins of the Trump Investigation," *New York Times*, May 16, 2018, https://www.nytimes.com/2018/05/16/us/politics/crossfire-hurricane-trump-russia-fbi-mueller-investigation.html.

10. Greg Miller, Adam Entous, and Ellen Nakashima, "National Security Adviser Flynn Discussed Sanctions with Russian Ambassador, Despite Denials, Officials Say," *Washington Post*, Feb. 9, 2017, https://www.washingtonpost.com/world/national-security/national-security-adviser-flynn-discussed-sanctions-with-russian-ambassador-despite-denials-officials-say/2017/02/09/f85b29d6-ee11-11e6-b4ff-ac2cf509efe5_story.html.

11. Michael S. Schmidt, "In a Private Dinner, Trump Demanded Loyalty. Comey Demurred," *New York Times*, May 11, 2017, https://www.nytimes.com/2017/05/11/us/politics/trump-comey-firing.html.

12. Jessica Taylor, "President Trump Fires FBI Director James Comey," *NPR*, May 9, 2017, https://www.npr.org/2017/05/09/527663050/president-trump-fires-fbi-director-james-comey.

13. Susan B. Glasser, "Russia's Oval Office Victory Dance," *Politico*, May 10, 2017, https://www.politico.com/magazine/story/2017/05/10/james-comey-firing-trump-lavrov-putin-215124/.

14. Jeff Stein, "Former FBI Director Robert Mueller Was Just Appointed Special Counsel to Investigate Trump and Russia," *Vox*, May 17, 2017, https://www.vox.com/2017/5/17/15655934/robert-mueller-special-counsel.

15. Jo Becker, Adam Goldman, and Matt Apuzzo, "Russian Dirt on Clinton? 'I Love It,' Donald Trump Jr. Said," *New York Times*, July 11, 2017, https://www.nytimes.com/2017/07/11/us/politics/trump-russia-email-clinton.html.

16. Alex Horton, "The Magnitsky Act, Explained," *Washington Post*, July 14, 2017, https://www.washingtonpost.com/news/the-fix/wp/2017/07/14/the-magnitsky-act-explained/.

17. Josh Meyer, "Mueller Reveals Closer Manafort Ties to Russian Oligarch," *Politico*, June 27, 2018, https://www.politico.com/story/2018/06/27/paul-manafort-mueller-russia-oleg-deripaska-680630.

18. Maev Kennedy, "Heather Heyer, victim of Charlottesville car attack, was civil rights

activist," *Guardian*, Aug. 13, 2017, https://www.theguardian.com/us-news/2017/aug/13/woman-killed-at-white-supremacist-rally-in-charlottesville-named.

19. Katie Reilly, "President Trump Again Blames 'Both Sides' for Charlottesville Violence," *Time*, Aug. 15, 2017, https://time.com/4902129/president-donald-trump-both-sides-charlottesville/.

20. Lauren Fox, "Hill Republican Dilemma: Dash to Pass Tax Reform or Face Donor Backlash," *CNN Politics*, Nov. 13, 2017, https://www.cnn.com/2017/11/13/politics/tax-reform-republican-donor-backlash/index.html.

21. William Gale, "A Fixable Mistake: The Tax Cuts and Jobs Act," American Enterprise Institute, Sep. 23, 2019, https://www.aei.org/economics/a-fixable-mistake-the-tax-cuts-and-jobs-act/.

22. Ben Popken, "What Trump's Disclosure of His 500 LLCs Can and Can't Tell Us," *NBC News*, May 16, 2018, https://www.nbcnews.com/business/taxes/what-trump-s-disclosure-his-500-llcs-can-can-t-n874391.

23. Anand Giridharadas, *The Persuaders: At the Front Lines of the Fight for Hearts, Minds, and Democracy* (Vintage Books, 2023), https://www.anand.ly/the-persuaders.

24. Alex Seitz-Wald, "Democrat Ralph Northam Wins Virginia Governor Race," *NBC News*, Nov. 7, 2017, https://www.nbcnews.com/storyline/2017-elections/election-results-virginia-new-jersey-n818406; Emily Tillett, "Virginia Election Results 2017: Republican David Yancey Wins Virginia House Seat," *CBS News*, updated Jan. 4, 2018, https://www.cbsnews.com/news/virginia-election-results-lottery-drawing-house-of-delegates-david-yancy-winner-virginia-house-seat/.

2018

1. Michael Alison Chandler and Joe Heim, "Protesters Gather for a Second Women's March in Nation's Capital," *Washington Post*, Jan. 20, 2018, https://www.washingtonpost.com/local/protesters-gather-for-a-second-womens-march-in-nations-capital/2018/01/20/c641bf16-fdef-11e7-ad8c-ecbb62019393_story.html.

2. Elizabeth Chuck, Alex Johnson, and Corky Siemaszko, "17 Killed in Mass Shooting at High School in Parkland, Florida," *NBC News*, Feb. 14, 2018 (updated Feb. 15, 2018), https://www.nbcnews.com/news/us-news/police-respond-shooting-parkland-florida-high-school-n848101.

3. "Maryland Primary Election Results," *New York Times*, June 28, 2018, https://www.nytimes.com/interactive/2018/06/26/us/elections/results-maryland-primary-elections.html.

4. Nick Miroff, "Trump's 'Zero Tolerance' at the Border Is Causing Child Shelters to Fill

Up Fast," *Washington Post*, May 29, 2018, https://www.washingtonpost.com/world/national-security/trumps-zero-tolerance-at-the-border-is-causing-child-shelters-to-fill-up-fast/2018/05/29/7aab0ae4-636b-11e8-a69c-b944de66d9e7_story.html.

5. McKay Coppins, "The Outrage Over Family Separation Is Exactly What Stephen Miller Wants," *Atlantic*, June 19, 2018, https://www.theatlantic.com/politics/archive/2018/06/stephen-miller-family-separation/563132/.

6. Brian Naylor, "Fact Check: Trump Wrongly States Obama Administration Had Child Separation Policy," *NPR*, Apr. 9, 2019, https://www.npr.org/2019/04/09/711446917/fact-check-trump-wrongly-states-obama-administration-had-child-separation-policy.

7. Jasmine Garsd, "U.S. Government Agrees to Settlement with Migrant Families Separated at the Border," *NPR*, Oct. 16, 2023, https://www.npr.org/2023/10/16/1206135260/u-s-government-agrees-to-settlement-with-migrant-families-separated-at-the-borde.

8. "Trump, Putin Held a Second, Undisclosed Meeting at G20 Summit," Reuters, July 18, 2017, https://www.reuters.com/article/idUSKBN1A32H0/.

9. Matthew Nussbaum, "Trump Publicly Sides with Putin on Election Interference," *Politico*, July 16, 2018, https://www.politico.com/story/2018/07/16/trump-russia-putin-summit-722418.

10. Dan Mangan, "Sen. John McCain says Trump gave 'One of the most disgraceful performances by an American president' at Putin summit," *CNBC*, July 16, 2018, https://www.cnbc.com/2018/07/16/john-mccain-says-trump-abased-himself-before-putin-at-summit.html.

11. Meghan Keneally, "Airbnb Warns That It May Expel 'Unite the Right' Rally Participants on Charlottesville Anniversary," *ABC News*, Aug. 9, 2018, https://abcnews.go.com/US/airbnb-warns-expel-unite-rally-participants/story?id=57121537.

12. Eric Tucker (Associated Press), "What Is Antifa? A Look at the Movement Trump Is Blaming for Violence at Protests," *PBS*, June 1, 2020, https://www.pbs.org/newshour/nation/what-is-antifa-a-look-at-the-movement-trump-is-blaming-for-violence-at-protests.

13. Emma Brown, "California Professor, Writer of Confidential Brett Kavanaugh Letter, Speaks Out About Her Allegation of Sexual Assault," *Washington Post*, Sep. 16, 2018, https://www.washingtonpost.com/investigations/california-professor-writer-of-confidential-brett-kavanaugh-letter-speaks-out-about-her-allegation-of-sexual-assault/2018/09/16/46982194-b846-11e8-94eb-3bd52dfe917b_story.html.

14. Jia Tolentino, "After the Kavanaugh Allegations, Republicans Offer a Shocking Defense: Sexual Assault Isn't a Big Deal," *New Yorker*, Sep. 20, 2018, https://www.newyorker.com/news/our-columnists/after-the-kavanaugh-allegations-republicans-offer-a-shocking-defense-sexual-assault-isnt-a-big-deal.

15. Nancy Cordes and Ed O'Keefe, "Senate Republicans Hire Female Prosecutor to Question

Accuser and Kavanaugh," *CBS News*, Sep. 26, 2018, https://www.cbsnews.com/news/chuck-grassley-rachel-mitchell-question-brett-kavanaugh-dr-christine-blasey-ford/.

16. Adam Serwer, "The Cruelty Is the Point," *Atlantic*, Oct. 3, 2018, https://www.theatlantic.com/ideas/archive/2018/10/the-cruelty-is-the-point/572104/.

17. Clare Foran and Daniella Diaz, "Democrats Win Control of the House in 2018 Midterms, CNN Projects," *CNN Politics*, updated Nov. 7, 2018, https://www.cnn.com/2018/11/06/politics/house-control-midterm-election/index.html.

2019

1. Tess Conciatori, "Mueller's Case Against Paul Manafort, Explained," *PBS*, Mar. 7, 2019, https://www.pbs.org/newshour/politics/muellers-case-against-paul-manafort-explained.

2. Erica R. Hendry, "Read Mueller's Full Indictment Against 12 Russian Officers for Election Interference," *PBS*, July 13, 2018, https://www.pbs.org/newshour/nation/read-muellers-full-indictment-against-12-russian-officers-for-election-interference.

3. Pete Williams, Julia Ainsley, and Gregg Birnbaum, "Mueller Finds No Proof of Trump Collusion with Russia; AG Barr Says Evidence 'Not Sufficient' to Prosecute," *NBC News*, Mar. 24, 2019, https://www.nbcnews.com/politics/donald-trump/mueller-report-conclusions-trump-congress-attorney-general-william-barr-n986611.

4. Robert S. Mueller IIII, "Report on the Investigation into Russian Interference in the 2016 Presidential Election," US Department of Justice, Mar. 2019, https://www.justice.gov/archives/sco/file/1373816/dl.

5. CNN Newsource, "List: The 172 House Democrats Calling for an Impeachment Inquiry into Trump," *KOAA News5*, Sep. 24, 2019, https://www.koaa.com/news/national/list-the-172-house-democrats-calling-for-an-impeachment-inquiry-into-trump.

6. Greg Miller, Ellen Nakashima, and Shane Harris, "Trump's Communications with Foreign Leader Are Part of Whistleblower Complaint That Spurred Standoff Between Spy Chief and Congress, Former Officials Say," *Washington Post*, Sep. 18, 2019, https://www.washingtonpost.com/national-security/trumps-communications-with-foreign-leader-are-part-of-whistleblower-complaint-that-spurred-standoff-between-spy-chief-and-congress-former-officials-say/2019/09/18/df651aa2-da60-11e9-bfb1-849887369476_story.html.

7. "Read the Trump-Ukraine Phone Call Readout," *Politico*, Sep. 25, 2019, https://www.politico.com/story/2019/09/25/trump-ukraine-phone-call-transcript-text-pdf-1510770.

8. Heidi Przybyla and Adam Edelman, "Nancy Pelosi Announces Formal Impeachment Inquiry of Trump," *NBC News*, Sep. 24, 2019,

https://www.nbcnews.com/politics/trump-impeachment-inquiry/pelosi-announce-formal-impeachment-inquiry-trump-n1058251.

9. Kevin Breuninger and Christina Wilkie, "Trump Ordered Ukraine 'Quid Pro Quo' Through Giuliani, Key Witness Sondland Testifies," *CNBC*, Nov. 20, 2019, https://www.cnbc.com/2019/11/20/trump-ordered-ukraine-quid-pro-quo-through-giuliani-key-witness-sondland-testifies.html.

10. Nicholas Fandos and Michael D. Shear, "Trump Impeached for Abuse of Power and Obstruction of Congress," *New York Times*, Dec. 18, 2019, https://www.nytimes.com/2019/12/18/us/politics/trump-impeached.html.

11. Michael D. Shear, "Trump Will Withdraw U.S. from Paris Climate Agreement," *New York Times*, June 1, 2017, https://www.nytimes.com/2017/06/01/climate/trump-paris-climate-agreement.html; Mark Landler, "Trump Abandons Iran Nuclear Deal He Long Scorned," *New York Times*, May 8, 2018, https://www.nytimes.com/2018/05/08/world/middleeast/trump-iran-nuclear-deal.html.

2020

1. Kyle Cheney, John Bresnahan, and Andrew Desiderio, "Republicans Defeat Democratic Bids to Hear Witnesses in Trump Trial," *Politico*, Jan. 31, 2020, https://www.politico.com/news/2020/01/31/murkowski-to-vote-against-calling-witnesses-in-impeachment-trial-109997.

2. Dylan Scott, "With All the Votes Counted, Pete Buttigieg Won the Iowa Caucuses—But Bernie Sanders Is Challenging," *Vox*, Feb. 9, 2020, https://www.vox.com/policy-and-politics/2020/2/9/21125703/iowa-caucuses-2020-final-results-pete-buttigieg-wins; Daniel Strauss, "Bernie Sanders Wins New Hampshire Primary with Buttigieg Second," *Guardian*, Feb. 12, 2020, https://www.theguardian.com/us-news/2020/feb/10/new-hampshire-primary-bernie-sanders-pete-buttigieg; David Siders, Laura Barrón-López, and Marc Caputo, "Bernie Wins Again," *Politico*, Feb. 22, 2020 (updated Feb. 23, 2020), https://www.politico.com/news/2020/02/22/nevada-caucuses-biden-sanders-116719.

3. Domenico Montenaro, "4 Takeaways From Joe Biden's Big Win in South Carolina," *NPR*, Mar. 1, 2020, https://www.npr.org/2020/03/01/810813892/4-takeaways-from-joe-bidens-big-win-in-south-carolina.

4. Dan Merica and Kate Sullivan, "Biden Racks Up Buttigieg, Klobuchar, O'Rourke Endorsements on Same Night," *CNN Politics*, Mar. 2, 2020, https://edition.cnn.com/2020/03/02/politics/joe-biden-endorsements/index.html.

5. Marc Silver, "My Hand-Washing Song: Readers Offer Lyrics for a 20-Second Scrub,"

NPR, Mar. 17, 2020, https://www.npr.org/sections/goatsandsoda/2020/03/17/814221111/my-hand-washing-song-readers-offer-lyrics-for-a-20-second-scrub.

6. Ashley Parker, Yasmeen Abutaleb, and Lena H. Sun, "Squandered Time: How the Trump Administration Lost Control of the Coronavirus Crisis," *Washington Post*, Mar. 7, 2020, https://www.washingtonpost.com/politics/trump-coronavirus-response-squandered-time/2020/03/07/5c47d3d0-5fcb-11ea-9055-5fa12981bbbf_story.html.

7. Official release, "NBA to Suspend Season Following Wednesday's Games," *NBA.com*, Mar. 11, 2020, https://www.nba.com/news/nba-suspend-season-following-wednesdays-games; "NHL to Pause Season Due to Coronavirus," *NHL.com*, Mar. 12, 2020, https://www.nhl.com/news/nhl-coronavirus-to-provide-update-on-concerns-316131734.

8. Fred Imbert, "Dow Drops Nearly 3,000 Points, as Coronavirus Collapse Continues; Worst Day Since '87," *CNBC*, Mar. 15, 2020 (updated Mar. 16, 2020), https://www.cnbc.com/2020/03/15/traders-await-futures-open-after-fed-cuts-rates-launches-easing-program.html.

9. Official release, "Important Community Update: MCPS Schools to Close March 15-27," MontgomerySchoolsMD.org, Mar. 12, 2020, https://ww2.montgomeryschoolsmd.org/departments/publicinfo/community/school-year-2019-2020/coronavirus-update-20200312.html.

10. Devan Cole, "Maryland's GOP Governor Closes Non-Essential Businesses Amid Coronavirus Pandemic," *CNN Politics*, Mar. 23, 2020, https://www.cnn.com/2020/03/23/politics/larry-hogan-coronavirus-closes-businesses.

11. Lauren Hirsch, "Trump Says, 'Anybody Who Wants a Test Gets a Test' After Pence Says U.S. Can't Meet Coronavirus Testing Demand," *CNBC*, Mar. 6, 2020, https://www.cnbc.com/2020/03/06/trump-anybody-who-wants-a-test-gets-a-test-amid-shortage-for-coronavirus.html.

12. Heather Long, "Over 10 Million Americans Applied for Unemployment Benefits in March as Economy Collapsed," *Washington Post*, Apr. 2, 2020, https://www.washingtonpost.com/business/2020/04/02/jobless-march-coronavirus/.

13. Kevin Liptak, Maegan Vazquez, Nick Valencia, and Jim Acosta, "Trump Says He Wants the Country 'Opened Up and Just Raring to Go by Easter,' Despite Health Experts' Warnings," *CNN Politics*, updated Mar. 24, 2020, https://www.cnn.com/2020/03/24/politics/trump-easter-economy-coronavirus/index.html.

14. "How George Floyd Died, and What Happened Next," *New York Times*, July 29, 2022, https://www.nytimes.com/article/george-floyd.html.

15. Richard A. Oppel Jr., Derrick Bryson Taylor, and Nicholas Bogel-Burroughs, "What to Know About Breonna Taylor's Death," *New York Times*, Dec. 13, 2023, https://www.nytimes.com/article/breonna-taylor-police.html.

16. Richard Fausset, "What We Know About the Shooting Death of Ahmaud Arbery," *New York Times*, Aug. 8, 2022, https://www.nytimes.com/article/ahmaud-arbery-shooting-georgia.html.

17. Tom Cotton, "Send In the Troops," *New York Times*, June 3, 2020, https://www.nytimes.com/2020/06/03/opinion/tom-cotton-protests-military.html.

18. Garrett Graff, "The Story Behind Bill Barr's Unmarked Federal Agents," *Politico*, June 5, 2020, https://www.politico.com/news/magazine/2020/06/05/protests-washington-dc-federal-agents-law-enforcement-302551.

19. Tom Gjelten, "Peaceful Protestors Tear-Gassed to Clear Way for Trump Church Photo-Op," *NPR*, June 1, 2020, https://www.npr.org/2020/06/01/867532070/trumps-unannounced-church-visit-angers-church-officials.

20. Christopher Cadelago and Caitlin Oprysko, "Biden Picks Kamala Harris as VP Nominee," *Politico*, Aug. 11, 2020, https://www.politico.com/news/2020/08/11/joe-biden-vp-pick-kamala-harris-393768.

21. Nina Totenberg, "Justice Ruth Bader Ginsburg, Champion of Gender Equality, Dies at 87," *NPR*, Sep. 18, 2020, https://www.npr.org/2020/09/18/100306972/justice-ruth-bader-ginsburg-champion-of-gender-equality-dies-at-87.

22. Domenico Montanaro, "Trump Derails 1st Presidential Debate with Biden, and 5 Other Takeaways," *NPR*, Sep. 30, 2020, https://www.npr.org/2020/09/30/918500976/trump-derails-first-presidential-debate-with-biden-and-5-other-takeaways.

23. Kathryn Watson and Grace Segers, "President Trump and First Lady Melania Test Positive for COVID-19," *CBS News*, Oct. 2, 2020, https://www.cbsnews.com/news/trump-covid-positive-first-lady-melania-coronavirus-2020-10-02/.

24. Sarah Ellison, "Trump Campaign Was Livid When Fox News Called Arizona for Biden—and Tensions Boiled Over On-Air," *Washington Post*, Nov. 4, 2020, https://www.washingtonpost.com/lifestyle/style/fox-news-election-night-arizona/2020/11/04/194f9968-1e71-11eb-90dd-abd0f7086a91_story.html.

25. William Cummings, Joey Garrison, and Jim Sergent, "By the Numbers: President Donald Trump's Failed Efforts to Overturn the Election," *USA Today*, Jan. 6, 2021, https://www.usatoday.com/in-depth/news/politics/elections/2021/01/06/trumps-failed-efforts-overturn-election-numbers/4130307001/.

26. Miles Bryan, "From Obscure to Sold Out: The Story of Four Seasons Total Landscaping in Just 4 Days," *NPR*, Nov. 11, 2020, https://www.npr.org/2020/11/11/933635970/from-obscure-to-sold-out-the-story-of-four-seasons-total-landscaping-in-just-4-d.

27. Bess Levin, "Rudy Giuliani's Hair Dye Melting Off His Face Was the Least Crazy Part of His Batshit-Crazy Press Conference," *Vanity Fair*, Nov. 19, 2020, https://www.vanityfair.com/news/2020/11/rudy-giuliani-hair-dye-press-conference.

28. Todd J. Gillman, "17 States and Trump Join Texas Request for Supreme Court to Overturn Biden Wins in Four States," *Dallas Morning News*, Dec. 9, 2020, https://www.dallasnews.com/news/politics/2020/12/09/trump-says-hell-join-texas-lawsuit-asking-supreme-court-to-block-62-biden-electors-from-four-states/.

2021

1. Berkeley Lovelace Jr., "FDA Approves Pfizer's COVID Vaccine for Emergency Use as U.S. Reaches Pivotal Moment in the Pandemic," *CNBC*, Dec. 11, 2020, https://www.cnbc.com/2020/12/11/pfizer-covid-vaccine-approved-fda-emergency-use.html; Berkeley Lovelace Jr., "FDA Approves Second COVID Vaccine for Emergency Use as It Clears Moderna's for U.S. Distribution," *CNBC*, Dec. 18, 2020, https://www.cnbc.com/2020/12/18/moderna-covid-vaccine-approved-fda-for-emergency-use.html.

2. Amy Gardner, "'I Just Want to Find 11,780 Votes': In Extraordinary Hour-Long Call, Trump Pressures Georgia Secretary of State to Recalculate the Vote in His Favor," *Washington Post*, Jan. 3, 2021, https://www.washingtonpost.com/politics/trump-raffensperger-call-georgia-vote/2021/01/03/d45acb92-4dc4-11eb-bda4-615aaefd0555_story.html.

3. Devlin Barrett and Josh Dawsey, "Trump to Acting AG, According to Aide's Notes: 'Just Say the Election Was Corrupt + Leave the Rest to Me,'" *Washington Post*, July 31, 2021, https://www.washingtonpost.com/national-security/trump-rosen-phone-call-notes/2021/07/30/2e9430d6-f14d-11eb-81d2-ffae0f931b8f_story.html.

4. Barbara Sprunt, "Here Are the Republicans Who Objected to the Electoral College Count," *NPR*, Jan. 7, 2021, https://www.npr.org/sections/insurrection-at-the-capitol/2021/01/07/954380156/here-are-the-republicans-who-objected-to-the-electoral-college-count.

5. Marissa J. Lang, Emily Davies, Peter Hermann, Jessica Contrera, and Clarence Williams, "Trump Supporters Pour into Washington to Begin Demonstrtating Against Election," *Washington Post*, Jan. 5, 2021, https://www.washingtonpost.com/dc-md-va/2021/01/05/dc-protest-trump-supporters-election/.

6. Steve Peoples, Bill Barrow, and Russ Bynum, "Warnock, Ossoff Win in Georgia, Handing Dems Senate Control," *AP*, Jan. 6, 2021, https://apnews.com/article/georgia-election-results-4b82ba7ee3cc74d33e68daadaee2cbf3.

7. Associated Press and Aaron Glantz (The Center for Investigative Reporting), "Read Pence's Full Letter Saying He Can't Claim 'Unilateral Authority' to Reject Electoral Votes," *PBS*, Jan. 6, 2021, https://www.pbs.org/newshour/politics/read-pences-full-letter-saying-he-cant-claim-unilateral-authority-to-reject-electoral-votes.

8. WBUR Newsroom, "Transcript: 'It's Not Protest, It's Insurrection': Biden Delivers

Remarks on 'Siege' upon U.S. Capitol," *WBUR*, Jan. 6, 2021, https://www.wbur.org/news/2021/01/06/transcript-joe-biden-capitol-chaos.

9. "'We Love You, You're Very Special': President Trump Tweets Message, Later Removed, to Rioters Storming the U.S. Capitol," *CBS News*, Jan. 6, 2021, https://www.cbsnews.com/baltimore/news/its-time-to-go-home-now-president-trump-tweets-message-to-supporters-storming-the-u-s-capitol/.

10. Associated Press, "Watch: Video Shows Capitol 'Mob Calling for the Death of the Vice President,' Plaskett Says," *PBS*, Feb. 10, 2021, https://www.pbs.org/newshour/politics/watch-video-shows-capitol-mob-calling-for-the-death-of-the-vice-president-plaskett-says.

11. Alana Wise, "House Approves 25th Amendment Resolution Against Trump, Pence Says He Won't Invoke," *NPR*, Jan. 12, 2021, https://www.npr.org/sections/trump-impeachment-effort-live-updates/2021/01/12/955750169/house-to-vote-on-25th-amendment-resolution-against-trump.

12. Lisa Mascaro, Mary Clare Jalonick, Jonathan Lemire, and Alan Fram, "Trump Impeached After Capitol Riot in Historic Second Charge," AP, Jan. 13, 2021, https://apnews.com/article/trump-impeachment-vote-capitol-siege-0a6f2a348a6e43f27d5e1dc486027860.

About the Author

Chris Pickett is an organizational leader and data analyst with a passionate interest in improving the conduct and culture of the American biomedical research enterprise. He lives in Silver Spring, Maryland, with his amazingly talented wife, Katherine, and their awe-inspiring daughters, Nancy and Hazel. Each year, they work together to support Democrats in state and federal elections.